AUSTRALIA

Published by Thomas Cook Publishing
A division of Thomas Cook Holdings Ltd
PO Box 227, Thorpe Wood
Peterborough PE3 6PU
United Kingdom

Telephone: 01733 503571
E-mail: books@thomascook.com

Text: © 2000 Thomas Cook Publishing
Maps: © 2000 Thomas Cook Publishing

ISBN 1 841570 66 4

Distributed in the United States of America by the Globe Pequot Press,
PO Box 480, Guilford, Connecticut 06437, USA.

Distributed in Canada by Whitecap Books, 351 Lynn Avenue,
North Vancouver, British Columbia, Canada V7J 2C4.

Distributed in Australia and New Zealand by Peribo Pty Limited,
58 Beaumont Road, Mt Kuring-Gai, NSW, 2080, Australia.

Publisher: Stephen York
Commissioning Editor: Deborah Parker
Map Editor: Bernard Horton

Series Editor: Christopher Catling

Written and researched by: Cathy Bolt, Bina Brown, Rick Eaves, Kerry
Fisher, Jacob Greber, Deborah Howcroft, Damien Murphy, Sue Neales and
Robin Taylor.

Cover photograph: Ethel Davies

must-see AUSTRALIA

CATHY BOLT, BINA BROWN, RICK
EAVES, KERRY FISHER, JACOB
GREBER, DEBORAH HOWCROFT,
DAMIEN MURPHY, SUE NEALES
and ROBIN TAYLOR

Getting
to know
Australia

5

GETTING TO KNOW AUSTRALIA

Discovering Australia

As long ago as the 1850s, Australian unions were campaigning for an 8-hour working day, with the slogan '8 hours' labour, 8 hours' recreation, 8 hours' rest'. That fiercely guarded balance between work and play still holds true today, which, for the tourist, means that Australia's possibilities for fun and R&R are endless.

Australia is one of those places that instantly conjures up vivid images in the mind's eye. Endless swathes of blue sky, long golden beaches, rugged red rocks and arid outback deserts. The white sails of the Sydney Opera House framed against the bright blue harbour with its tiny yachts. The bright underwater coral and flashing fish of the Great Barrier Reef, and the lush green tropical rainforests of far North Queensland tumbling down to white-sand coves and bays. And bounding red kangaroos, cuddly koalas clinging to gum trees and the glorious bright rainbow colours of the parrots, lorikeets and rosellas.

Most of all, Australia is about a sense of space, timelessness, and untamed lands. This, the sixth biggest country in the world, has a population of just 18 million. It's a land of extreme contrasts, with snow-covered mountains in the south and rocky red gorges in the north, vineyards laden with luscious grapes in the far west and pounding surf beaches in the east. Farms are measured in thousands of hectares, roads stretch far into the distance, towns are hundreds of kilometres apart, and in some remote communities traditional Aboriginal people still live a life not that far removed from that of their ancestors hundreds of generations ago. This country has

more than 2 000 National Parks and 13 World Heritage-listed wonders, from ancient fossil fields and impenetrable rainforests to the glistening white sands of Fraser Island and the Aboriginal rock art of Kakadu National Park.

Surprising as it may seem to some visitors, Australia, with its urban roots, is as much about thriving, modern and exciting cities, teeming with cutting-edge festivals, major sporting events, sophisticated restaurants and a well-developed theatre and arts scene, as it is about the bush and the outback.

It takes many Australians a lifetime just to get to know their own state – and, when they've done that, there are still six other states waiting to be discovered. The choice is seemingly endless – pottering around the vineyards of the Barossa or Hunter Valleys, tasting wine amid magnificent countryside; eating fresh cheese direct from the factory in Victoria's mellow northeast; seeking out a lesser known golden beach on the NSW north coast; finding the relaxing natural spas of Hepburn Springs, or a cosy bed and breakfast in the Blue Mountains; exploring some of the national parks and their walking trails, and seeing the country's unique native animals in the wild; skiing or fly-fishing in the soaring Snowy Mountains of southern NSW; horse-riding or whitewater rafting in the Victorian Alps.

> " Australians all let us rejoice,
> For we are young and free;
> We've golden soil and wealth for toil;
> Our home is girt by sea;
> Our land abounds in nature's gifts
> Of beauty rich and rare;
> In history's page, let every stage
> Advance Australia Fair. "

Australia's national anthem,
Advance Australia Fair

The trick with planning any holiday to Australia is to realise that it's impossible to do it in one go. This is one of the world's most ancient lands, where many of the natural wonders have been around for millions of years, and they will probably wait for your next time Down Under.

Life in Australia

Today's modern Australian cities may have their fair share of harassed-looking executives, but as a visitor you never shake off the feeling that work is peripheral and that this country's population conserves most of its energy for an attractive outdoor lifestyle and a huge amount of post-work fun.

A Sydneysider's typical day might go something like this:

0700 A brisk trot along the scenic Bondi to Coogee coastal path, or the Manly to Spit walkway. Back for a shower (every house or apartment has at least one).

> " *Leisured multitudes all in shirt sleeves and all picnicking all the day.* "
> **Rudyard Kipling (1865–1936) on the Australians**

0800 A flat white or a short black caffeine hit or a ginger and carrot juice and a flick through the *Sydney Morning Herald* at a favourite café.

0830 The Central Business District (CBD) starts to buzz with suited financiers, while ferries are crowding into Circular Quay with commuters from across the water.

1230 A free lunchtime concert in Martin Place, or a *focaccia* sandwich under the shady trees in Hyde Park.

1430 Bondi's beach, cafés and juice bars are busy with office workers throwing 'sickies' and lucky tourists.

1730 A pack of VB beers or a chilled Chardonnay from the 'bottle shop' on the way home, or a little something from David Jones Food Hall.

1900–midnight The possibilities are endless: dinner overlooking the harbour, or on one of the

restaurant-lined streets of Kings Cross and Darlinghurst, or at trendy new Cockle Bay Wharf; cocktails with a view; outdoor live music in The Domain; cinema under the stars; a play at one of dozens of theatres; a cold beer in a pub in The Rocks … the list goes on and on …

2330 The first trickle of tightly trousered butts wends its way to the nightclubs around Oxford St and the CBD.

Of course, life in Australia's cities – and especially Sydney – is lived at a much faster pace than in rural areas. There, socialising is very different – it wasn't *that* long ago that pubs closed at six in the evening. However, there's still a strong sense that enjoyment is all-important, and you'll encounter friendliness and a refreshing lack of pretention almost everywhere you go outside urban areas. Australians are proud of the egalitarianism and classlessness that they claim is still the backbone of the Aussie character. 'Mateship' is another vital part of their make-up, and one of the things that makes travelling in Australia so pleasurable. The locals' instant friendliness is endearing but, be warned, it may take you aback at first.

" *Australia is a weird, big country. It feels so empty and untrodden … even Sydney, which is huge, begins to feel unreal, as if life here really had never entered in: as if it were just sprinkled over and the land lay untouched.* "

D H Lawrence's impression of Australia in the 1920s

This country is informal to a fault, and there's little point in packing anything more than jeans, T-shirts and shorts, and a 'cossie' (swimming costume), unless you're planning to spend most of your time in the swanky restaurants of the big cities. Remember, this is a nation in which *everyone* used to call the head of state 'Bob', and where one of the most famous icons is an 11m-high banana.

Yesterday and tomorrow

Just over 200 years ago, Australia was an untamed wilderness, populated by Aborigines who had lived there undisturbed for around 60,000 years.

In the beginning

The Aborigines existed in nomadic family groups and moved land according to the seasons. Their children were taught from an early age that they belonged to the land. According to Aboriginal legend, powerful spirits created the land and people during the Dreamtime; rock paintings throughout the country depict this period.

The penal colonies

Between 250,000 and 500,000 Aborigines were living a nomadic bush lifestyle when Australia was first settled by Europeans, in 1788. The arrival of the white people was to bring an end to the traditional Aboriginal way of life.

Sitting on Sydney's Campbell's Cove, watching the ferries weave in and out of Circular Quay, it's hard to imagine that just over 200 years ago, the whole area was bushland, populated by indigenous tribes. Eighteen years after Australia's east coast was claimed by **Captain Cook**, Britain decided that the answer to its overcrowded jails lay in a far-flung penal colony.

In 1788, the First Fleet, under the command of **Captain General Phillip**, landed at Sydney Cove with 736 convicts and around 200 marines. The captain, impressed by the deep harbour and good water supply, described Sydney Cove as 'a noble and capacious harbour, equal, if not superior to any known in the world'.

Free settlers began to trickle in from 1793, lured by the promise of cheap land and convict labour. Under the vision of **Governor Macquarie** (1810–21), the colony of New South Wales began to prosper.

Van Diemens Land (Tasmania) was established as a second penal settlement in 1803, followed by settlements on the Brisbane River in 1824, on the Swan River in 1829, on Port Phillip Bay in 1835 and

on Gulf St Vincent in 1836. The capital cities of five
Australian states have grown from these sites.

Exploration and gold

In the 19th century, the urge to explore inland and find new
grazing land opened up the country in all directions. In
1801–3, **Matthew Flinders** circumnavigated Australia and
completed the mapping of the coastline; **Burke
and Wills** were the first Europeans to cross
the continent from south to north, in 1860;
Edward John Eyre crossed the continent
from Streaky Bay in South Australia to
Albany in Western Australia; **Charles Sturt**
discovered the Murray River. In the early
1850s, gold was discovered at a number of
sites across the country, bringing a fresh influx of immigrants
from Europe, China and America. The gold rush was followed
by a building boom and continuing growth of wool and
cattle wealth.

Into the 20th century

Australia was declared a **commonwealth**, a federation of
six founding states, on 1 January 1901. In 1902, it was the
second nation to give women the vote. In the 1920s, 300,000
'Brits' emigrated to Sydney, and the construction of the
Harbour Bridge began. Australia's involvement in the Second
World War was followed by a massive post-war British and
European **immigration boom**. In the 1970s, the Labour
party came to power after an absence of over 20 years.

Today

Australia remains a **federation of states**, with its own
federal parliament based in Canberra. Voting is compulsory
for all citizens aged 18 and over. The Queen of England
currently remains the nominal Head of State, although
the debate on whether to become a full and independent
Republic is gathering momentum.

All state capital cities are built either on or very near water
(even Canberra, although an inland city, is dominated by Lake
Burley Griffin), and Australians embrace a **beach culture**.
Their weekend attire reflects an outdoor lifestyle, so that it's
hard to believe that, at the turn of the 20th century, bathing
in daytime was prohibited on the grounds of public decency.

People and places

Australians are straightforward people who are generally unimpressed by wealth, success or status. Indeed, very successful people are known as 'Tall Poppies', ripe for being chopped down. However, there are a few key movers and shakers who've dared to poke their noses above the parapet.

The media men

Australia was the birthplace of **Rupert Murdoch**, one of the most prolific media moguls in the world. His extensive empire includes the *New York Post*, the English newspapers the *Sun* and *The Times*, the satellite Fox Network and Star TV. He also owns the Los Angeles Dodgers baseball team and tried (and failed) to buy the English football team, Manchester United. His arch rival **Kerry Packer**, who owns an enormous TV and magazine empire, is one of the richest men in Australia.

The creative creatures

Australia has a vibrant arts scene, with many artists, designers, actors and writers gaining inspiration from the country's natural beauty. The current star of the Sydney fashion scene is **Collette Dinnigan**, famed for wispy feminine creations which are popular with celebrities such as Jerry Hall and Paula Yates. Her reputation was assured when Australian supermodel **Sarah O'Hare** commissioned a Dinnigan dress for her marriage to Murdoch's son, **Lachlan**.

Australian artist **Ken Done** has achieved immense commercial success by translating bright, simple images on to everyday objects such as murals, T-shirts and table mats.

> *If you inherit wealth you're lucky. If you accumulate wealth, you're a crook, and if you win a fortune, you're a national hero … When it comes to the crunch there is only one thing the Aussies value – having a good time.* **"**

Ken Hunt,
***The Xenophobe's Guide to the Aussies,* 1993**

In the past, many writers (**D H Lawrence**, **Jack London**, **Rudyard Kipling** among them) visited Australia from overseas. Back in the 1890s, the *Bulletin* was famous for encouraging Australian bushmen to contribute literary offerings about life in the outback. Two of NSW's poets, **Banjo Paterson** (1864–1941), best known for writing the words to *Waltzing Matilda*, and **Henry Lawson** (1867–1922; buried in Waverley Cemetery, Bronte, Sydney), competed with each other through its pages.

Ardent feminist **Miles Franklin** (1879–1954), author of *My Brilliant Career* (1901), is now remembered in the name of the most prestigious literary award in Australia. Equally ardent **Germaine Greer**, who studied at Sydney University, found worldwide fame with her book *The Female Eunuch* (1970). In 1973, **Patrick White** (1912–90) won the Nobel Prize for Literature with *The Eye of the Storm*.

Australian stars of the silver screen include **Nicole Kidman**, who grew up in Sydney, **Mel Gibson**, **Paul Hogan** of *Crocodile Dundee* fame and the latest hot property, actress **Cate Blanchett** (star of *Elizabeth*).

The politicians

Gough Whitlam was the first Labour Prime Minister since 1949 when he came to power in 1972. His government

introduced a programme of social reform such as free university education and a national health system. However, amidst rising inflation and accusations of loan mismanagement, Whitlam's government was sacked in 1975 by the Queen's representative in Australia, the Governor-General, a crisis which is often pinpointed as the catalyst for a serious republican movement. Currently, Australia's Prime Minister is **John Howard** (Liberal), popular with the country's middle classes for his conservative policies and squeaky-clean image, although many feel that he lacks the excitement of his predecessor, the charismatic republican **Paul Keating** (Labour) who was particularly vocal on the subject of Australia becoming a republic. This issue is now high on the agenda again.

Getting around

Although Australia is a vast continent, it is easily explored by plane, rail, coach and car or campervan. The country's transport system evolved rapidly, and it now has excellent long-distance networks. For most travellers, a good option is to hire a car to explore each chosen region, and then to link these regions with a internal flight.

Air

All major airlines fly to Australia, with many using Singapore or Bangkok as a mid-flight stop. Of the domestic airlines – **Qantas** and **Ansett** – Qantas, the world's safest airline, now offers daily Australia–Europe flights. Sydney and Cairns are the most popular entry points, but it worth thinking about starting at Darwin, Perth or Alice Springs, and then proceeding south or east. Internal flights are not cheap, but there are significant discounts for most flights booked 21 days in advance, and special fares for holders of international flight tickets.

Coaches

Major coach companies such as **Greyhound Pioneer** and **McCaffertys** drive daily and nightly between all major cities and are an efficient – if not always comfortable – way of covering long distances quickly and relatively cheaply.

Driving

Australia is ideally suited to car touring by **independent travellers**. There are about 810,000km (503,010 miles) of sealed roads (except in the remote Outback), the road rules are familiar, the driving is safe, and navigation is easy. Far-distant regions can be linked by internal flights, with a car being hired in each one. Alternatively, driving between major destinations – along the coastal Pacific Highway between Sydney and Brisbane, or over the Snowy Mountains and the Alpine Way via Canberra between Sydney and Melbourne – is an invigorating way to see the country.

Victoria: RACV
Tel: 13 1955 (enquiries);
13 1111 (breakdown)

NSW: NRMA
Tel: 13 2132 (enquiries);
13 1111 (breakdown)

Queensland: RACQ
Tel: 13 1905 (enquiries);
13 1111 (breakdown)

Tasmania: RACT
Tel: 13 2722 (enquiries);
13 1111 (breakdown)

538·317
N.T. · OUTBACK AUSTRALIA ·

Western Australia: RACWA
Tel: (08) 9421 4444 (enquiries);
13 1111 (breakdown)

South Australia: RAASA
Tel: (08) 8202 4600 (enquiries);
13 1111 (breakdown)

NT: AANT
Tel: (08) 8981 3837 (enquiries);
13 1111 (breakdown)

For car hire, either go with one of the four major car-rental companies (*Hertz: 1800 550 067 or 133 039*; *Avis: 1800 225 533 or 136 333*; *Budget: 1300 362 848 or 132 727*; *or Thrifty: 1300 367 227*), or look at smaller local companies, whose rates for day hire may be cheaper.

For an extended period of travel, hired campervans are well equipped, and can be parked in camping grounds, national parks and by the roadside. The main rental company is **Britz Australia** (*free call 1800 331 454* or *www.britz.com*). For places off the beaten track, such as the more remote parts of Kakadu, consider hiring a 4-wheel drive (4WD) vehicle. All the major car companies rent out 4WDs, often with the option of hiring camping equipment too.

Camping is a great way to explore the real Australia, and to manage a limited travel budget. In more remote parts of Australia, it is normal to pitch a tent by the side of a road or river for free. In the more settled states of Australia, one of the many camping grounds and caravan parks should be used. Most national parks have serviced campsites; in some of the more popular ones, it is necessary to book in advance. Facilities everywhere are generally good. Guides are available from caravan and camping associations and motoring organisations.

Tips for drivers

- Tourists may drive in Australia with a valid overseas driver's licence.
- Australians drive on the left.
- The maximum speed limit in cities and towns is 60 km/h (35mph) and on country roads and highways 100 km/h (62mph) to 110km/h

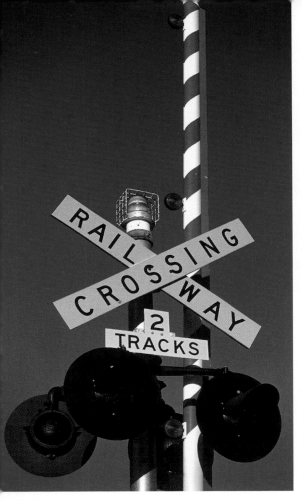

drivers. Thorough preparation is essential. Advise someone of your route, destination and arrival time. Stay on recognised routes and check road conditions and fuel availability before proceeding. Re-fuel whenever possible. Carry two spare tyres, as well as a first-aid kit, spare parts, detailed maps, enough food and water for one extra week (at least 20 litres/5–6 gallons of water per person). In the case of a breakdown, stay with the vehicle, which offers protection from the heat.

● Respect the distances in Australia – plan trips carefully and allow for regular stops. The road-safety authorities have a saying: 'Drowsy Drivers Die'.

(68 mph), unless signs indicate otherwise. In the Northern Territory there is no speed limit on open roads.

● Strict drink-driving laws apply in Australia; police have the right to carry out random breath testing.

● Most roads and highways in Australia are free, with the exception of a few bridges and recently built roads, including the Sydney Harbour Bridge and the new private CityLink tollway system in Melbourne.

● Driving in the immense Outback can be hazardous for inexperienced

Maps

Maps of all parts of Australia can be bought from most major newsagents or bookshops, but a visit to state tourist offices usually yields some good free maps and high-quality brochures. State automobile clubs, which have reciprocal rights for members of major motoring organisation worldwide, give away excellent free regional maps and touring guides.

Public transport in cities

Almost all of the capital cities have excellent bus and train networks, while Melbourne also has its outstanding tram system, and Sydney its entertaining harbour ferries. Most city councils and transport systems operate public transport information booths; day and weekly passes are also available.

Taxis

Metered taxis operate in all major cities and towns; they can be picked up from taxi ranks or hailed in the street, or ordered via the Yellow Pages. Small additional charges are made for luggage and telephone reservations, otherwise the account shows on the meter. Taxi drivers do not expect to be tipped, but appreciate gratuities.

Trains

Australia is served by 40,000km (24,840 miles) of railway lines, in all states except Tasmania. Interstate, there are some exciting journeys: the **trans-continental Indian Pacific**, between Sydney and Perth, includes the world's longest straight stretch of railway – 475 kilometres (297 miles) – across the Nullarbor Plain. The **Ghan** runs between Adelaide and Alice Springs, while the **Orient Express Company** operates a de luxe nostalgia service between Brisbane and Cairns.

Austrail passes, which should be purchased before leaving home, are great value. UK residents should call 01733 502808, or e-mail *railpassdirect@thomascook.com*.

Don't miss

1 Sydney Harbour

Fresh oysters and champagne on the waterfront of Circular Quay, on Sydney Harbour, as the sun goes down, contemplating your BridgeClimb, before heading off to a night of theatre or music under the magical white sails of the Opera House. **Pages 24–7**

2 Wineries

Touring the wineries and gourmet restaurants in the NSW Hunter Valley (**Pages 60–1**), SA's Clare Valley, McLaren Vale or Coonawarra regions (**Pages 172–3**), or in the luscious Margaret River area of WA (**Pages 198–9**).

3 Byron Bay

Climbing to the top of Mount Warning near Byron Bay at dawn, to watch the first rays of the sun strike the continent's most easterly point. Then a quick surf at Byron before an outdoor breakfast. **Pages 69–70**

4 Eating in Melbourne

Breakfast in avant-garde St Kilda or at the Queen Victoria markets, followed by coffee in bustling Brunswick Street, pasta for lunch on Carlton's Lygon St, afternoon tea at the café on the end of elegant St Kilda Pier, and a cheap Vietnamese dinner down Victoria St in Richmond. **Pages 134–6**

5 Great Ocean Road

Two or three days driving along Victoria's spectacular coast road, exploring Cape Otway, the Twelve Apostles, the rugged Shipwreck Coast and the quaint village of Port Fairy, before returning to Melbourne for a couple of days' walking in the Grampians. **Pages 148–9**

6 WA wildflowers

Luxuriating amid millions of wildflowers and blooming native plants in Australia's southwest corner, and revelling in the laid-back atmosphere of WA's surfing towns.
Pages 206–7

7 Fraser Island

Exploring this World Heritage Site near Noosa – swimming in its blue mirror lakes with their clear white sands surrounded by rolling sandhills and giant satinay forests.
Pages 216–17

8 Great Barrier Reef

Snorkelling, sailing and fishing on the Reef and around its coral cays and tropical islands. The sea is unbeatable blue and the fish and corals flash with colour. **Pages 236–7**

9 The Red Centre

Uluru-Kata Tjuta National Park in the Red Centre. Allow three to four days to drive from Alice Springs, preferably in a hired 4WD vehicle equipped with camping gear, to marvel at the real outback of King Canyon, Finke Gorge and the MacDonnell Ranges as well as the awe-inspiring Rock itself.
Pages 240–5

10 The Top End

An adventure week driving through the wild and remote rocky gorge Kimberley country of northern WA and relaxing in the little pearl and beach resort town of Broome. Or outdoor eating at the Mindil Beach Markets under the palm trees in Darwin, before heading off for a tour of Kakadu National Park. **Pages 246–9**

Sydney

Australia's largest city is built around the hills and coves of a brilliant blue harbour that is perpetually dotted with boats. On central Circular Quay, 200 years separate the colonial buildings of The Rocks area and the iconic Sydney Opera House. Today, this lively, vibrant city offers endless possibilities for fun and R&R, both on and off the water.

SYDNEY

BEST OF
Sydney

*Information: Sydney Visitor Centre, 106 George St,
The Rocks.* Tel: (02) 9255 1788.
NSW Tourism: www.tourism.nsw.gov.au

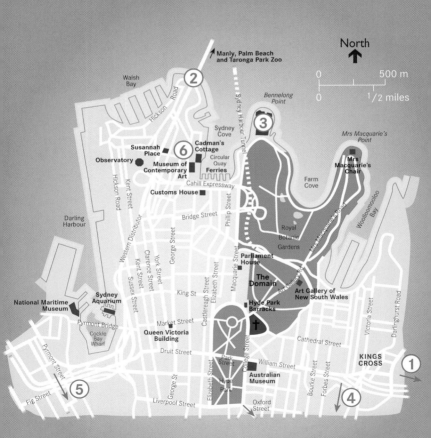

① Bondi to Coogee

The coastal walk from Bondi Beach to Coogee is the ultimate soul-soothing scene – a rugged coastline, clear sky, golden beaches, a profusion of wildflowers and a chance to observe Sydney's city dwellers at play.
Page 28

② The Harbour Bridge

Be sure to walk or cycle across it, take the train or, better still, climb up to the arch's mid-point for a top-of-the-city view. **Pages 26–7**

③ The Opera House

With its white shells reaching up into a blue NSW sky, it's as innately Australian as the kangaroo and the koala. The harbourside walk from this unique symbol of Sydney to Mrs Macquarie's Chair is one of the best in the city. **Pages 50–1**

④ Paddington

Known to Sydneysiders as 'Paddo', this bohemian suburb houses the city's best examples of wrought-iron colonial 'lacework', as well as independent art galleries, a plethora of coffee shops, quirky fashion boutiques and a wonderful Saturday craft market.
Pages 43–4

⑤ Powerhouse Museum

Forget stodgy and staid displays – this vibrant museum puts the fun into the past and present with an interactive kaleidoscope of Australia's social history, triumphs, inventions, transport and more. **Page 39**

⑥ The Rocks

The site of the birth of the Australian nation over 200 years ago, this 19th-century village combines heritage and history with excellent restaurants, great pubs and souvenirs.
Pages 25–6

Getting around

Sydney has a network of inexpensive buses, trains and ferries, detailed on the excellent *Sydney Public Transport Map*. The main terminals for the **Sydney Buses** are at Alfred St by Circular Quay, York St at Wynyard and by the QVB and Elizabeth St (*info kiosks at Circular Quay, QVB, Manly Wharf and Bondi Junction*). In addition, the red **Sydney Explorer** hop-on, hop-off buses take in 24 main sights, from the Opera House to Darling Harbour, while the **Bondi & Bay Explorer** follows a coastal route to Watson's Bay and Bondi. Both depart from Alfred St, Circular Quay. **Ferries** are a fun way to sightsee; all depart from Circular Quay. **Sydney Ferries** also runs good-value harbour cruises (*info: (02) 9207 3170, and opposite wharf 4 at Circular Quay*). The **monorail** is a raised scenic loop linking the city centre with Darling Harbour. **Taxis** are metered, relatively inexpensive, and can be flagged down in the street. **One-day passes** and the weekly **TravelPass**, for unlimited bus, ferry and rail travel, are available from stations, bus kiosks and some newsagents. The three-, five- or seven-day **SydneyPass** offers unlimited travel on Sydney Buses and Ferries and the Explorer buses, plus Sydney Ferries cruises, the JetCat and the CBDCityRail network.

On the waterfront

Circular Quay

The vibrant area around the U-shaped Circular Quay throngs with tourists taking in the splendour of the Opera House (see Profile, pages 50–1), the majestic Harbour Bridge and the sheer beauty of a city that lives so close to the water. If a cool beer at a harbourside café, watching buskers and cosmopolitan crowds, isn't entertainment enough, beautiful gardens, intriguing museums and spectacular colonial buildings are a short walk away.

Sydney ferries

Information line: 131 500. Between 0600–2200 daily.

Circular Quay is the hub for the perpetual to-ing and fro-ing of the basic little green ferries and more modern catamarans used by Sydney commuters. The ferry services also offer visitors one of the best ways to see Sydney, with trips upstream to pretty Balmain and Hunters Hill, across the harbour to Manly (1 hour), Mosman, Taronga Park Zoo, Kirribilli, and towards the open sea to Rose Bay and Watson's Bay, with its famous seafood restaurants. One ferry runs regularly to the Homebush Bay for access to the site for the 2000 Olympic Games. All ferries and catamarans leave from well-marked jetties. Tickets are cheaper in a 'book' of ten.

The Rocks

This is where the First Fleet set foot on Australian soil, way back in 1788, when the shores were home to Aborigines. Today, it's a lively, vibrant area, a beautifully preserved 19th-century village with a labyrinth of streets lined with old sandstone storehouses, historical buildings, colonial hotels and pubs, as well as interesting one-off shops and gourmet restaurants.

Cadman's Cottage Historic Site
National Parks & Wildlife Service

Cadman's Cottage (1816), at 110 George St, is the oldest house in Sydney. It was originally a waterfront cottage for the government's coxswain, although land down to the water has been reclaimed since then. Next door is the **Visitors' Centre**, the main information centre for Sydney and NSW, originally the Sydney Sailors' Home designed to provide cheap, safe accommodation for visiting sailors. Off to the right, at **Campbell's Cove**, you can indulge at one of the excellent waterfront restaurants housed in the beautiful sandstone **Campbell's storehouses**, dating from 1839. They originally stored tea, sugar and cloth imported from India; the pulleys that hauled the cargo up from the docks are still there.

Under the bridge pylons, **Lower Fort St** is an attractive road lined with lacework houses. To the left, on the corner of Windmill St, the **Hero of Waterloo Hotel** has been a favourite drinking hole since 1844. Underneath it is a cellar, where men more than a little the worse for wear would be taken and led to the docks through connecting underground tunnels as extra hands for the ships. At the end of Lower Fort St is the **Garrison Church**, the first military church in Australia, built in 1840 and enlarged by architect Edmund Blacket 15 years later. A right turn takes you to Argyle Place, Sydney's only village green, and a beer at the oldest pub in the city, the **Lord Nelson Hotel** (1842) on Kent St. Turn left through the **Argyle Cut**, hacked out of the sandstone by convicts over a 24-year period from 1843, to go back to the centre of the village. On Harrington St, a flight of steps leads up to the historic houses of **Susannah Place** in Gloucester St (*see below*). The Missionary Steps lead down to **Nurses Walk** where the first makeshift hospitals were set up. At the far end is one of the narrowest streets in the area, **Suez Canal**, which used to be an open sewer running down to the harbour.

Best Rocks Tour

Tue, Thur–Sun, departing 1830. Tel: (02) 9555 2700. $$. History, Convicts and Murder Most Foul … Dressed as a pirate and wielding a cat o'nine tails, ball and chain and lantern, Chris O'Neill walks the Rocks, combining a love of storytelling and drama with factual detail. Tours last 2¹/₂ hours, ending up in the Hero of Waterloo for a spooky finale and a free drink.

Susannah Place

*58–64 Gloucester St. Tel: (02) 9241 1893. Open Sat–Sun 1000–1700. $.
Five-minute walk from Circular Quay station/ferry, Sydney Explorer.*

This row of 1840s working-class terraced houses belonged to Irish immigrants Edward and Mary Riley. They ran the corner shop, renting out the other houses for £26 per year to fellow immigrants. Now a museum, the buildings are a mixture of decorative styles reflecting the different eras of occupancy.

Sydney Harbour Bridge

Second only to the Opera House as the symbol of Sydney, this 503m-long single-arch bridge, 'the coathanger', is an integral part of the city's landscape.

The building of the Harbour Bridge provided so many jobs in Sydney during the years 1923–32 that it was known as the **Iron Lung**. Sixteen people died during its construction – and nine of those were minding their own business on the ground. It provided a welcome alternative to ferry rides and long detours to reach the north shore and today supports eight traffic lanes, bicycle paths and railway lines. The southeast pylon houses the ever-improving Harbour Bridge Museum (*via Cumberland St, Miller Point; tel: (02) 9247 3408; open daily 1000–1700; $*).

Getting there: Circular Quay ferry and station.

In ribbons

Amid much pomp and ceremony, Jack Lang, Premier of New South Wales, was supposed to cut the ribbon to mark the official opening of the Harbour Bridge. However, ardent royalist Francis de Groot galloped up on his horse and slashed the ribbon with his sword in protest because a member of the royal family hadn't been invited to do the honours.

BridgeClimb

5 Cumberland Place, The Rocks. Tel: (02) 9252 0077. Tours daily every 20 minutes. Night climbs Thur–Sat. $$$.

It took Paul Cave, chairman of BridgeClimb, six years and $12 million to overcome all the objections to allowing people to climb to the top of the Harbour Bridge. A harness, a special suit and breath-testing for alcohol levels ensure that the three-hour experience – a mixture of knee-trembling vertigo and total exhilaration – is safe. The views, as far as the **Blue Mountains** in the west, are breathtaking.

Museum of Contemporary Art

Enter from the front at Circular Quay or from George St, The Rocks. Tel: (02) 9252 4033. Open daily 1000–1800. $.

On the water's edge at Circular Quay, the MCA is a cutting-edge establishment in a classic 1930s art-deco building. Contemporary art shows are complemented by related film and lecture series, and the MCA shop, which has some original merchandise. Facing north, so it gets the winter sun, its pleasant café-style restaurant provides plenty of people-watching.

The Great Outdoors

Coastal walks

The coastal walk from **Bondi** to **Clovelly** is spectacular. Populated with power-walkers, joggers, dog-walkers and people just watching the sea, it's a real celebration of outdoor life. Join the path at the southern end of Bondi, which leads

along the coast to **Tamarama** and **Bronte**. After Bronte, take the coastal road through the sandstone cliffs, a favourite spot for rock climbers trying out their techniques. Continue through **Waverley Cemetery**, where there are huge family vaults and graves dating back to the mid-1800s. It's hard to imagine a more idyllic place for eternal rest – on the cliff tops, surrounded by wildflowers, and cooled by the sea breeze. This will lead you to Clovelly and on to **Gordon's Bay**, which has a 620m underwater nature trail marked by chains and drums for divers. After Gordon's Bay, the walk is mostly through suburban streets to the long sweep of pale sand at **Coogee**, where you can enjoy a swim in **Wiley's Baths**, an Olympic-size pool cut into the rocks, or at the secluded women and children only pool.

Rooms with a view

So prized are Sydney's harbour views that no one ever dreamed that developers would manage to secure planning permission for a luxury apartment block just along from the Opera House on East Circular Quay. Amid huge outrage and controversy, the $750 million, 237-apartment project was given the go-ahead in the mid 1990s.

The beautiful 10-km **Manly Scenic Walkway** is one of the best coastal walks in Sydney. It takes in panoramic views of Sydney Harbour, Aboriginal shell middens and suburban city life, pockets of rainforest, native bushland and a myriad of wildflowers and colourful birds. It's a mixture of easy walking and rough, steep slopes with plenty of secluded beaches and bays to refresh yourself along the way. Pick up the *Guide* from the tourist office.

Sydney Harbour National Park

National Parks and Wildlife Service: Cadman's Cottage, The Rocks. Tel: (02) 9555 9844. Open daily 0900–1700. Small fee to visit the islands, and parking meters for cars at all the harbour parks.

Sydney's natural harbour is one of the most glorious in the world. It's the soul of Sydney, creating a feeling of space and freedom right at the heart of the city.

The indented coastline is studded with beautiful coves and secluded bays, doubling up as the city's playground with swimming, windsurfing, yachting and an armada of pleasure cruisers. It's the top spot for watching the annual New Year's Eve **firework bonanza** and the starting point for the fiercely competitive annual **Sydney to Hobart (Tasmania) race**, which leaves from Rushcutter's Bay on Boxing Day.

The Sydney Harbour National Park incorporates the majestic entrance to the harbour (the North and South Heads), natural bushland, secluded sandy beaches, harbour islands and rugged sandstone cliffs, with cosmopolitan Sydney in stark contrast in the background. Several sections of the park are dotted around Sydney Harbour; most are accessible by public transport. Take a water taxi to Shark Island off Rose Bay for a special picnic spot. Nielsen Park on the southern foreshore in Vaucluse is also beautiful for picnics and swimming (shark-netted during summer). South Head provides spectacular views and walks (and wonderful sunsets). Discovery walks, talks and tours are available in all the parks.

Given the spectacular views, it comes as no surprise that the most **prestigious property** clusters around the harbour shores. Areas such as Point Piper, Double Bay and Rose Bay on the south shore and Kirribilli and Mosman on the north shore boast wonderful waterfront dwellings. Rose Bay is the location for the exclusive Royal Sydney

Golf Club, which has a 20-year waiting list; the sea-plane service to Palm Beach operates from here.

The harbour is dotted with tiny islands. The best known is **'Pinchgut' Island**, so called because Captain Phillip would dump prisoners here for a week with very meagre rations. In 1796, convicted murderer Francis Morgan was hanged in chains, and his body left to rot for three years as an *aide-mémoire* to potentially disobedient convicts. The tiny **Fort Denison** was built in the 1850s to protect the city from the distant threat of invasion after the discovery of gold, but a shot has never been fired.

Mrs Macquarie's Chair and The Domain

This sandstone rock on the headland above Farm Cove was fashioned for Governor Macquarie's wife, Elizabeth, soon after the first settlement; she would sit on the rock, surveying the wild, empty harbour, waiting for ships carrying letters to arrive from England. It's now a favourite vantage point to enjoy panoramic views of the Harbour Bridge. The magnificent harbour view north takes in Garden Island, a large naval base. Most of the navy ships are berthed in Woolloomooloo Bay. Further round from Mrs Macquarie's Chair is the superbly located, outdoor **Andrew 'Boy' Charlton Swimming Pool**. Mrs Macquarie's Rd leads to the **Art Gallery of NSW** (*see page 34*) and the public parkland of **The Domain**, where outdoor concerts and opera nights are often held during summer. The Domain is also on the route of the **Sydney Sculpture Walk** (*tel: (02) 9265 9775*), a trail around 20 contemporary artworks by Australian and international artists.

Manly

Information Centre, Ocean Beach, North Steyne, Manly. Tel: (02) 9977 1088; fax: (02) 8966 8123. Open daily 1000–1600.

Manly is a unique part of Sydney, with a wide, pristine ocean beach on one side and a serene, sandy harbour cove on the other. Manly Wharf has an eclectic collection of shops and cafés, and **Oceanworld** (*West Esplanade, Manly Wharf; tel: (02) 9949 2644; open daily 1000–1730; $$*), with its giant underwater aquarium. The colourful **Corso**, with a mixture of shops and restaurants, links the harbour side of Manly to the ocean. Pick up some fish and chips and head for the promenade along the beach and beneath an avenue of Norfolk Pines heading north.

Famous for its fabulous surf, Manly was the first beach in Sydney to allow surfing and daylight swimming, in 1903. Nearly three-quarters of a century later, liberalism triumphed again when the first legal topless and nude beach was established at **Reef Beach**, on the way to the Spit. Today a host of **surf competitions** and **life-saving carnivals** (January) take place at Manly Beach, as well as **volleyball championships** (January), and the **Ironman** and **Ironwomen Championships** (February).

Palm Beach

The most northern of the Sydney beaches, this wonderful terracotta stretch of sand is the backdrop for the Australian TV soap *Home and Away*. Well known as a playground for the rich and famous, it's a big holiday-home area, with wealthy families building million-dollar houses, which they occupy for just a couple of weeks a year. The **Pittwater** inlet to the west is a great spot for cruising, boating and fishing.

The Palm Beach Ferry Service (*tel: (02) 9918 7247*) runs hourly from Palm Beach wharf to The Basin, where there is a 2.8-km walk through scrubland and forest, past a site of Aboriginal rock engravings.

No to *Baywatch*

Avalon beach, a glorious stretch of sand a few kilometres south of Palm Beach, was top choice for American TV series Baywatch. *Despite support from NSW Premier Bob Carr, locals protested that it would cause traffic congestion and infringe on their freedom to use the beach, and sent all those bronzed bods to film elsewhere.*

Back to nature

Royal Botanic Gardens

Mrs Macquarie's Rd. Tel: (02) 9231 8111. Open daily 0800–1700 in winter, to 2000 in summer. Visitors' centre (maps, books, self-guide audio tours) open 0930–1630. Guided walks daily at 1030, except public holidays. Martin Place/Circular Quay station, Sydney Explorer, Bus 438.

The exceptional views and beautiful walks are reason enough to visit these gardens. Keen gardeners will be thrilled by the variety of 7 500 plants, some so rare they have to be locked in a cage. It's also the setting for a series of evening classical concerts around the end of November, beginning of December. The best way to explore is on foot, but a trackless train with a commentary runs every 15 minutes from the visitors' centre. The **Tropical Centre** (*open daily 1000–1600; $*) is a glass pyramid housing native plants from misty mountains and distant rainforests. The neighbouring glass arc houses non-native exotic species. The nearby **Fernery** (*open daily 1000–1600*) is home to subtropical, warm and cool temperate climate ferns from all over the world, whilst the shady **Palm Grove** has the rarest palm collection in the world, with over 180 species. The central lake supports a variety of birdlife including the native Australian ibis bird.

Wollemi pine

The rare Wollemi pine specimen in the botanic garden is one of only 38 trees known in the wild, and is rare enough to be kept in a cage. It was thought to be extinct until 1994, when it was discovered in an almost impenetrable sandstone gorge in Wollemi National Park, 150km northwest of Sydney.

Sydney Aquarium

Aquarium Pier, Darling Harbour. Tel: (02) 9262 2300; fax (02) 9290 3553. Open daily 0900–2200. $$. Monorail: Darling Park station, Sydney Explorer, walk from city centre down Market St, ferry/charter boat from Circular Quay to Aquarium Pier, train to Town Hall station.

Fascinating displays of all that's weird and wonderful in the world beneath the sea combine with hands-on rock pools and underwater walkways to make this an exciting trip for any age. The newest oceanarium, **Jewels of the Great Barrier Reef**, which allows you to stand nose (to glass) to nose with sharks, stingrays, sea turtles and a host of brightly coloured tropical fish is spectacular, but check out the **Sydney Harbour Oceanarium**, seal sanctuary and crocodile pool too.

Taronga Park Zoo

Bradleys Head Rd, Mosman. Open daily 0900–1700, with some twilight openings in January. $$.

Some of the 3 000 animals in Taronga Zoo have the best views in the world, looking across Sydney Harbour towards the Opera House. Located on the edge of the North Shore, the zoo has an extensive collection of Australian animals, including koalas, kangaroos, echidnas, dingoes, Tasmanian Devils and the nocturnal possums, all in spacious, leafy environments. During the day there are various keeper talks, plus feeding, seal shows and koala encounters. The free flight bird show is a spectacular display of birds flying over the Harbour.

Getting there: Ferry to Taronga Zoo, Bus 247. Aerial safari ride (cable car) to the top. A good-value Zoo Pass ticket (available at Circular Quay ferry) includes return ferry and bus trips, zoo admission and the cable car.

Historic & cultural Sydney

Art Gallery of New South Wales

The Domain. Tel: (02) 9225 1744. Open daily 1000–1700. Admission to special exhibitions $, general collection free.

This wonderful gallery is the sort of place you can dip in and out of – it's free, well laid out and knowledgeable volunteers run excellent guided tours. It is housed in a superb sandstone building, overlooking **The Domain** parkland and the **Royal Botanic Gardens**. Its strength lies in its 19th- and 20th-century **Australian collection**, with some good European works and the interesting **Yiribana Gallery** of Aboriginal and Torres Strait Islander art.

Australian highlights: There are several excellent examples of **colonial art** in which the artists are strongly influenced by London's painting styles – the works of **John Glover**, who arrived in Australia in 1832, show the clarity of light in the southern hemisphere.

Among the Australian **Impressionist** paintings is the famous *Shearing at Newstead (The Golden Fleece)* by **Tom Roberts**, a tribute to the men who worked so hard to create an industry. **Frederick McCubbin** was best known for his depiction of the textures of the Australian bush, as in his painting *On the Wallaby Track* (1896).

Brett Whiteley was among the most famous of Australian contemporary artists, famed for his match sculpture representing old and new Australia on the edge of The Domain. One of his most attractive paintings is *Balcony 2*, a view of Sydney Harbour at night painted from Lavender Bay.

Yiribana Gallery: this is a lovely airy gallery on the lower floor. Highlights include the atmospheric **Pukumani** grave posts, in which carved forms and painted motifs represent the transition between life and death. There's also a fine collection of heads painted on sandstone.

The Art Gallery of NSW also hosts touring blockbuster exhibitions and shows, and has a courtyard **café**, **restaurant** and **shop**.

Australian Museum

Founded in 1827 as a natural history showcase, today it's a museum with a mission – to help people understand the impact humans have on the natural environment. A mixture of the fascinating and the forgettable.

A guided tour helps visitors make sense of the **bird, spiders and reptile collection**, the **human evolution** displays, and the **Albert Chapman** collection of over 67,000 minerals, rocks and meteorites. The museum's newest collection, **Biodiversity**, is an interactive display to help people understand the interdependency between plants, animals and humans.

'Eric' the **opalised pliosaur**, a fast-swimming marine predator over 110 million years old, was delivered to the museum as a box of bones. A radio appeal easily raised the half a million dollars needed to buy him. Children will also enjoy the 130-million-year-old, 9m-long **Afrovenator**, discovered in Africa in 1993.

The excellent **Aboriginal section** offers fascinating insights into indigenous culture, documenting the Aborigines' close relationship with the land. Particularly interesting are the personal video testimonies from the 'stolen generation' – from the Second World War to 1969, the government separated Aboriginal children from their parents and placed them with white families, so that they could learn to think and act 'white'.

Getting there: 6 College St. Tel: (02) 9320 6000. Open daily 0930–1700. Tours on the hour 1000–1500 Mon–Fri, 1100–1300 Sun. $$. Martin Place station, Bus 311/12, 441, Sydney Explorer.

" *If you want to use a hard term to describe the impact that removal of Aboriginal children from Aboriginal families has had – attempted cultural genocide is a good phrase.* **"**

Carol Kendal, *Indigenous People and the Law*, 1995

Customs House

Alfred St, Circular Quay. Tel: (02) 9247 2285. Open daily 0930–1700. $.
Circular Quay rail, ferry and bus station. Something for everyone in this
architecturally superb building. Galleries, hands-on exhibitions, great views,
cafés, bar.

Fronting the Circular Quay area, **Customs Square**, the entrance to Customs House, is a piece of history. Paving in the square depicts the original tidal zone as it was at the time of the First Fleet landing, long before the construction of the quay itself. The imposing **Customs House** has undergone a number of transformations, both inside and out, since it was built in 1885. The first customs collection point in NSW, it was constructed on the land of the traditional owners, the Eora People. Five floors built around a stunning glass atrium house some of Sydney's best art exhibitions, history displays, art and craft shops and eating places.

Djamu Gallery on the second floor is the Australian Museum's new indigenous and Pacific Island gallery, with a fabulous collection of art (*open daily 0930–1700*). In the **Object Galleries** (*open daily 1000–1600*) the Centre of Contemporary Craft showcases innovative contemporary craft, design and 3D art through its galleries on the ground and third floors. The fourth floor serves as an information centre about **Sydney's urban development**. On display is a permanent model of Sydney, including buildings that are yet to be built. **Café Sydney** (*$$*) on the fifth floor has some of the best views of the bridge and the harbour.

Convict labour

Lachlan Macquarie's governorship of 1810–21 was a turning point for the penal colony of New South Wales. He was an even-handed man who saw in Australia a world of opportunity rather than just a dumping ground for unwanted Brits. His vision was to create a prosperous colony populated by emancipated convicts rehabilitated through work and rewards. To this end, he began an extensive building programme of public institutions constructed by convict labour.

Hyde Park Barracks

Queen's Square, Macquarie St. Open daily 0930–1700. $$.

Considered to be among the finest works of the convict architect **Francis Greenway**, these beautiful buildings were originally conceived as convict barracks from 1819–48. During the latter half of the 19th century, the building housed an immigration depot for women, then courts and legal offices. Refurbished in 1990, Hyde Park Barracks is now a museum about its various occupants over 180 years.

Among the displays there are interesting personal histories of women who emigrated to the colony from Britain and Ireland to balance the male population. There's a fascinating display of material discovered under the floorboards during renovation in the 1980s, which had been stored away by rats. Upstairs is a convict dormitory plus a convict database where you can check for any dodgy ancestors.

National Maritime Museum

Murray Street, Darling Harbour. Tel: (02) 9552 7777. Open daily 0930–1700. $$. Sydney Light Rail: Pyrmont Bay, Monorail: Harbourside, Sydney Explorer, Bus 456.

This indoor and outdoor museum gives an insight into how the sea has shaped life in Australia. The leisure gallery examines aspects of Aussie beach culture, with quirky exhibitions about the 1930s seaside battles over skimpy swimsuits alongside boats that have made history such as Ken Warby's *Spirit of Australia*. It broke the world speed record in 1977 and again in 1978; it still stands, at 511.11km/h.

The Passenger exhibition recalls the experiences of people who made the journey to Australia by sea, in luxury, as penniless immigrants and as desperate refugees. Voice recordings, diary snippets, personal mementoes, letters and clothing evoke the courageous – and sad – adventures of travellers from the convict era to the Indo-Chinese boat people of modern times.

SYDNEY

Observatory

Observatory Hill. Tel: (02) 9217 0485. Open weekdays 1400–1700, weekends 1000–1700. $. Planetarium show at weekends at 1130 and 1530.

Built in 1858, the Sydney Observatory offers spectacular views of the harbour to the west of the bridge, and is a great spot to stop and rest for a quiet hour in the sun, the bustle of the city just a quiet hum in the background. It is now used as a museum of astronomy, with planetarium shows at weekends.

Parliament House

Macquarie St. Open Mon–Fri 0930–1600. Free guided tours run at 1000, 1100 and 1400.

The magnificent colonnaded building (1816) which houses the legislative assemblies of New South Wales was once a wing of the neighbouring convict-built Sydney Hospital, known as the 'Rum Hospital' because it was built on the

proceeds of rum importation and resale. A visit here is informal and a guided tour will help you understand the intricacies of state government. If Parliament is in session, you might catch a combative question time.

The highlight of the building is the spectacular book-lined **Jubilee Room**, built in 1905 as the main reading room of the Parliamentary Library. It has a beautifully ornate stained-glass window, as well as displays and photographs tracing the history of the building and Parliament since 1770. In the front lobby are the opal-encrusted scissors used by **Jack Lang**, the Premier of New South Wales, to cut the ribbon on the opening of Sydney Harbour Bridge in 1932 (*see pages 26–7*).

Powerhouse Museum

Harris St. Tel: (02) 9217 0111. Open daily 1000–1700. $$. Free highlight tours daily at 1330 (also 1115 at weekends), book at the counter on level 4. Haymarket Monorail/Sydney Light Rail, Sydney Explorer, Bus 501.

This fun interactive museum housed in a former power station is positively uplifting. It's a genuine something-for-everyone museum, an eclectic mix of social history with transport, space, technology and decorative arts thrown in.

Its exhibits include a 1928 Bugatti motor car, a full-sized Catalina flying boat, a spacesuit worn by one of the Apollo 13 team and a replica 1930s art-deco cinema (with interior fittings from the QVB), while interactive displays on award-winning Australian designs range from the frivolous to the essential.

Among the engineering displays, **Locomotive No 1**, built in England in 1854 by Robert Stephenson, pulled the first passenger train into Sydney a year later. The **Boulton & Watt steam engine** is the oldest surviving rotative steam engine in the world. It dates from 1784 and worked the malt grinder at the Whitbread Brewery in London for over 100 years, the first machine to replace people in industry. Regular demonstrations are given throughout the day.

See and be seen

Bondi and the beaches

This big sweep of golden sand has been the focus of Aussie beach culture for over 100 years. Whatever bad publicity Bondi might have received for its drugs culture and loutish tourists drinking in the sun, it's still a stunning sight.

Once the domain of the working classes, today **Bondi**'s atmosphere is cosmopolitan, with upmarket restaurants and trendy shops. Frequented by locals and backpackers, and home to a large immigrant community, it's a tableau of outdoor living with tanned torsos heading surfwards and micro bikinis flouting the 'safe tanning' rules. Topless bathing is tolerated around South Bondi – a change from the 1960s when beach inspectors measured women's bikinis to check that their bottom halves conformed to the four-inch rule.

Tamarama Beach: a 20-minute walk from Bondi, this attractive sandy cove is nicknamed 'Glamarama' because of its popularity with beautiful people, particularly handsome men and body-conscious gays. When the wind's blowing in the right direction, it's a top surfing spot.

Bronte Beach: nicknamed 'the thinking man's Bondi' because it tends to attract creative types – actors, writers and several celebs. It's also a popular family spot with a convenient swag of cafés just over the road. *Bus 378 from Oxford St.*

Clovelly Beach: the least beautiful of the five beaches, it's good for novice swimmers as it's more like a creek. It's an excellent area for snorkellers (look out for giant groper) and for those who live in fear of being coshed on the head by a surfboard – surfing is banned for most of the day. *Bus 339 from Circular Quay.*

Coogee: a few kilometres south of Bondi, similar in atmosphere (with less ferocious surf), but not so crowded. This beach tends to be a backpackers' hang-out and, consequently, pretty lively in the evenings, with busy pubs selling schooners of beer at knock-down prices. *Buses 373, 374 from Circular Quay, train to Bondi Junction then 314 or 315.*

Getting there: Train to Bondi Junction then/or bus 380, 382 or 389 from Circular Quay, Bondi & Bay Explorer. Craft and second-hand market Sun.

Kings Cross

Kings Cross station, Bus 311, 333 or both Sydney Explorer buses.

Kings Cross is an 'in yer face' area of Sydney, famed for its dusk-till-dawn nightlife, excellent restaurants and bars and seedy red-light district. At night time, neon bosoms and bottoms light up Darlinghurst Rd while broad-shouldered bouncers shout out the merits of their 'adult shows'.

> " *I would stay [in the Cross] briefly on visits from Melbourne in the late 60s – it was a tapestry of rock and roll, flared clothes, underground publications, communal experiments and being kind to each other over sitar music and herbal tea.* "
>
> **Graeme Blundell, actor, writer and director,** *Places in the Heart*

However, it's not all tack. The area boasts some fabulous late-1800s architecture, and just a short walk from the sleazy 'Strip' – along Bayswater Rd and Victoria St – are some of the best restaurants Sydney has to offer, offering all styles of cuisine.

Oxford St

Museum station, then/or Bus 378, 380, 382 or L82 up Oxford St.

Oxford St is central to Sydney's gay scene, a colourful area of outrageous transvestites and taut T-shirted muscle men. It's a focal point for the month-long gay and lesbian **Mardi Gras** in February, which has been commemorating the Greenwich Village Stonewall Riots since 1978. The festival culminates here in a 600,000-strong parade of feather boas, sequins, glitter and glamour, which takes three hours to snake its way from Hyde Park to the Old Showground. In recent years, Mardi Gras organisers have had to struggle to keep it a celebration of gay rights rather than a funky free-for-all. During the rest of the year, some Oxford St nightclubs such as **DCM** (*31–33 Oxford St*) are all things to all people, with strong links in the gay community, but still attracting a partly heterosexual crowd; others, such as the **Beauchamp Hotel** (*267 Oxford St*), **Midnight Shift** (*85 Oxford St*) and the dragshow hotspot, the **Albury Hotel** (*6 Oxford St*), are exclusively gay.

Paddington

Paddington, at the far end of Oxford St, is a mixture of the bohemian, arty and relentlessly trendy. It's the hub of the city's fashion industry and home to many local artists. This, along with its excellent Saturday market, makes it the ultimate browse-and-buy area.

While Oxford St has variety, colour and character, a meander off into the side roads displays a prettier side of Paddington with some of Sydney's best examples of 1900s lacework (elaborate wrought-iron) balconies.

43

A walking tour of Paddington

Although Paddington was originally one of the slummiest areas of Sydney, a stroll around the beautiful back streets shows why it's now one of Sydney's most desirable addresses.

Paddington's terraces

Paddington's terraces were constructed by small-time builders who bought plots of land at auction, built a house for their family, then another one to let. The elaborate lacework on the façades was an exercise in one-upmanship. To give the impression of opulence, they competed with each other, adding ever more ornate ironwork and extravagant tiling and plasterwork.

Head down **Glenmore Rd**, past some lovely lacework iron balconies to **Liverpool St**, well known for its long rows of Victorian terraces and more lacework. Turn right into **Spring St**, then left into **Prospect St** and **Gipps St**. These are the oldest streets in Paddington with single-storey brick houses and two-storey, four-room dwellings built in the

1840s to house the workers who were building the Victoria Barracks. A right turn into **Shadforth St** takes you past buildings with corrugated-iron roofs and offers a good view over the convict-built Victoria Barracks.

Walk along Oxford St to the **Town Hall** (1891), with its arches and balustraded balconies. It now houses a theatre, cinema and library. On the other side of the road on the corner of **Ormond St** is the ornate **Post Office** (1885) and **Juniper Hall**, the oldest example of a Georgian villa in Australia. Completed in 1824, it was built by convict settler Robert Cooper, a distiller publican and self-confessed smuggler. He named the house after the berries used to distil his gin.

Festival!

Sydney likes to enjoy itself: in January, the Sydney Festival is a month-long arts jamboree; in February, the month-long gay and lesbian Mardi Gras culminates in the famous parade and all-night party; in May, the Writers' Festival attracts Australian and international writers; June's Film Festival is hosted by the State Theatre; in August, thousands of fun-runners jostle their way from the Town Hall to Bondi in the City to Surf Run; for three weeks in September, multicultural music and dance is celebrated throughout NSW in Carnivale, and on the second Sunday, kite fliers take over Bondi for the Festival of the Winds; Manly's huge international Jazz Festival is a major celebration in October.

Turn down Ormond St. Between 56a and 56b, there's a small fragment of a Georgian mansion, called **Engerhurst**, which was built in 1835.

Take a right turn into **Olive St**, where you can just see an early colonial home dating from 1869 above the drawings of a children's nursery. Follow the road down to the **Five Ways** roundabout, the hub of village life, with the lovely **Royal Hotel** (1888) with cast-iron balconies. Head straight over into Gurner St, then right into **Cascade St**, which is lined by beautiful 1880s two-storey terraces. Turn left into the lacework-decorated **Hargrave St**, then right into Elizabeth St. A right turn takes you into **Underwood St**, named after Thomas Underwood, a convict from the First Fleet who sold the land granted to him and headed back to Britain a richer man. Underwood St is intersected by **William St** – take a detour here to quirky shops or pop in for a beer at the attractive blue and white **London Tavern** (1875) on the corner of Underwood St and William St. Finally, you'll come out at Paddington Inn on the corner of Oxford St.

Getting there: Museum station, then/or Bus 378, 380, 382 or L82 up Oxford St.

Queen Victoria Building

Cnr George St and Market St. Guided tours leave from information desk, daily 1130 and 1430. Tel: (02) 9264 9209. Town Hall station, many buses including 431–8.

The **Queen Victoria Building (QVB)**, built in the 1890s to replace the original Sydney markets, is an architectural gem with a domed roof and cupolas. It's currently home to over 190 individual shops built into ornate archways. It hasn't always been a prized historical building. In 1963, the original cupolas were sold for scrap and, by the 1980s, it was earmarked for demolition. A Malaysian company stepped in and restored it. Turn-of-the-century features include a beautiful stained-glass cartwheel window and original mosaic floors. Gallery 2 contains royal 'curios' such as a hanging royal clock with moving British monarchs, a replica of the British Crown Jewels and a tableau of Queen Victoria's coronation in 1838.

The QVB

With a biting recession squeezing Sydney's craftsmen at the end of the 19th century, the Romanesque architecture of the QVB was deliberately elaborate in order to provide jobs for the unemployed stonemasons, plasterers and stained-glass window artists.

Eating and drinking

Pavilion on the Park
1 Art Gallery Rd. Tel: (02) 9232 1322. Café open daily 0900–1700. $$. Restaurant, lunch Sun–Fri, dinner Thur–Sat. $$$. The pleasant outdoor café serves delicious brunch-style food all day, plus wonderful coffee and cakes. The excellent restaurant alongside is floor-to-ceiling glass with a view over The Domain, serving modern Australian dishes.

Cockle Bay Wharf
Darling Park monorail, Town Hall station. The latest 'in' place for Sydney's body beautifuls to hang out for dinner with harbourside views.

The historical **Campbell's Storehouses** in **The Rocks** house an array of superb waterfront restaurants, from Chinese to modern Australian (*all $$$*).

Philip's Foote
101 George St. Tel: (02) 9241 1485. Open daily lunch and dinner. $$. Located in the heart of The Rocks, with a lovely leafy garden, dinner here is do-it-yourself – pile on the salad, then pick your prime cut and head off to the communal barbecue.

Beluga on Oxford Street
340 Oxford St. Open daily 1030–2100. $. Pick any freshly caught creature of the sea and they will cook it for you, to take away with chips or salad.

La Mensa
257 Oxford St. Tel: (02) 9332 2963. Open Mon–Thur 1100–2200, Fri 1100–2300, Sat 0900–2300, Sun 0900–2200. $$. Aromatic Italian dishes are served at long communal metal tables to trendy young things about town. Or opt for an antipasto take-away from the fabulous adjoining deli. Visit the adjoining contemporary photography gallery too (*open Tue–Sun 1100–1800*).

Micky's
268 Oxford St. Open daily 0900–2400. $$. The sunny garden is great for a lunchtime bagel, or a robust dinner of sausages, mash and onion gravy.

Venice Beach
3 Kellett St. Tel: (02) 9326 9928. Open daily till late. $. A couple of minutes' walk from the Cross, decent dinners are served for a tiny fistful of dollars on the glorious candlelit garden terrace.

La Galerie
The Corso, Manly. $. Large food court serving a range of take-aways, including Indian, seafood, sushi and health food.

Bondi Tratt
34b Campbell Parade, Bondi. Tel: (02) 9365 4303. Open daily for breakfast, lunch and dinner. Licensed and BYO. $$. Always busy, so you need to book. Delicious dishes range from roasted tomato risotto with parmesan and rocket to pork and pistachio nut sausages, with a choice of lively indoor atmosphere or a backdrop of the starry night sky.

Doyles, Watson's Bay
Ferry to Watson's Bay, Doyle's water taxi from Circular Quay (weekday lunchtimes only), Bus L24, 324, 325, Bondi & Bay Explorer. Picturesque Watson's Bay is famous for its long-established fish restaurant, **Doyles**, of which there are now three variations. The original restaurant, Doyle's on the Beach, founded in 1885, attracts a mixed crowd for its mouth-watering seafood dishes. Doyles on the Wharf offers a similar menu. For speed and economy, there's an adjoining take-away fish and chip shop. The views of the city are wonderful.

Doyle's on the Beach
Tel: (02) 9337 2007. Open daily lunch and dinner. $$$.

Doyles on the Wharf
Tel: (02) 9337 1572. Open Wed–Sat, lunch and dinner, Mon and Tue evenings in Jan. $$$.

Cafés

Art Gallery Café
Art Gallery of NSW, Art Gallery Rd. Open daily 0900–1700. $. Dainty light lunches served on a beautiful flower-filled terrace overlooking Sydney. A lovely place to linger over a book or newspaper.

The Chocolate Factory
8 Elizabeth St. Open daily until 1700. $. This quaint café serves up spectacular sandwiches and biscuits with a home-cooked twist.

Café Brioni
Cnr Paddington market. Open daily 0700–1800. $$. It's bursting at the seams on Saturday, with customers enjoying the bands busking nearby over an all-day breakfast or speciality sandwich.

Belly Dance Café
210 Oxford St. Open Wed–Sun 0900–1800. $. John serves up *focaccia* melts, fabulous lemon meringue and chocolate cake; wife Rosalind gives belly-dancing lessons. Chill out over a light lunch in the wonderful back garden.

Tropicana
227b Victoria St, Darlinghurst. Open 0500–2400. $. The original formica café, famed for its huge portions, value for money and colourful clientele. Popular for early morning frothy coffee and late-night pastas by the mega bowlful.

The Strand Mall on Pitt St has some excellent cafés – try the olde-worlde **Harris Coffee Shop**, the **Strand Café** for light lunches, or **The Olive Italian Food Bar** for take-away sandwiches with a fabulous choice of breads.

Greens Eatery
1–3 Sydney Rd, just off the Corso, Manly. Open daily 0800–1800. $. A super-wholesome lentil, rissole and rice café. Eat in or take away. There's a little terrace outside for newspaper perusing.

Late-night snacking

Pie, peas and chilli dogs, anyone? Those in the know head to a Sydney institution, **Harry's Café de Wheels** (*Cowper's Wharf Rd, Woolloomooloo Bay*), where Harry has been serving the drunk and the famous from his take-away van since 1945. Open 0730 until the wee hours, it's plastered with pics of celebrities who've joined his colourful clientele.

Boozing and bands

The Rocks is home to many British-style pubs: the **Lord Nelson** (*cnr Kent St and Argyle St*) the **Hero of Waterloo** (*81 Lower Fort St*), and, on George St, the **Mercantile Hotel**, the **Fortune of War** and the **Orient**. Most pubs in The Rocks have live bands on Sunday afternoons, and often on Friday and Saturday nights.

Shopping

The Rocks is famed for its opals and souvenir shops – try **Designed and Made: Contemporary Arts and Crafts** (*cnr George St and Playfair St*) and **Australian Craftworks** (*127 George St*) for contemporary ceramics and arty souvenirs, **Flame Opals** (*119 George St*) for unset or mounted gems. For a bargain, head to level two at **Market City** for big-name factory outlets.

Paddington market
Cnr Newcombe St and Oxford St. Saturday 1000–1600. Paddington's craft market is a commercial outlet for some of Sydney's most innovative contemporary designers.

Pitt St shopping malls

Centrepoint Shopping Centre: clothing, costume jewellery and real gems. The Wilderness Society Shop has books on bushwalking, didgeridoo CDs and Aboriginal artefacts.

Skygarden for upmarket fashion, homewares and fabulous roof-garden food court.

The Strand for Victorian architecture, fancy boutiques and jewellery, and **Strand Hatters** for the best bush hats.

David Jones: Sydney's premier department store.

For 'Australiana' souvenirs, head to the **QVB** (*cnr George St and Market St*). Check out **Blue Gum Designs** for Aboriginal artefacts, **Best of Australiana** for quality souvenirs, and **Heaven & Earth** for creative, humorous paintings and prints.

Sydney Opera House

Billed as the eighth wonder of the world, Sydney Opera House, with its grand white sails, is the internationally recognised symbol of Sydney.

Bennelong Point, the site of this unique building, is historically significant. In January 1788, Captain Arthur Phillip began to set up Sydney's first farm nearby, in what are now the Royal Botanical Gardens. Phillip soon befriended an Aboriginal called Bennelong, and had a dwelling built for him on the point. Bennelong's hut became something of a social centre for the Aborigines who frequented the settlement. In March 1791, Bennelong Point hosted its first-ever concert, when Bennelong provided an evening of Aboriginal song and dance for the Governor and his party.

Unhappy architects

The Sydney Opera House was designed by a Danish architect, **Jørn Utzon**, who beat the opposition from 233 contenders in a 1957 design competition. The public's unenthusiastic response to an appeal for funds led to the setting up of the Australian lottery, in order to cover the estimated $7 million needed.

Inspiration

According to legend, Utzon's idea for the unique design of the Opera House came from a pile of orange peel.

Building started in 1959, yet the complexity of the design and resulting engineering problems meant that the building took 14 years and sent costs spiralling to a final total of $102 million. Utzon stormed away from the project in 1966 over a disagreement over his fees and preferred suppliers. When the building opened in 1973, the grandeur of the outside, clad in over a million tiny tiles, outshone the less imaginative interior.

Modern-day theatre

The Opera House is one of the busiest performing art centres in the world, hosting around 3 000 events a year for two million visitors. It's a labyrinth of nearly 1 000 rooms comprising 60 dressing rooms and five rehearsal studios. Of the five main theatres, the largest, the **Concert Hall**, with seating for over 2 600 people, lends itself to musical events. The **Opera Theatre**, under the largest 'shell', tends to show performances of ballet, dance and, of course, opera. **The Studio** was opened in 1999 for the production of experimental and contemporary arts.

Walk around the front of this extraordinary building for unencumbered views of the Harbour and the Harbour Bridge. A café on the front promenade is a perfect place to soak up the ambience of the harbour.

In the wings

For a first-hand insight to how the scenery rises up from under the stage in the Opera Theatre, or how the light and sound booths operate in the Drama Theatre, take the Opera House's backstage tour. Tours (for ages 12 plus) run on selected mornings, depending on who is rehearsing what. Tel: (02) 9250 7250 for information. $$$.

Getting there: Bennelong Point, Circular Quay station, then walk east along the harbour, Sydney Explorer, Bus 438. Opera House Information, tel: (02) 9250 7111. Box office, tel: (02) 9250 7777, open Mon–Sat 0900–2030, or Ticketek, (02) 9266 4800. Hour-long guided tours of the theatres and foyers run continuously between 0900–1600, from the lower concourse. $$.

West and north of Sydney

Head west from Sydney to the Blue Mountains for a wander around spectacular sandstone gorges. Or meander north up to the lush green vineyards of the Hunter Valley to taste superb wines over a gourmet lunch. Further up the coast, spot some dolphins at Port Stephens before carrying on up the Pacific Coast Highway to discover eucalyptus forests, the banana port of Coffs Harbour and the surfing paradise of Byron Bay.

BEST OF

West and north of Sydney

Getting there from Sydney: *For organised day trips to the* ***Blue Mountains*** *and the* ***Hunter Valley:*** ***ATS*** *(* tel: (02) 9555 2700 *);* ***AAT Kinga*** *(* tel: (02) 9252 2788 *);* ***Murrays*** *(* tel: 13 2251 *).*

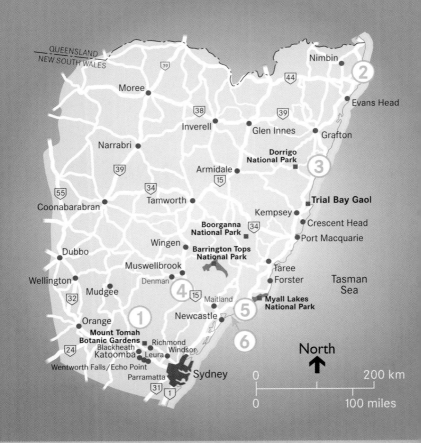

QUEENSLAND
NEW SOUTH WALES

Nimbin

39

44

2

Moree

Evans Head

38

39

Inverell

Glen Innes

Grafton

Narrabri

Dorrigo National Park

3

39

Armidale

15

Trial Bay Gaol

55

34

Tamworth

Kempsey

Crescent Head

Coonabarabran

34

Port Macquarie

Boorganna National Park

Wingen

Barrington Tops National Park

Dubbo

Muswellbrook

Taree

Wellington

Denman

Forster

Tasman Sea

Mudgee

4

15

Maitland

32

Myall Lakes National Park

5

Orange

1

Newcastle

Mount Tomah Botanic Gardens

6

24

Richmond

Blackheath

Windsor

North

Katoomba

Leura

Wentworth Falls / Echo Point

Parramatta

Sydney

0   200 km

31

1

0   100 miles

① Blue Mountains

Even if you 'don't do walking', the only way to get a true feel for the vast wilderness of the Blue Mountains is on foot. Head to Echo Point or Govetts Leap (Blackheath) to choose from 20-minute strolls to several hour-long hikes. Top choices: the Prince Henry Cliff walk and Pulpit's Rock.
Pages 56-9

② Byron Bay

The tourist literature claims that Byron Bay is 'one of the few places in the world where you can sit amongst native wildflowers and grasses on the edge of the rainforest and listen to a whale breathe'. When there's no wind, that's true. What more incentive do you need to visit this laid-back, surfing mecca of the north coast?
Pages 69-70

③ Coffs Harbour, Bellingen and Dorrigo

Nothing can prepare you for the abundance of fish life in the underwater paradise that surrounds the Solitary Islands in the marine reserve by **Coffs Harbour**. If you want to swim with the sharks, this is your chance. The sleepy little town of **Bellingen** makes you want to sit on a wall, kicking your heels and dreaming. The World Heritage rainforest of **Dorrigo** is one of the most rewarding national parks to visit, with vine-strewn trails over cascading falls and views over the lush Bellinger Valley. **Pages 68, 71-2**

④ Hunter Valley

Family-run, city-slick, spit-and-sawdust … Hunter Valley's vineyards are as varied as the wines themselves, so sip your Shiraz, swirl the Chardonnay and find out for yourself why NSW wines account for 21 per cent of Australia's exported wine. For an entertaining tour, head to Tyrells; for informative and generous wine tasting, choose Rosemount. **Pages 60-1**

⑤ Port Stephens

If your only experience of dolphins is in a tank at the zoo, enjoy the true beauty of these sleek intelligent animals roaming wild, riding the bow waves of the boats in Port Stephens. In migrating season, just beyond the harbour, you might even spot a humpback or southern right whale on their yearly trip to the tropics and back.
Pages 64-5

⑥ Stockton Beach

It's easy to become blasé about NSW's beautiful beaches but Stockton Beach is superlative, a series of giant windblown dunes deposited on the shore over 6 000 years ago. In fact, 'beach' seems a little tame when the other end is over 30km away, and the mobile sand mounds are marching steadily inland at a rate of 10m a year. **Page 65**

Blue Mountains National Park

After the bustle of cosmopolitan Sydney, the Blue Mountains, just a 90-minute drive west, provide a wilderness atmosphere and fresh air by the lungful. So named for the blue-tinged haze shimmering in the valleys as the sun reflects off oil droplets from the eucalyptus trees, the mountains proved to be an impenetrable barrier to the fertile western plains during early colonial days.

In 1813, a route was discovered through to valuable new grazing pastures. Present-day explorers can enjoy a mixture of stunning cliffs and gorges, wildlife and waterfalls and arty-crafty villages, dotted about on a series of plateaux divided by deep valleys.

Bell's Line of Road

Named after 19-year-old Archibald Bell, who discovered the route in 1823, the Bell's Line of Road links the historic towns of Richmond and Windsor with the Blue Mountains. Originally built by convicts in 1841, the road winds its way along the ridge of the spectacular Grose Valley, meandering north from Richmond, through the historic Kurrajong Village. It then passes through the Bilpin apple orchards, where there are many fruit and pie stalls, and carries on to the Mount Tomah Botanic Garden. Near Bell is the entrance to Pierce's Pass. Walk for about half an hour from the car park to the pass for stunning views of the Grose Gorge and the Grose River.

Blackheath

National Parks and Wildlife Service/Heritage Centre, end of Govetts Leap Rd, Blackheath. Tel: (02) 4787 8877. Open daily 0900–1630. Excellent collection of maps of walking trails in the area.

So named in 1815 because of its charred, open, heath-like appearance, the town of Blackheath is the starting point for some of the Mountains' best bushwalking and views. North of the highway are superb views of the **Grose Valley**. Walls Cave Road leads to the beautiful spot of **Wall Cave**, occupied by Aboriginals at least 12,000 years ago. Govetts Leap Road, off the highway, leads to **Govetts Leap Lookout** for stunning views of basalt tops. Less crowded, **Evans Lookout** offers equally breathtaking views, and walks to **Neates Glen**, the **Grand Canyon** and **Beauchamp Falls**; walk there from Govetts Leap (*3km one way, medium walk along the* **Cliff Top Track** *through dense heathland of trees and wildflowers*). Other walks from Govetts Leap include **Perrys Lookdown** and **Pulpit Rock** (*allow 3hrs return – waterfalls, wildflowers, lush rainforest, flowing streams*), and the walk to the base of the 180m **Bridal Veil Falls** (*1.5hrs return straight down and up, taking in a historic stone stairway*).

57

Echo Point

A panoramic cliff drive from Leura weaves its way to **Echo Point**, home to the Blue Mountains' most famous rock formation, the Three Sisters, a cluster of 240-million-year-old sandstone outcrops. A strenuous 896-step walk takes you to the valley floor via the Giant Stairway. From here, an hour's walk through giant ferns and forest brings you to the Scenic Railway for a lift back up. Various bushwalks start from Echo Point, including the scenic Prince Henry Cliff walk along the escarpment edge in either direction – east to the Leura cascades or west to Katoomba Falls.

Information:

Echo Point, Three Sisters, Katoomba. Tel: (02) 4739 6266. Open daily 0900–1700. www.bluemts.com.au

Blue Mountains Heritage Centre, Govetts Leap Rd, Blackheath. Tel: (02) 4787 8877. Open daily 0900–1630. Excellent programme of guided walks.

Katoomba

Katoomba is a Blue Mountains centre, with second-hand shops, cafés and activity gear shops. Agents for booking abseiling, guided mountain walks, horse-riding excursions, 4WD exploring and the latest extreme sport of canyoning: **Aussie Tours** (*238 Main St; tel: (02) 4782 1866, or 1300 300 915 outside Blue Mountains area*), **Blue Mountains Adventure Company** (*84a Main St; tel: (02) 4782 1271, www.bmac.com.au*), or **Cox's River Escapes** for environmentally friendly expeditions in small groups (*tel: (02) 4784 1621*).

For a quick thrill, take the nearby **Scenic Skyway**, a panoramic cable-car ride across the Jamison Valley, or plunge into the valley on the **Scenic Railway**, on the site of a disused coal-mining operation that was closed in 1895, and now the world's steepest railway with a vertical descent of 229m (*Violet St; both open daily 0900–1650; $*).

Leura

A quaint village with some upmarket galleries, restaurants and souvenir shops, Leura hosts an annual **garden festival**, when private gardens are opened to the public on the second weekend in October. Just south of the village is **Leuralla** (*36 Olympian Parade; tel: (02) 4784 1169; open daily 1000–1700; $*), a grand family home with elegant 1920s furnishings, a toy museum and a collection of 1920–1950s clockwork, electric and steam model trains and figures. Over the road, the amphitheatre in the gardens is the perfect panoramic picnic spot. A few kilometres east of Leura is **Sublime Point** where a steep walk to the lookout offers a fabulous view over the dense valley below.

Mount Tomah Botanic Gardens

On Bell's Line of Road, past Bilpin. Open daily 1000–1600; $ per car. Award-winning restaurant overlooking the gardens.

Mount Tomah Botanic Gardens is best known for its collection of cool-climate plants. There is also an extensive array of native trees, including the Wollemi Pine, a rare species of tree only discovered in 1994.

Wentworth Falls

Apart from the magnificent 300m cascade of water and superb views of the Jamison Valley, the village of Wentworth Falls is the starting point for a network of fabulous walking tracks, including the **Charles Darwin Walk** – allow plenty of time. On Tableland Road, a short drive south leads to Queen Elizabeth Drive and a track that takes you to the haunting **Kings Tableland Aboriginal site**, which has artefacts dating back 22,000 years. **Wentworth Falls Lake** is extremely picturesque and an ideal picnic area.

Hunter Valley Wineries

Hunter Valley Wine Country Information Centre: Turner Park, Aberdare Rd, Cessnock (approx 1km before Cessnock). Tel: (02) 4990 4477; www.winecountry.com.au. Open Mon–Fri 0900–1700, Sat 0930–1700, Sun 0930–1530.

Centred around the village of **Pokolbin**, the lower **Hunter Valley** is home to over 60 wineries. They range from internationally acclaimed outfits to small family businesses brewing a few bottles in their backyard. In almost all of them, you can turn up for a free cellar-door tasting without obligation.

Broke Rd is home to some interesting wineries such as **Peterson's Champagne House** on the corner (*tel: (02) 4998 7881; open daily 0900–1700*) which specialises in sparkling wines. A little further along, **McGuigan's** (*tel: (02) 4998 7402; open daily 1000–1650; tours daily 1200*)

is a slick outfit offering a whole range of wines, from inexpensive Chardonnays to the prestigious Personal Reserve Tawny Port. The complex encompasses several restaurants, an excellent souvenir shop and the Hunter Valley Cheese Co, where you can buy a selection of cheeses (try Mount Buffalo Blue goat's cheese) or antipasto plate, uncork a bottle of fine wine and enjoy the ultimate picnic at an outside table. Next door is the picturesque

Small is beautiful

Try Rosemount's premium red wines – GSM or Traditional – as the smaller quantities produced means it's largely squirreled away for the domestic market.

Peppers Creek Winery (*tel: (02) 4998 7532; open Wed–Sun 1000–1700*), where you can sample traditional handmade wines and enjoy a delicious *bruschetta* snack on the rose-filled terrace at the adjoining Café Enzo.

One of the oldest Hunter vineyards, still owned by the original founding family, **Tyrell's** (*tel: (02) 4993 7000; open Mon–Sat 0800–1700*) offers a wonderfully entertaining vineyard tour (*open Mon–Sat 1330*). It culminates in a plentiful wine tasting – try the inexpensive, wonderfully rich Long Flat Red.

At the far end of Gillards Rd (off Macdonalds Rd) is **Constable and Hershon** (*tel: (02) 4998 7887; open daily 1000–1700; free garden tours Mon–Fri 1030*). At this unusual 'boutique' vineyard, a rose garden, a herb garden, croquet lawn and contemporary sculpture garden border the vines.

In the **Upper Hunter Valley**, there are fewer than ten wineries, spread out in a wide circle from Denman. Rolling pastures are set against a backdrop of scrub-covered mountains and sandstone cliffs. In recent years, the Upper Hunter Valley has been recognised as a prime grape-growing region. (*Note that many cafés and tours operate at weekends only.*)

The largest producer is the **Rosemount Estate** (*Rosemount Rd, Denman; tel: (02) 6547 2467; open Mon–Sat 1000–1600, Sun 1030–1600*), with some of the region's most prestigious wines. There are no tours, but the wine tasting is generous, with welcoming, knowledgeable staff. An attractive drive north leads to **Cruickshank Callatoota** (*Wybong Rd, Wybong; tel: (02) 6547 8149; open daily 0900–1700*), a spit-and-sawdust vineyard specialising in red wines (Cabernet Sauvignon and Cabernet Franc) plus an excellent *rosé*. A further 8km leads to **Reynolds Yarraman** (*Yarraman Rd, Wybong; tel: (02) 6547 8127; open Mon–Sat 1000– 1600, Sun 1100–1600*), a picturesque convict-hewn sandstone building dating from 1837. Try the award-winning Sémillon wines and a selection grown in the cooler climate of Orange district.

Barrington Tops National Park

Visitor Information Centre, Denison St, Gloucester. Tel: (02) 6558 1408.

Rugged untamed mountains, cool-climate rainforest, gorges, cliffs and waterfalls make the 280,000 hectares of Barrington Tops National Park a wilderness paradise. The park was declared a World Heritage Area in 1986, and contains some of Australia's tallest and oldest trees. Every shade of green is represented, from the light green of the thick moss that glows between the lacy tracery of tree-fern fronds to the blue-green of the forest of huge eucalypts. Nestled among the trees just outside the national park is the unique **Barrington Guest House** (*tel: (02) 4995 3212; $$*), as much as refuge for native animals as for visitors.

Maitland

Visitors' Centre, High Street. Tel: (02) 4933 2611.

On the **Hunter River**, Maitland has been central to the development of the Hunter Valley since it was established in the 1820s by emancipated convicts and free settlers. The wealth of the town is reflected in some of its grand heritage buildings, including the **Courthouse** (1895) and the **church of St Mary the Virgin** (1860). Town walk maps are available from the Visitors' Centre.

Mudgee

Visitor Information Centre, 84 Market Street. Tel: (02) 6372 5875; fax: (02) 6372 2853; www.mudgee.nsw.gov.au. Open Mon–Fri 0900–1700, Sat 0900–1530, Sun 0930–1400.

Mudgee is a magnificent old rural town, with classic landscapes, fine wines, good eating and a sense of history. The 150-year-old township is set amid rolling blue hills, green pastures, red-dirt side tracks and valleys of vineyards. Grand buildings line its main street, largely protected by the National Trust.

The volcanic soils of the region around Mudgee produce some of the best Shiraz and Chardonnay wines in Australia. The labels to look for – and buy at local cellar doors – are Poets Corner, Rosemount, Huntington, Botobolar, Craigmoor and Montrose. Mudgee also hosts a wine festival each September, featuring its wines and local gourmet foods such as yabbies, trout, lamb, peaches and asparagus.

Newcastle

Visitor Information Centre, The Old Station Master's Cottage, 92 Scott St. Tel: (02) 4929 9299. Open weekdays 0900–1700 and weekends 1000–1530.

With the closure of the steel mill in 1999, Newcastle has had to transform itself from an industrial centre to a bustling, cosmopolitan city by the sea. With some of the most beautiful beaches on the east coast, vineyards to the west, wilderness to the northwest and the picturesque **Lake Macquarie** to the south, tourism was one obvious solution. After an earthquake in 1989, which destroyed 70,000 properties, the authorities decided to restore the city and its heritage rather than re-shape it with modern developments. **Newcastle Beach** is only a few minutes' walk from the city centre, across the plaza from Hunter Street, through the 'time tunnel'.

Port Stephens to Port Macquarie

The attractions of Port Stephens and Port Macquarie are completely natural – beautiful surfing beaches, national parks, and an abundance of wildlife and flowers. They're the ultimate seaside playgrounds, brimming with Australia's wild and wonderful treasures, sandy havens for those who want to fish, swim and sail while becoming acquainted with a dolphin or two.

Port Stephens

Visitors' Centre, Victoria Parade, Nelson Bay. Tel: 1800 808 900; www.portstephens.org.au. Open Mon–Fri 0900–1700, weekends 0900–1600.

Five escaped convicts from Sydney were the first Europeans to live in the Port Stephens area after they were shipwrecked in 1790. Taken in by Worimi Aborigines, they must have thought they'd swum to paradise.

The large, sheltered natural harbour of Port Stephens, with its beautiful beaches and scenery, is now a weekend playground for Sydneysiders and a great spot to relax.

Nelson Bay, on the southern side, is the most 'commercialised' town, and the departure point for an armada of boats running **dolphin- and whale-watching tours**. From January to April, Nelson Bay is a prime spot for **game fishing**; Port Stephens' exceptionally deep water makes for some of the best marlin fishing in the world. All bookings for water activities can be made at the **Boat Hire** floating office at D'Albora Marinas (*tel: (02) 4984 3843*). The marine sanctuary between **Nelson Head** and **Fly Point** offers excellent snorkelling and scuba diving, with many underwater shipwrecks. **Pro Dive** (*D'Albora Marina; tel: (02) 4981 4331*) runs courses for all levels.

The freshest fish

Stockton is one of the best fishing beaches in NSW, and whatever is in season will grace local restaurant menus. Look out for jewfish (Feb–Apr), bream (Apr–May), whiting and dusky flathead (Oct–Feb). Port Stephens oysters are also particularly good.

Bushwalkers can stretch their legs with a walk up to the volcanic rock peninsula, **Tomaree Head**, or stroll over **Fingal Spit** at low tide, a narrow sandbank connecting the glorious Fingal Beach (*off Marine Drive*), a fantastic surfing spot, to the rocky reef of **Point Stephens**.

For sun worshippers, **Little Beach**, north of the lighthouse, is safe and child-friendly, **One Mile Beach** offers the best surf, and **Samurai Beach** gives nudists a chance to let it all hang out. However, the must-visit beach is **Stockton** (*turn left down James Paterson St*), which has golden dunes, 30m high, as far as the eye can see. **Horizon Safaris** (*tel: (018) 681 600*) run 4WD dune adventures, and **Sahara Trails** (*tel: (015) 290 340*) offers coastal horseback rides.

Port Macquarie

Visitor Information Centre, cnr Clarence St and Hay St, Port Macquarie. Tel: (02) 6581 8000, toll-free: 1800 025 935. Open Mon–Fri 0830–1700, weekends 0900–1600.

The ultimate holiday destination, and a brilliant base for day trips. Within an hour of Port (as it's known to the locals), you can tuck yourself away in a peaceful paradise of dense rainforest, tumbling waterfalls and national parks thronging with wildlife.

Appreciate the scenery from **the lighthouse**, south of the town. This is prime whale-spotting territory during the migration season and dolphins frolic here all year round. A two- to three-hour **coastal walk** leads from the lighthouse back to Town Beach. Take the track off to the left at the Miner's Beach 0.8km sign, through the forest to a semicircle of near-deserted golden sand. Walking north, you come across

the long **Shelly Beach**, the epitome of Australian beach culture. **Lighthouse Beach**, down Matthew Flinders Drive, can be explored by **camel safari** (*tel: (02) 6583 7650/mobile: 0412 566 333*).

The **Koala Hospital** (*Lord St; open daily; donation*) is dedicated to the rescue of injured koalas and their release back into the wild. Koalas are notoriously difficult to spot, so aim for feeding time (*daily 1500–1530*). If you're heading north for bushwalking in the national parks, take a trip to the **Sea Acres Rainforest Centre** (*Pacific Drive; open daily 0900–1630; $$*). In this rare area of coastal rainforest, volunteer rangers will help you identify the walking stick palm, strangler fig and python trees, as well as the spectacled monarch bird and the brush turkey.

Out and about around Port Macquarie

Getting there: Turn off the Pacific Highway following signs to Gladstone, then South West Rocks.

Activities

Port has plenty of activities to choose from. The Port Marina Complex (opposite McDonald's on Park St *) houses Graham Seers bike hire (* tel: (02) 6583 2333; closed Sun *); Port Macquarie Dive Centre (* tel: (02) 6583 8483 *) and Hastings River Boat Hire (* tel: (02) 6583 8811 *). The Town Wharf, north of Town Beach, is the booking and departure point for boat-based activities such as scenic river and dolphin-watching cruises MV Port Venture (* tel: (02) 6583 3058/after hours (018) 65 6522 *); Waterbus Everglade Tours (* tel: (02) 6582 5009 *) and Fanta-Sea II (* tel: (015) 256 742/after hours (02) 6582 2037 *).*

Take the spectacular drive **southwest** up to the sleepy village of **Comboyne** (*turn left off the Oxley highway 32km from Port Macquarie*) on a steep winding road along rocky, forested road. You eventually spill out on to a fertile green plateau, reminiscent of the English countryside in spring. Continue on to **Boorganna Nature Reserve**. Despite partial logging of the area during the 1950s, many of the surviving trees are thousands of years old. The 2.7-km walk down to the bottom of Rawson Falls is a misty, fragrant, almost eerie trail, weaving between enormous plank buttresses, brush boxes, water gums and the smooth white trunks of pigeon berry ash. At the bottom of the fall is a freezing cold rock pool – only for the very brave. A further 15-minute drive takes you to **Ellenborough Falls** (*85km from Port Macquarie*), the longest single-drop waterfall in the southern hemisphere. It's a great place for picnicking and meandering bush walks.

A trip **south** from Port Macquarie towards Laurieton takes you past Christmas Bell Plain, which is a carpet of red Christmas Bell flowers around December and January. For more flora and fauna, turn off to the **Kattang Nature Reserve** at Dunbogan. An undemanding 2-km circular walk called the

Flower Bowl takes you through small pockets of rainforest and wildflower heaths, with panoramic views south to Diamond Head and north to Port Macquarie. In August and September the wildflowers are in bloom. Further south on the coastal road is **Diamond Head**, another wonderful stretch of white sand. To see a kangaroo at close quarters, head to the campsite here. The visitors' information centre (*open daily 0800–2000*) has maps of headland walks. Back towards Laurieton is **North Brother Mountain** (*off Ocean Drive*) where look-out platforms offer an eagle-eye view of the labyrinth of waterways, rivers and lakes. The scenery is magnificent in all directions, with views over Queen's Lake, the Middle and South Brothers, the Camden Haven River and the broad sweep of Crowdy Bay, plus the many hang-gliders who use the summit as a launch pad.

North of Port is **Crescent Head** (*turn right off the Pacific Highway just before Kempsey*), one of the best surfing beaches along this part of the coast, with stunning views. Further north still is the partly demolished **Trial Bay Gaol** (*open daily 0900–1700; $$*), standing majestically on the South West Rocks headland. After visiting the gaol, and wandering through Cell Block A (where a couple of the 4m x 2m cells have life-sized dummies re-creating prison life), head along the beautiful **Monument Trail**, where a hillside monument commemorates the Germans who died during internment. Sea eagles duck and dive over the water, butterflies dart backwards and forwards, and the trail criss-crosses beautiful heathland with views over both sides of the headland.

Myall Lakes National Park

North of Port Stephens, the **Myall Lakes National Park** runs along the coast from Hawk's Nest to Seal Rocks. It's a network of coastal lakes, golden beaches and wild scenery with spectacular multi-hued swamps and trees growing straight out of the water. In spring the area is dotted with wild roses and white lilies. **Mungo Brush Rainforest** walking trail (*badly signposted – far right-hand side of Mungo Brush campsite*) is an undemanding palm-shaded trail, which meanders down to the edge of Bombah Broadwater. At dusk, keep your eyes open for a flying fox or ring-tailed possum.

Coffs Harbour to Byron Bay

The coast offers the surfing paradise of Byron Bay, vibrating to the sound of the bongos and the didgeridoo. The hinterland has eucalyptus forests and fertile plains, dotted with sleepy old timber towns. The escarpment encompasses rainforest, ice-cool swimming holes and slopes thick with wildlife. This most northerly chunk of New South Wales offers an unrivalled diversity of experience.

Bellingen

Signposted off the Pacific Highway.

Bellingen offers low-level tourism, jazz festivals and a strong arts tradition. It's the perfect place to spend an afternoon 'fossicking' in some of the best craft shops in NSW before chilling out in one of the quaint cafés. On the third Saturday of the month there's a large country market; in August there's a three-day jazz festival (*infoline: (02) 6655 9345*); in October, a long weekend for the Global Festival of Arts. If you have time, drive out towards the delightfully named **Promised Land** (*via Gleniffer*). Situated on the banks of the Never Never River, the locals head here on hot days, for a 'refreshing' swim in freezing cold spring-fed water holes.

Byron Bay

Named by Captain Cook as he sailed past in 1770, Byron Bay, was, until recently, home to several industries – dairy production, sand mining and then whaling.

Recently, it's found its niche as a 'new age' holiday spot. Surfers flock here for the excellent waves around Cape Byron, while others revel in the laid-back, patchouli-perfumed atmosphere. Byron's repertoire is quite sophisticated these days, with excellent restaurants, shops and a myriad of activities, from hang-gliding to trapeze. High-rise buildings are banned, and there are no fast-food chains.

Byron's beaches

There's something about the wildness of Byron's beaches that makes you want to fling your clothes in the air and turn a series of cartwheels. Should you want to do so, the 7-km **Tallow** beach, south of the cape, is 'clothing optional', as is **Belongil** beach to the north. The **Pass** and **Watego** offer some of the best surfing on the east coast, while a family-safe natural lagoon often forms at **Clarks** beach. **Main Beach** is popular with kite fliers.

Byron is the most easterly point in Australia, so be the first to see the **sunrise** from **Cape Byron** and drink the dawn in with a champagne breakfast. Or brunch at the café on Clarks Beach before **walking** the 3.5-km lighthouse circuit. **Cape Byron** is tops for whale-spotting from May to August. If you want the panorama without the exercise, drive up to Cape Byron. *The area around the lighthouse is open daily 0800–1730.*

Byron Visitor Centre

Jonson St, by the railway station. Tel: (02) 6685 8050; www.byronbay.com

Other close-to-nature excursions include **horse-riding** on the beach (*Byron Beach Rides, tel: (02) 6684 7499; Pegasus Park Equestrian Centre, tel: (02) 6687 1446; $$*), **sea kayaking** with curious dolphins who pop their noses up and swim alongside (*Byron Bay Ocean Kayaking, tel: (02) 6685 7651; $$*), and **snorkelling** and **diving** at the Julian Rocks Marine Reserve, 2.5km off shore (*Bayside Scuba, cnr Lawson St and Fletcher St; tel: (02) 6685 8333/toll-free: 1800 243 483; $$$*).

If you want to learn how to stand on those slippery little sucker **surfboards** (*$$*), Byron's the place to try it. The instructors at **Swell Surf Co** (*tel: (02) 6685 5352*) guarantee small groups. Other options are **East Coast Surf School** (*tel: (02) 6685 5989*) and **Byron Bay Surf School** (*tel: 1800 707 274*).

Alternative times

Byron Bay is the centre of all that is spiritual, soulful and downright whacky. If you need to find yourself, the new-age shop, **Focus** (*cnr Marvell St and Jonson St*) is a good place to start. The sign on the front door of **Osho's House** (*1/30 Carlyle St; tel: (02) 6685 6792*) reads, 'Step inside and leave your shoes and mind behind'. The place offers soul-soothing flotation tanks, reflexology, tarot card readings and aura soma sessions.

Flying high in Byron

The opportunities to **fly high** in Byron are many. For unparalleled views, fly over Byron Lighthouse in a two-seater plane, then glide back with the engine off (*Byron Power Gliding Club, tel: (02) 6684 7627; $$$*) or forget the mechanics and go tandem hang-gliding (*Joe Scott, Byron Bay Hang-gliding Club, tel: (02) 6684 3711/0415 717 141; $$$*). The action takes place around Cape Byron and nearby Lennox Head, depending on the wind.

" *Even if you're not into all this new age stuff, you can't help being sucked in – there's something magical about the place.* **"**
Teresa Valentine, first-time English visitor to Byron

Coffs Harbour

Tourist information, cnr Rose Ave and Marcia St. Tel: (02) 6652 1522/toll-free: 1800 025 650.

Main town of the banana-growing region, Coffs Harbour isn't quaint, but it certainly offers variety. Set around a man-made harbour between inland subtropical rainforests and golden coastal beaches, Coffs is the place to come for an active, sporty holiday with good food and interesting day trips.

Getting active in Coffs

For the low-down on every activity, from cruises, horse-riding, deep-sea fishing, parasailing and 4WD trips, the one-stop shop is the **Marina Booking Office** (*near Muttonbird Island; tel: (02) 6651 4612*).

Highlights include: some of the best **diving** on the NSW coast, at Solitary Islands Marine Park (*Jetty Dive Centre, 398 High St; tel: (02) 6651 1611; $$$*); a three-hour **kayaking** tour (*Coffs Sea Kayaking, tel: (02) 6658 0850; $$*) to see dolphins, sea turtles and manta rays, or **canoeing**, to explore the backwaters of Coffs Creek (*Promenade Leisure Hire, Coffs Promenade; tel: (02) 6651 1032; open daily 0900–1600; $$*); glorious **walks** around Coffs including Muttonbird Island, and a 6-km relaxing stroll along Coffs Creek (starting from Coffs St); **whale-watching** – Coffs claims to be the 'number one' spot from June to October (*Pacific Explorer sailboat tours, tel: 0418 663 815; $$; or Spirit of Coffs Harbour summer cruises, tel: (02) 6650 0155; $$*); **whitewater rafting** on the Nymboida River in Dorrigo's hinterland, or on the swirling Gwydir River in summer, when water crashes down from an upstream dam (*Wildwater Adventures, tel: (02) 6653 4469; $$$*); or, finally, **tandem skydiving** (*Coffs City Skydivers (tel: (02) 6651 1167*).

The Big Banana

Australians seem to have a strange penchant for huge landmarks: Coffs Harbour's version is an enormous Big Banana, marking the entrance to the theme park.

Dorrigo National Park

60km from Coffs Harbour, via Bellingen and Waterfall Way. Dorrigo Rainforest Centre, Dorrigo National Park. Tel: (02) 6657 2309.

Southwest of Coffs Harbour, the outstanding Dorrigo National Park encompasses both a high, cool plateau and steep rugged escarpment. It has been a World Heritage site since 1986 for its magnificent rainforests. **The Skywalk**, a boardwalk suspended over the trees, offers a rare view down on to the rainforest canopy. The 5.8-km subtropical rainforest **Wonga Wonga walk** is one of the most picturesque, with 600-year-old yellow carabeens, strangler figs, and the Crystal Shower and Terania waterfalls.

Red gold

Loggers opened up the Bellinger Valley in the 1840s for the lucrative red cedars known as 'red gold'. By the end of the century, the red cedars were almost extinct and the inhabitants turned to dairy farming. Although the Dorrigo plateau was cleared for cattle and potato crops, the precious rainforest was saved because the slopes were too steep to clear.

Nimbin

Nimbin Ecotourist Connexion, 80 Cullen St. Tel: (02) 6689 1764. Open Mon–Fri 1200–1700, Sat–Sun 1200–1400.

A stroll through Nimbin is a surreal experience. It's been the alternative capital of Australia since 1973, when a myriad of politically correct groups came here for the Aquarius Festival. Communal living in harmony with the land is its mission. Many people come here to fill up on drugs – and you don't have to be Inspector Clouseau to find those – but even for chemical virgins, the shops and cafés with colourful characters make it an interesting place. The off-the-wall 'stream of consciousness' **Nimbin Museum** (*open daily, no fixed hours*) displays some psychedelic 'exhibits', ranging from camper vans, environmental articles and an informative 'Say Know to Drugs' section.

Cool waters

For the most scenic swimming hole imaginable, head to the tumbling Protestor's Falls (access from the Channon, dirt road *), which cascade over the rocks, tucked away in a palm-filled gorge among bird's-nest ferns and huge rainforest trees.*

Eating and drinking

Blue Mountains

The Mall in **Leura** has some excellent restaurants and cafés. Try **Café Bon Ton** (*192 The Mall; tel: (02) 4782 4377; open daily breakfast, lunch and dinner; closed Tue evening; $$*). Modern Australian dishes served in the lovely shady garden or light airy indoor café. BYO. **Loaves and The Dishes** (*180a The Mall; $*) deals in wholesome fare: pumpkin and parmesan risotto, potato, leek and sorrel soup, Mediterranean salads, and huge chunks of chocolate/date/orange cake and fruit muffins. **Silk's Brasserie** (*128 The Mall; tel: (02) 4784 2534; open daily lunch and dinner; $$$*) is smart, yet traditional, offering hearty portions of modern Australian 'mountain' food in relaxing surroundings.

Among **Katoomba**'s many reasonably priced art-deco cafés are the bright, airy **Savoy** (*26–28 Katoomba St; open daily breakfast–dinner; $*), the friendly, funky **Café Zuppa** (*36 Katoomba St; $*) and **The Blues Café** (*$*), over the road at number 57, which is a veggie and vegan haven.

Hunter Valley

The **Hunter Valley**'s best cafés and restaurants are usually attached to wineries. **The Cellar**, at McGuigan's (*Broke Rd; tel: (02) 4998 7584; open daily lunch and dinner, closed Sun evening; $$$*) serves dishes ranging from BBQ duckling to smoked kangaroo in a candlelit garden room, with log fires in winter. Best to book. **Rosemount Vineyard Restaurant** (*Rosemount Rd, Denman; tel: (02) 6547 2467; open Tue–Sun lunchtime; $$*) serves a limited but interesting menu, and cream teas from 1000. Indulge at the excellent **Roberts**, at the Pepper Tree vineyard (*Halls Rd, Pokolbin; tel: (02) 4998 7330; open daily lunch and dinner; $$$*). At the century-old vineyard of **Craigmoor**, in Mudgee (*tel: (02) 6273 4320; $$*), there is a gourmet restaurant.

Port Stephens and Port Macquarie

Kaleidoscope
Nelson Towers Arcade, Nelson Bay. Open breakfast–lunch. $. Light bites – pumpkin soup, Mediterranean *focaccia*, gourmet sandwiches – on an upstairs panoramic balcony.

Robs on the Boardwalk
D'Albora Marina, Nelson Bay. Open daily breakfast–dinner. $$. A mellow waterfront spot for robust breakfasts and mod Oz lunch and dinners with delights such as ravioli of plump scallops and blue-eyed cod with truffle-infused mash.

Rocklobster
D'Albora Marina, Nelson Bay. Tel: (02) 4981 1813. Open daily. $$–$$$. This bright, light restaurant serves exquisite fish dishes such as prawns in beer batter and red Thai fish curry, on an outdoor terrace with beautiful views. Licensed and BYO.

Café 66
Clarence St, Port Macquarie. Open Tue–Sun, breakfast–dinner. $$. Busy and buzzing, this friendly café serves tasty Italian fare with a flourish. BYO.

Family Buffet
14 Clarence St, Port Macquarie. Open daily lunch and dinner. $. Despite the uninspiring name, this eat-as-much-as-you-want diner, with oriental, seafood, salad and roasts, is great value and good, if not gourmet.

Pottsy's Place
1 Hay St, Port Macquarie. Tel: (02) 6584 1143. Open daily from 1800, lunch Sun–Fri. $$. This lively rustic restaurant on the seafront serves dainty dishes of kangaroo, crocodile and venison, as well as seafood and steak. Licensed and BYO.

What to try

The Blue Mountains has so far managed to resist the fast-food invasion, and generally there's a strong leaning towards wholesome, organic 'slow food'. Bread is Leura's speciality, particularly sourdough, known locally as 'brickbread'. **Quinton's Bakery** (*179 The Mall; open daily 0730–1930*) offers a fine range of bread, gourmet sandwiches and cakes.

Shopping

Blue Mountains

Leura's high street (*The Mall*) has many art and craft shops: check out **Moontree Studio** (*157 The Mall*) for beautifully scented candles, lanterns, hand-cut soaps and candleholders, and the gloriously eclectic **Cinnamon Road** (*181 The Mall*) for beautiful wood crafts and mirrors. **Breewood** (*169 The Mall*) sells some upmarket ceramics and china. The **Leura Fine Woodwork Gallery** (*130 The Mall*) is a kaleidoscope of shiny woods, from red cedar mirrors to black-wood clocks, sculptures and simple Aboriginal art.

In **Katoomba**, **Summit Gear** (*88 Katoomba St*) offers all the climbing, cycling and bushwalking togs needed for an active holiday. The Hatter's Shop near by (*171 Lurline St*) has Akubra hats in every style.

Australia's National Parks

For visitors from small, densely inhabited countries, one of the most striking features of Australia is its vastness. With a total of 6.2 million people, New South Wales is one of the most heavily populated states, yet off the main coastal roads, you can feel like you're the only person on the planet.

But this surplus of land does not mean that it is taken for granted. As far back as 1863, laws were passed in Tasmania to protect Australia's evocative landscape, with the first national park (the **Royal**) established south of Sydney in 1879. Since then, a protected status has been granted to more than 50 million hectares encompassing over 3 400 sites of particular interest for their wildlife and vegetation.

There are more than 70 national parks in NSW, taking in over four million hectares of land. Some of these are within the city of Sydney such as the **Sydney Harbour National Park**, others are rugged wilderness areas such as **Barrington Tops**.

Many national parks have marked walking trails and barbecue and picnic facilities, and some of the larger ones have visitors' centres, cafés and campsites, but they are very low key and uncommercialised – you won't find McDonald's outlets and ice-cream vans. Very few national parks in NSW charge a fee, except for camping – notable exceptions are **Kosciuszko**, **Ku-ring-gai Chase** and **Jervis Bay**.

The parks vary tremendously in flora and fauna, from the moist sub-tropical rainforests in the north to the eerie alpine snow gums in the south. However, whether you find yourself tiptoeing across the tops of waterfalls, clambering over massive plank buttress roots in a 6 000-year-old rainforest or plunging into crystal clear coastal waters, the natural treasures of NSW parks are not to be missed.

Here are a few to savour.

North of Sydney

Myall Lakes, near Hawk's Nest. Sand dune upon golden sand dune against a backdrop of mangrove lakes.

Boorganna, 60km southwest of Port Macquarie. An eerie, atmospheric rainforest surrounding Rawson Falls with plentiful bird life.

Dorrigo, west of Coffs Harbour. A World Heritage listed rainforest.

> " *I love a sunburnt country,*
> *A land of sweeping plains,*
> *Of ragged mountain ranges,*
> *Of droughts and flooding rains,*
> *I love her far horizons,*
> *I love her jewel sea,*
> *Her beauty and her terror,*
> *The wide brown land for me.* "
> **Dorothea Mackellar, poet and novelist, *My Country* (1911)**

South of Sydney

Kosciuszko, Snowy Mountains. The highest mountain in Australia plus stunning alpine scenery.

Jervis Bay, 25km south of Nowra. Spectacular white sandy beaches and plentiful bird and animal life.

Canberra and southern NSW

Southern NSW is a wonderfully kept secret, with quaint villages rooted in the 1830s, the highest mountain in Australia, beaches where kangaroos play in the surf and national parks where parrots and wallabies outnumber tourists. There are long sweeping beaches of virgin sand and the cooler climate keeps the lush southern highlands a velvety shade of green. In the middle of the region is the tiny state of ACT, with the highly unusual capital city of Canberra at its heart.

CANBERRA AND SOUTHERN NSW

BEST OF

Canberra and southern NSW

*Getting around: The **Canberra Explorer Bus** (tel: 132 251) does a two-hour tour of the city, or you can purchase a pass ranging from four hours to three days, which allows you to hop on, hop off. Buses depart from platform 11, City Bus Interchange, East Row (tel: 131 710).*

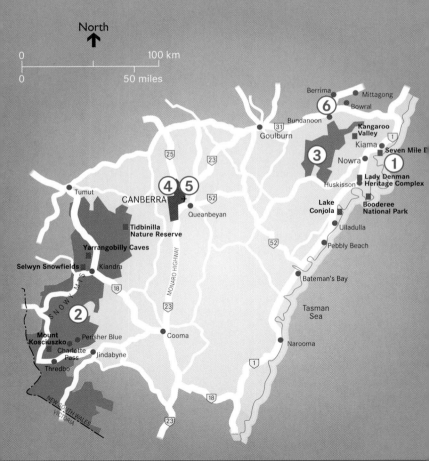

CANBERRA AND SOUTHERN NSW

① Jervis Bay

There are few places in New South Wales that are more rewarding to the senses than Jervis Bay. Deserted white sandy beaches with crystal clear water, beautiful forests, a colourful bird population and a spectacular underwater world make this a relaxing retreat for a peaceful few days. **Pages 98–100**

② Kosciuszko National Park

Australia's semi-arid landscape possesses only 250 square kilometres of alpine land and half of those lie in NSW on the section of the Great Dividing Range north of Mount Kosciuszko. Named after a Polish general by Paul Strzelecki, who climbed the mountain in 1840, Kosciuszko offers Australia's best skiing in winter and hearty, bracing mountain air and activities in summer. **Pages 103–4**

③ Morton National Park

Deep in the heart of the Southern Highlands, this is sandstone scenery at its best, peppered with fabulous walks through rainforest gullies, the magnificent Fitzroy Falls and the bizarre Glow Worm Glen, sparkling at night with the blue luminescence emitted from gnats' larvae.
Page 97

④ National Gallery of Australia, Canberra

According to Colin Madigan, the gallery's architect, 'a gallery is supposed to act like a cathedral to lift the spirits of the people'. That's exactly what this spacious building does. From Australian impressionism to international master-pieces and Aboriginal bark paintings, each room has its own charm. But perhaps the true gem is the lakeside sculpture garden – art, air and the lunchtime chimes of the 53-bell carillon.
Pages 88–9

⑤ Parliament House, Canberra

Described by writer Mark Lawson as having 'all the original Aussie brio of the Sydney Opera House', Parliament House stands majestically at the southern tip of the Parliamentary Triangle, formed by Capital Hill, Commonwealth and Kings Avenues. Burrowed so far into the side of the hill, you can walk over its roof, the architecture alone is reason enough to visit, although a glimpse of parliamentary question time is comforting proof that politicians are the same everywhere. **Pages 90–1**

⑥ Southern Highlands

The Southern Highlands sleepy villages, such as Bundanoon and Berrima, seem to have sidestepped development, depending on curious tourists and a burgeoning afternoon tea and arts and crafts industry to keep them on the map. They won't get your adrenalin pumping – quite the opposite – but an afternoon browsing through their artistic treasures might make you question the merits of big-city living. **Pages 96–7**

Tourist information

Canberra Visitors' Centre, 330 Northbourne Ave, Dickson. Tel: (02) 6205 0044/toll-free 1800 026 166; www.canberratourism.com.au. Open daily 0900–1800.
Fitzroy Falls Visitors' Centre, Fitzroy Falls. Tel: (02) 4887 7270.
Cooma Visitors' Centre, 119 Sharp St, Cooma. Tel: (02) 6450 1742/toll-free 1800 636 525.

Canberra

The deserted sheep station of 'Canberry', at the foothills of the Snowy Mountains, was chosen in 1908 as the unlikely location for a brand-new city, to be the seat of Australia's government. Ultra-modern Canberra has received some fierce criticism, but its plus points are many. Planned as a city within a garden, there's lots of lush green space, a backdrop of mountains and thousands of gum trees, as well as excellent restaurants, a magnificent art gallery and impressive museums.

When the six colonies of Australia united in a federation in 1901, the country needed somewhere to house its government. Both Sydney and Melbourne staked their claim, but the site of Canberra, within its own tiny state, the **Australian Capital Territory (ACT)**, was eventually chosen as a compromise, halfway between the two.

An international design competition was held, and the plans of American architect **Walter Burley Griffin** were selected. His vision was to create a symbolic and symmetrical city centred around a man-made lake, in harmony with the surrounding landscape. When work began, in 1913, the city was built out rather than up, resulting in a bright, airy capital, stretching 35km north to south. All properties are on a 99-year lease so that the government retains tight control over the city's development.

For many years the city remained practically empty of people, with just 5 000 inhabitants after the Second World War. Today, there are around 300,000, with the vast majority employed in government offices. Moves are currently afoot to build an international **airport** at Canberra to rival Sydney's. If they go according to plan, this spacious city could find itself nearly half full.

Australian War Memorial

Bus 901 and Canberra Explorer. Open daily 1000–1700, but an extensive redevelopment programme means that some exhibits may be closed. A bugle plays the last post at closing time. Guided tours roughly every hour 1000–1400.

Part memorial, part museum, this is a moving tribute to the Australians who died in 20th-century wars. Standing at the top of the monument-lined Anzac Parade, where the red gravel signifies the blood shed, the tranquil walls surrounding the **Pool of Reflection** are engraved with the 102,000 names of Australia's war dead. The **Tomb of the Unknown Soldier**, one of 46,000 Australians who died on the Western Front in the First World War, lies in the domed **Hall of Memory**. This peaceful building contains one of the world's largest mosaics, made from six million Italian tiles and painstakingly assembled by war widows (*under restoration until 2001, but still accessible*).

Downstairs is an impressive military museum, with excellent exhibitions spanning the many wars in which Australia has participated, from the Korean War and Vietnam to the two World Wars and the Gulf War. Displays include uniforms, weapons, mementoes and recreations of the battles, as well as rocket launchers, armoured personnel carriers and helicopters. The Second World War gallery, reopened in 1999 after a $20 million redevelopment, is particularly moving, brought alive by personal testimonies, love letters and diaries alongside the military memorabilia. The Bradbury aircraft hall includes the Lancaster Bomber 'G' for George, which serves as a reminder of the 4 000 Australians who died while flying with the RAF Bomber Command during the Second World War.

Embassy Row

Canberra Explorer and Bus 901.

If you're feeling homesick, head down to Yarralumla, the diplomatic precinct where all the foreign embassies and high commissions are based. Buildings range from the beautifully ornate and culturally distinctive (Thailand, Papua New Guinea, India) to the dull and dreary (Poland, Finland).

Lake Burley Griffin

A city built around a lake was central to **Walter Burley Griffin**'s original plan, although this only came to fruition in 1963, when the Molonglo River was dammed. Situated

between the triangle of Black Mountain, Capital Hill and Mount Ainslie, the lake's landmarks include the **Captain Cook Memorial Jet**, which spurts 147m high (*operates daily 1000–1200, 1400–1600*), and the **carillon** bells, a jubilee present from Britain in 1963, which ring out classical tunes along with the occasional *Pink Panther* theme. For a closer look, head to **Lake Burley Griffin Boat Hire** (*Ferry Terminal, Barrine Drive*) and explore in a canoe, paddle boat or aqua bike (*$$*). Nearby is **Mr Spokes** bike and rollerblade hire (*open Wed–Sun 0900–1700, daily during school holidays*). A cycleway runs right round the lake.

Mount Ainslie and Telstra Tower

Both the Canberra Explorer and Bus 904 go to the Telstra Tower.

Walter Burley Griffin planned Canberra around the Capital Hill–Mount Ainslie axis. At 843m high, Mount Ainslie's one of the best vantage points over the city (particularly at sunset), with views over the lake, Anzac Parade, Parliament House and the foothills of the Snowy Mountains in the distance. You can drive up, or hike up the pretty trail from behind the War Memorial, where you may bump into kangaroos, which live at the base of the mountain. The 195m-tall Telstra communications tower on **Black Mountain** (*open daily 0900–2200; $*) to the west also offers a splendid panorama, as well as a revolving restaurant.

National Capital Exhibition

Regatta Point, Commonwealth Park. Open 0900–1700 (until 1800 in summer). Canberra Explorer and Bus 901.

For an effortless understanding of Canberra's history, head to the National Capital Exhibition on the banks of the lake. Here, laser displays, short audio-visual shows and old photographs unravel the story behind this manicured city.

National Gallery of Australia

Parkes Place. Open daily 1000–1700. Free guided tours of Australian and International sections, daily 1100 and 1400. Tours of the Aboriginal section, Thur and Sun 1100. Self-guided audio tours are available. Canberra Explorer and Bus 901.

This spacious and uncluttered art gallery is a pleasure to visit, particularly in the company of a knowledgeable guide. The core of the collection is Australian, with a large selection of indigenous art. The strength of the international collection lies in contemporary paintings with a few important pre-1800 European works, while the beautiful lakeside gardens house a wonderful variety of sculptures.

The Australian collection: highlights include several impressionistic paintings from the Heidelberg School (there are others in the Art Gallery of NSW, Sydney), such as *Golden Summer, Eaglemont* (1889) by **Arthur Streeton** and **Tom Roberts**' beautiful bushland painting *In a Corner on the Macintyre* (1895). *Weighing the Fleece* (1921) by **George W Lambert** is one of the best-known pictures in Australian art, reflecting the prosperity of the farmers after the First World War.

An important contribution to post-war art is the *Ned Kelly series* (1945–7) by **Sidney Nolan**. It explores ideas about authority and violence in the direct aftermath of the Second World War, tracing the true story of an Irish immigrant's son who goes on the run, robbing banks and shooting policemen before meeting his end on the hangman's noose in 1880. **Fred Williams**, one of Australia's artistic stars in the 1960s, took landscape painting to another level, by portraying the countryside as a vast abstract space, not dominated by any one element; see his *Lysterfield triptych* (1967–8).

Move with the times

In the 1970s, modern paints and canvas were introduced by a teacher called Geoffrey Bardon to an isolated Aboriginal area in Papunya, Alice Springs, which became the birthplace of Aboriginal art on canvas. Until that time, their work had mainly been restricted to body art or carvings on the ground. The traditional bark paintings did not serve a decorative purpose but were designed to instruct, and were used mainly for initiation, funerals and festivals.

Aboriginal art: Aboriginal people depend heavily on pictures, dance and oral tradition to pass their culture down the generations, as they have no written language to record their knowledge.

Highlights here include the traditional eucalyptus bark painting, the *Wagilag Creation Story* (1963) by **Dawidi**, depicting social rules, while **Mick Namarari Tjapaltjarri**'s *Sunrise Chasing Away the Night* (1977–8) shows the recent trend of acrylic paints in indigenous art. **Robert Campbell**'s series of paintings tell the story of deaths in custody, black segregation at the cinema and land rights through a combination of the traditional dot technique and human figures, to enable westerners to understand. The poignant *Aboriginal Memorial* (1987–8) features 200 hollow log coffins, traditionally used in burial ceremonies. Each one marks a year of European settlement and commemorates the thousands of Aboriginals who have died defending their land.

International art: 20th-century contributions form the bulk of the collection, but important 18th-century works include **Giambattista Tiepolo**'s *Marriage Allegory* (1750), originally designed as a ceiling panel. The painting is rich in symbolism. **Jackson Pollock**'s *Blue Poles* (1952) is probably the most famous painting in the gallery, although its purchase for US$2 million in 1973 caused a tremendous public outcry. Other paintings to look out for include **Willem de Kooning**'s *Woman V* (1952–3), **Pablo Picasso**'s *Luncheon on the Grass*, **Andy Warhol**'s *Elvis* and the huge *Trapeze Artists* by **Fernand Léger**.

Old Parliament House

King George Terrace, Parkes. Tel: (02) 6270 8222. Open daily 0900–1600. $.
Canberra Explorer and Bus 901.

Intended as a 'temporary solution', this grand building housed the government for over 60 years until 1988, when the (new) Parliament House was opened. It's now home to the **National Portrait Gallery**, which exalts Australia's good and great, from sportsmen (Donald Bradman), to singers (Kylie Minogue), explorers, scientists and businessmen. There's also a brilliant light and sound show, 'Order, Order' in the **House of Representatives**, which maps out some of the defining moments in the building's history.

Situated on the lawns outside is the **Aboriginal tent embassy**. It was first established on Australia Day in 1972 and has remained there on and off for over 30 years providing a focus for Aboriginal campaigns for land rights and social justice. It was called an 'embassy' to symbolise the feeling of many indigenous people that they were essentially foreigners in their own country.

Parliament House

Capital Hill. Open daily 0900–1700. Recorded infoline: (02) 6277 2727.
Free tours run every half-hour. Canberra Explorer and Bus 901.

What does it mean?

Symbolism is rife at Parliament House. The Aboriginal mosaic in front of the entrance depicts a meeting place, and represents Australia's indigenous heritage. The ceremonial pool is the sea flowing around Australia, the red gravel the country's deserts. Australia's coat of arms has an emu and kangaroo – neither animal can walk backwards, and their use is said to represent Australia's progressive society.

Burley Griffin's desire to create a city within a garden, blending buildings into the landscape, is stylishly executed in the new Parliament House. Ninety per cent of the government's new home is underground, dug into the side of a hill and landscaped over the top. You can walk over the roof. It's a real people's palace, where the public can wander in and out at will, admire the huge contemporary art collection or watch parliamentary proceedings from the public gallery.

At a cost of over one billion dollars, the décor, stonework and wooden marquetry panelling are exquisite. Ninety per cent of the materials used were Australian, although the white marble of the veranda is from Carrara, Italy. Inside, the foyer's 48 green-grey marble pillars represent the eucalyptus forests of Australia, while water flowing over a slab of granite muffles the sound of ministers' voices in the central **Members' Hall**.

You can visit the **House of Representatives**, the **Senate** and the **Great Hall**, where a 20-m tapestry of a eucalyptus forest hangs, based on a painting by **Arthur Boyd**. It took 13 weavers two and a half years to complete, weaving in one small extra detail – a white teardrop representing Haley's Comet, which passed over Australia in 1986.

The **outside** is also impressive, with curved granite walls topped by a giant flagmast, the tallest four-legged structure in the world at 81m.

Question time is 1400–1500 when parliament is sitting; arrive very early for a chance to watch ministers at loggerheads or better still, book (*tel: (02) 6277 4899*).

Questacon

The National Science and Technology Centre, King Edward Terrace. 24-hour recorded infoline: 1800 020 603. Open daily 1000–1700. $$. Canberra Explorer and Bus 901.

A hi-tech spiral walkway leads through fascinating galleries brimming with temporary and permanent interactive exhibits and DIY experiments. In the permanent galleries, you can see three million volts of electricity crackling in a lightning display, rattle about on an earthquake simulator and understand how a hovercraft is propelled. The 'good vibes gallery' has appearance-altering mirrors, a delayed speech monitor, a bionic ear and, best of all, a frozen shadow section where you assume a silly pose, wait for the light to flash, then move away, leaving the shadow frozen to the wall. Education has never been such fun.

Sculpture garden

Joggers pass through, old men play boule, schoolchildren sketch here … and, in among the beautiful trees and shrubs, this lakeside garden is home to some wonderful contemporary and classical sculpture, including **Bert Flugelman**'s enormous mirror-surfaced *Cones* (1976–82) and *La Montagne* (1937) by French sculptor **Aristide Maillol**.

Parliamentary apologies

In June 1997, Bob Carr, the Premier of NSW, made a significant step towards recognising the injustices meted out to Australia's indigenous people. He called upon the NSW Parliament to apologise for its part in enacting the laws and policies that resulted in the separation of children from their families. The resolution was passed unanimously.

Festival!

One of Canberra's main festivals is the month-long Floriade, from mid-September in the lakeside Commonwealth Park, with over 1.3 million flower bulbs and annuals. From March to May, Canberra's Season of Festivals encompasses dance, music and multicultural events. In April, the National Folk Festival takes place in Exhibition Park, as well as the Chamber Music Festival at various venues. The Festival of Contemporary Arts takes place in October.

Tidbinbilla Nature Reserve

45km southwest of Canberra, via Paddy's River Rd.

This 5 500-hectare nature reserve offers the perfect opportunity to see native Australian animals in a semi-wild environment. Emus and eastern grey kangaroos roam the surrounding hills, while a loose enclosure is home to a band of red kangaroos. You might also glimpse one of the few hundred rock wallabies left in the world, or a wombat emerging from an underground tunnel. There's also a koala breeding area, where around 10 to 15 koalas are housed at any one time, gradually being released into the wild as numbers grow. They're difficult to see as they blend in so well with the gum trees, but rangers post an up-date of where they are hiding out every morning.

There's also copious birdlife at Tidbinbilla with ample opportunity to see kookaburras, galahs and the splendid red-crested gang-gang cockatoo. To ensure a good close-up, rangers feed the birds daily at 1430.

Guided tour: positively the best way to enjoy Tidbinbilla is with friendly native Canberran Sue White. Much wildlife slips past unnoticed, but if there are rock wallabies, echidnas or duck-billed platypus on the move, she'll spot them for you. The day tour also includes a picnic, sampling of bush tucker foods and a dip in a swimming hole at Cotter Dam. Tours run three times a week (*tel: (02) 6259 5999; $$$*).

CANBERRA AND SOUTHERN NSW

Southern Highlands

Berrima

A quaint 1830s village that time forgot, Berrima invites leisurely lunches and afternoons browsing in the many craft and antique shops. Originally intended as the manufacturing centre of the region owing to its good water supply and fertile soil, an imposing sandstone courthouse and gaol were built in 1838. However, it was bypassed by the railway and the grand plans – and population – dwindled away. Today the courthouse is a museum (*open daily 1000–1600; $$*) much of which is devoted to a re-creation of the famous trial of two immigrant convicts, **Lucretia Dunkley** and her lover **Martin Beech**, who were hanged in 1843 for murdering Lucretia's husband. There's also an interesting room that shows the parallel history of the world, Australia and Berrima throughout the 1900s.

Bowral

Nowhere near as quaint as Berrima, Bowral has two main claims to fame. One is the spectacular **Tulip Time Festival** at the beginning of October in Corbett Gardens. The other is the **Bradman Museum** (*St Jude St; tel: (02) 4862 1247; open daily 1000–1600; $$*), a shrine to Australia's most famous cricketer, Sir Donald Bradman, who began his career on the Bowral Oval in the 1920s. It traces the history of Australian and international cricket from the first match played in Sydney in 1804 to present day, with an upstairs section dedicated solely to Bradman's life. Cricket *aficionados* will love it and even those who don't know a wicket from a wide might muster some enthusiasm.

Bundanoon and Morton National Park

A top destination for honeymooners in the 1940s when newly weds packed out more than 50 guesthouses, Bundanoon, 'a place of deep gullies', has slipped into a slumber since then. It's now a picturesque olde-worlde village that makes an excellent base for exploring Morton National Park.

From Bundanoon, a steep 20-minute walk into the valley at the bottom of William St takes you to **Glow Worm Glen**. On a good day, glow worms cling to the rock face like little luminous clocks lighting up the darkness. You'll need a torch for the walk down but switch it off at the bottom – curious torch beams are killing them off.

One kilometre from Bundanoon is the entrance to the park. Interesting walks include the **Eris Coal Mine** trail across the top of waterfalls, down to a disued coal mine, with plenty of wildflowers such as boronia and honey flowers (*Sept–Dec*). The **Fairy Bower** trail, which follows a waterfall down into the valley, really does feel like a stroll through a magical glade along a path lined with king ferns. Bird life, particularly crimson and eastern rosellas, is plentiful.

The Brigadoon Festival

The Southern Highlands were popular with early settlers because of the cooler climate and four distinct seasons, which reminded them of Europe. The large immigrant Scottish populations of Bundanoon and nearby Sutton Forest celebrate in April in Bundanoon with the Brigadoon Festival, a tartan spectacle of Scottish dancing, caber-tossing and haggis-hurling.

On the eastern side of Morton, the spectacular **Fitzroy Falls** (*Nowra Rd*) plunge 81m into the Yarrunga Valley. The **West Rim** walk offers heart-stopping panoramas over the sandstone gorge, leading across the top of another gushing cascade, the **Twin Falls**, against a backdrop of yellow-tailed black cockatoos, eastern yellow robins and crimson rosellas dancing above the black wattle and peppermint gum forest.

The coast south of Sydney

South to Jervis Bay

The little town of **Kiama**, 120km south of Sydney, is a convenient stopping-off point. Its claim to fame is a big and little blowhole, where the sea comes whooshing through. The long sweeping golden-sand **Seven Mile Beach**, south of Gerringong, is a great place for a picnic, disturbed only by a few dog walkers and schoolboy surfers. From there, an attractive drive with ocean views and green hills leads to idyllic **Jervis Bay**, first sighted in 1770 by Captain Cook and finally named in 1791 after Rear-Admiral Sir John Jervis. Today it is famed for its clean waters and dazzling white sands.

CANBERRA AND SOUTHERN NSW

Booderee National Park

Jervis Bay Rd. $$.

Booderee National Park is a marine park and nature reserve (*with campsites*), second only to the Great Barrier Reef in terms of marine diversity. The beaches are spectacular – Hyams Beach, surrounded by sandstone cliffs, claims to have the whitest sand in the world. For seclusion, head to Scottish Rocks, at the base of a thick patch of forest. Green Patch beach is a favourite fishing and snorkelling spot, perfect for families and abundant with wildlife. The lorikeets, rosellas and kangaroos are very tame (feeding them is harmful). Picturesque Murrays Beach is a long sweep of golden sand, fringed by thick forest and deep sapphire water with a view over Bowen Island. The ruined Cape St George Lighthouse (*down the very rough Stony Creek Rd*) offers a stunning panorama over Wreck Bay, so called because of the many shipwrecks that occurred there in the 19th century.

The sleeping princess

In the early 1920s, D H Lawrence *spent several months in Thirroul on the south coast of NSW, writing his semi-autobiographical novel,* Kangaroo. *This was his impression: 'Australia has a marvellous sky and air and blue clarity and a hoary sort of land beneath it like a sleeping princess on whom the dust of ages has settled. Wonder if she'll ever get up.'*

Within the park, Jervis Bay Botanic Gardens (*Cave Beach Rd; open weekdays 0800–1600, Sun and public holidays 1000–1700, closed Sat*) are perfect for shady walks in the rainforest gully, among the orchids, rhododendrons and bottle brushes.

Huskisson

This tiny town is the closest you'll find to a commercial centre. Activities on offer include the extremely popular dolphin watch tours (*Dolphin Watch, 50 Owen St; tel: (02) 4441 6311; booking advisable; $$*), game fishing (*$$$*) and reel fishing (*$*) (*Jervis Bay Tackle Co., 57 Owen St; tel: (02) 4441 6377*). Snorkelling (*$$*) and scuba diving (*$$$*) are very pleasurable in Jervis Bay's sheltered, temperate waters, which deliver up rewards such as huge cuttlefish, weedy sea dragons, corals and Port Jackson sharks (*Pro Dive, 64 Owen St; tel: (02) 4441 5255*).

Lady Denman Heritage Complex

Dent St, Huskisson.

Enjoy a peaceful boardwalk through the mangrove swamps among the sea eagles or spend a while browsing in the **Lady Denman Maritime Museum** (*open Tue–Fri 1300–1600, weekends 1000–1600; $$*). It houses a fascinating display about the Aborigines, the original inhabitants of Jervis Bay, and includes items used for shelter, fishing and hunting. There's also a section on diving (including a suit from 1914), whaling and shipwrecks, as well as a collection of old barometers, compasses, seaman's boxes and ornate ships figureheads to delight old sea dogs.

Lake Conjola

North of Ulladulla.

Edged with lush green forest, the beautiful Lake Conjola is a popular stamping ground for families and fishermen. There's a public reserve at the end of the caravan park, with sandy beaches and a proliferation of king parrots and galahs. Like many natural beauty spots, facilities are fairly sparse, with the Post Office (*just before the tourist park*) fulfilling the functions of boat and canoe hire, fishing bait supplier, grocery store and newsagent.

Pebbly Beach

Take the turning to Depot Beach off the Princes Highway.

Halfway between the pretty little harbourside town of Ulladulla and Bateman's Bay lies wild, sandy Pebbly Beach, sandwiched between sandstone cliffs and thick forest. The road is terrible, through a forest of spotted gums that shine ghostly white, but it's worth the effort. A large kangaroo population lives around the campsite by the beach; they can sometimes be spotted playing in the waves, along with crimson rosellas and galahs. It's the perfect place for bushwalking, picnics, barbecues and swimming.

CANBERRA AND SOUTHERN NSW

Snowy Mountains

The Snowy Mountains are just one example of Australia's extraordinary geographical diversity. Part of the massive Great Dividing Range, they are covered with deep snow for four to five months of the year. Uplifted from the sea floor more than 250 million years ago, many of the landmark mountains are not jagged peaks but rounded mounds, with the country's only glacial lakes. Wildflowers carpet the alpine meadows in summer, while in winter gnarled snow gums bend with their snow burden and icy granite boulders stand out against clear blue skies.

Alpine Way

'Kosciuszko Alpine Way' brochure, available from the Snowy River Visitor Centre in Jindabyne. Tel: (02) 6450 5600.

One of the most spectacular routes through the Snowy Mountains runs from Cooma and Jindabyne in NSW through to Victoria, along the Alpine Way. This road, 111km long, is best in late spring, summer and early autumn. It passes along the beautiful Thredbo River valley, via Thredbo village and through Dead Horse Gap pass, before dropping over the steep western face of the 'Snowies' to the headwaters of the mighty Murray River, while Mount Kosciuszko and Mount Townsend tower above. A $14-a-day Kosciuszko National Park entry fee must be paid at the gates, and tyre chains must be carried by law during winter.

Cooma

Cooma Visitors' Centre, 119 Sharpe St, Cooma. Tel: 1800 636 525 or (02) 6450 1742.

Cooma, halfway between Canberra and the Snowy Mountains ski fields, has a colourful past of frontier-like shoot-outs in the main street, multi-cultural romance and bush mountain feats. Once the base for the Snowy Mountains Scheme, with

its thousands of European migrant workers, Cooma is now a busy rural town acting as the gateway to the NSW Snowy Mountains, Kosciuszko National Park and the ski fields. It has an abundance of ski shops and fly-fishing stores, as well as some splendid historic buildings and old pubs that can be visited on three heritage walks.

Kosciuszko National Park

Snowy River Visitor Centre and Kosciuszko National Park information centre, NSW National Parks and Wildlife Service, Kosciuszko Rd, Jindabyne. Tel: (02) 6450 5600; fax: (02) 6456 1249; e-mail: srvc@npws.nsw.gov.au

Kosciuszko, visited by more than three million people a year, is the state's largest national park, covering 690,000 hectares of thick bush wilderness, rocky mountain peaks, rushing thaw rivers and grassy mountain meadows. It contains NSW's only ski fields and half of the country's snow area, including Australia's highest mountain, Mount Kosciuszko, at 2 228m. It is protected under international regulations as a significant Unesco biosphere reserve, and is home to more than 200 plant, frog and animal species found nowhere else in the world.

Mount Kosciuszko

Many people use Thredbo (*see opposite*) as a base for their climb to the 'top of Australia'. Mount Kosciuszko is an easy 6.5-km walk (one way) on a metal walkway from the top of the **Crackenback chairlift** (*from Thredbo centre; $$*), which runs all year round. The views, as you would expect, are fabulous and the slopes are carpeted with wildflowers, especially in January and February. Further down, other beautiful walks include the 3.2-km Meadows Nature Track, which leads through alpine gums along the river.

Skiing

Perisher Blue ski resort (including Smiggin Holes, Guthega and Blue Cow). Tel: 1800 655 844. www.perisher.com.au

Selwyn Snowfields, Cabramurra Rd, via Kiandra. Tel: (02) 6454 9488.

Perisher Blue, which has combined the former resorts of Blue Cow, Guthega, Smiggin Holes and Mount Perisher, is now the largest ski resort in the Snowy Mountains. **Selwyn Snowfields** is a great resort for families and complete novices, while those who cannot find accommodation in the main resorts can stay in Jindabyne and Cooma, and travel in. The ski season runs from mid-June to October, with the best snow from July to September. Outside these months, the resorts are virtual ghost towns and even Thredbo will be snoring if you arrive before the Christmas rush.

Thredbo

$$$ per day.

Thredbo's wooden chalets nestle among the snow gums in an alpine valley, and are packed to the gills in winter with skiers from all over the state. In recent years, it's been marketing itself as a year-round resort with a brilliant programme of summer activities, ranging from canoeing, kayaking, horse-riding and fly-fishing to abseiling, mountain biking, bobsledding, tennis, golf and bushwalking. All activities can be booked through the Thredbo Centre (*tel: (02) 6459 4100*) at the bottom of the ski lift. Nearby, Raw NRG Thredbo (*tel: (02) 6457 6282*) runs mountain-bike courses and rents equipment.

Yarrangobilly Caves

Snowy Mountains Highway. Open daily 0900–1630. $$.

Information: Kosciuszko National Park, NSW National Parks and Wildlife Service. Tel: (02) 6454 9597.

A detour to Yarrangobilly gives a good sense of Australia's vastness. After Kiandra, the terrain becomes almost lunar-like, dotted with eerily twisted snow gums. There are six caves at Yarrangobilly. The largest is called the Glory Hole, a spring chicken in cave terms at less than 100,000 years old, which you can explore on your own. Of the others, the Jillebenan (*tours at 1100 and 1500*) and the Jersey (*tours at 1300*) are the most decorative. At the bottom of the valley is a glorious thermal pool surrounded by snow gums – a scenic setting for a (nearly) warm swim all year round.

Ghost town

Kiandra on the Snowy Mountains Highway is the original ghost town. A boom town for a few years after gold was discovered there in 1859, and a centre for local shepherds, skiers and small-scale miners in the late 19th century, it now sits spookily in the middle of nowhere undisturbed by a single inhabitant, except for the occasional amateur treasure hunter hoping for an overlooked nugget.

Eating and drinking

Canberra

Canberra, with its fat-cat politicians (with large expense accounts) and a young affluent population, is blessed with a huge number of wide-ranging restaurants. Top eating turf includes the smart, fashionable suburb of Manuka, and Garema Place in the city centre.

Antigo
Petrie Plaza. Tel: (02) 6249 8080. Open daily all day and dinner. $$. An outdoor terrace under the trees, laid-back blues music, and a menu peppered with cajun spices, slow-roasted tomatoes and delicacies such as kangaroo fillets. There's live jazz every Friday 2130–2330; book for this and Saturday nights.

Lemon Grass Thai
71 London Circuit. Tel: (02) 6247 2779. Open Mon–Fri for lunch, Mon–Sat for dinner. $$. This polite, family-friendly restaurant serves a spicy selection of dishes with plenty of choice for vegetarians.

Red Back Café
15 Garema Place. Tel: (02) 6247 1236. Open daily 0900–1030. $$. Modern Australian cuisine encompassing all the specialities – emu, crocodile and kangaroo – plus a fine selection of gourmet sandwiches.

My Café
Franklin St, Manuka. Open daily till late. $$. This relaxed arty café incorporates native bush foods into the menu in the guise of mint, hazelnut and macadamia pesto and lemon myrtle sauce, concentrating on low-fat, low-cholesterol – but still tasty – nosh. BYO.

Timmy's Kitchen
Furneaux St, Manuka. Tel: (02) 6295 6537. Open daily for lunch and dinner. $. Small and serviceable, what this restaurant lacks in glamour is made up for by the delicious Chinese and Malaysian food. BYO.

The Tryst
Bougainville St, Manuka. Tel: (02) 6239 4422. Open daily 1800–2230. $$$. Buzzing with the affluent young and old, this is sophisticated food with an oriental twist.

The Southern Highlands

Berrima Bakery
Wingecarribee St, Berrima. $$. Pick up a picnic of tomato bread, pumpkin damper or leek pie, as well as some delightful cakes. There's also a little coffee shop to the side.

The Surveyor General Inn
Old Hume Highway, Berrima. Tel: (02) 4877 1226. Open daily lunch and dinner. $$. Opened in 1835, this is the oldest continuously licensed hotel in Australia, serving plenty of ale as well as traditional barbecue food and roasts.

The Post Office Café
27 Railway Ave, Bundanoon. Tel: (02) 4883 6354. Open Wed–Sun for lunch, Wed–Sat for dinner. $$. The service can be snail-like, but the innovative modern Australian dishes are excellent, served in pretty plant-filled surroundings.

Snowy Mountains

Royal Hotel
Cooma. Tel: (02) 6452 2132. $. Typical budget country pub with its wide two-storey veranda and cosy bar.

Café Avalanche
At the bottom of the ski lift, Thredbo. Simply the best raspberry muffins in the southern hemisphere.

T-Bar
Mowamba Mall, Thredbo. Tel: (02) 6457 6355. Open daily from 1800. $$. This fully licensed restaurant serves chargrilled steaks and seafood in cosy surroundings. Children's menu available.

The **Alpine Hotel**, Thredbo, encompasses a variety of restaurants ranging from the upmarket **Cascades** (*open breakfast, lunch (winter only) and dinner*) to the self-service **Bistro** (*open all year 1000–2400*). Après-skiers head to the **Schuss Bar** which has live music (*open Mon–Sat 1600–1930, weekends in summer*), followed by the **Keller Bar** which parties until 0300 (*closed in summer*).

Shopping

The huge **Canberra Centre** in the capital city houses the major department stores, David Jones and Grace Bros, as well as a myriad of fashion, jewellery, shoe and gift shops. For one-off shops and designer boutiques, **Manuka** is the place. For arts and crafts and tempting food stalls, head to the **Old Bus Depot Markets** (*Wentworth Avenue, Kingston; Sun 1000–1600*).

In the Southern Highlands, the **Bundanoon Art Gallery** (*cnr Railway Ave and William St; open daily 1000–1600*) has unusual handmade jewellery, mosaics, glassware, sculpture and paintings within every price range. **Bundanoon Memorial Hall** (*Railway Ave*) hosts a country fair on the first Sunday of each month (*open 0900–1500*).

A myriad of art and crafty shops line Berrima's main street, the Old Hume Highway. **Berrima Galleries** sells upmarket watercolours, jewellery, ceramics and glass, while the **Little Hand-stirred Jam Shop** is a gourmet's delight of unusual marinades, sauces and pickles as well as way-out jams and honey.

Nightlife

Canberra has some good pubs and a strong music and arts scene. See the Canberra Times *entertainment section on Thursday or the free* bma *magazine.*

Pubs to try include the Irish theme pubs, **P J O'Reillys** (*cnr West Row and Alinga St*), which has bands on Saturday nights. Across the way is the **Wig & Pen**, which serves real ale and brews its own beer. Named after a 1940s Sydney madame, **Tilley Devine's** (*cnr Brigalow St and Wattle St, Lyneham; tel: (02) 6247 7753*) is a bar/coffee shop/restaurant and small music venue, revered for its repertoire of big-name ticketed shows and free musicians' practice nights.

PROFILE
The Aborigines

When the First Fleet landed in Sydney in 1788, there were probably around 300,000 Aborigines living in the whole of Australia. They lived in small, scattered groups, mainly along the coast where the sea provided a rich source of food and the rainfall was higher.

Jervis Bay south of Sydney was home to several such groups, described by **Governor Macquarie** in 1811 as 'well-made good-looking men, perfectly at their ease and void of fear'. Like many indigenous tribes in the early days of European settlement, they acted as guides to the impenetrable bushland. They did not realise that the white settlers would dispossess them of their land, claiming *terra nullius* – that the territory belonged to no one. As land is the very core of Aboriginal ancestral origins and culture, the Aboriginals could not have suffered a worse fate, likened by **Robert Hughes** in *The Fatal Shore* to condemning them to 'spiritual death'.

Almost all over the country, the introduction of sheep and cattle drove out the kangaroos and native game, causing the breakdown of their hunting environment. European diseases such as smallpox, influenza and measles wiped out large numbers. Violent clashes with the settlers and the introduction of alcohol killed many more. Within 100 years of settlement, total numbers had declined to around 50,000.

" I thought, that's a real indictment upon Australia that Aboriginal people living in an advanced country have third-world health problems. "

Dr Sandra Eades, Aboriginal Medical Service, in *My Kind Of People: Achievement Identity and Aboriginality*, 1994

Throughout the 19th and 20th centuries, the Aborigines were subjected to discrimination at all levels and omitted from the population census until the 1960s. Many children were taken from their parents and placed with white families to learn to think and act 'white' under the government's policy of 'assimilation'.

However, by the 1970s, Aboriginal issues were creeping on to the political agenda. A land-rights movement gathered momentum, publicised by the **Aboriginal tent embassy** (*see page 90*) outside Canberra's Parliament House. Several steps have been taken to hand back land to indigenous tribes as part of a reconciliation process, particularly in the Northern Territories. On the south coast, Jervis Bay's national park was transferred to the Aboriginal community in 1995 and renamed **Boodereeb**, meaning 'plenty of fish'.

Despite some progress, great inequality remains. Indigenous people have a higher infant mortality rate, and poorer housing, sanitation and food supplies than other Australians. On the positive side a strong Aboriginal culture of writers, dancers and artists has emerged, receiving widespread recognition.

" I could tell you of heartbreak, hatred blind,
I could tell of crimes that shame mankind,
Brutal wrong and deeds malign,
Of rape and murder, son of mine.
But I'll tell instead of brave and fine,
When lives of black and white entwine,
And men in brotherhood combine,
This would I tell you, son of mine. "

***Son of Mine*, 1964, by Aboriginal poet
Oodgeroo Noonuccal**

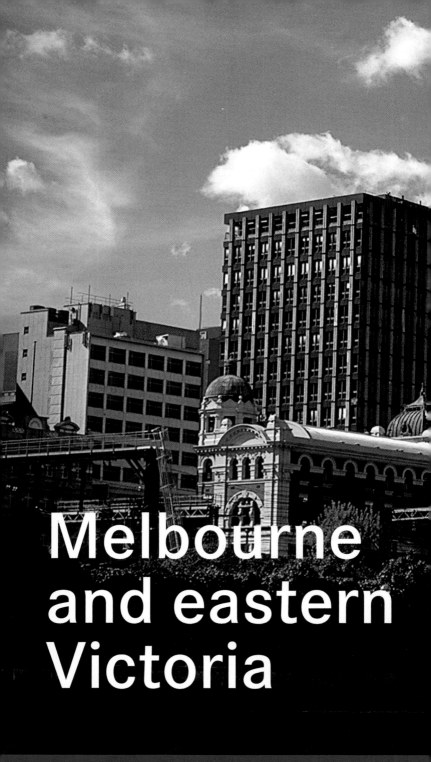

Melbourne and eastern Victoria

Melbourne's multi-cultural population is fortunate indeed. They live in one of the most agreeable and easy-going cities in the world, and on their doorstep is an area of great natural beauty, with fertile valleys producing treasures of food and wine, sandy beaches, rocky headlands, and an abundance of animals and birdlife. Add to that delightful snowy mountains within easy reach, and covered in dramatic ghost gums, and you have a tourist area of unparalleled charm.

MELBOURNE AND EASTERN VICTORIA

BEST OF
Melbourne and eastern Victoria

Getting around: A great way to see **Melbourne** is from the free City Circle Tram, refurbished and decked out in burgundy and gold. Trams operate every 10 mins daily, from 1000 to 1800, touring the city in both directions, with 25 stops along the route.

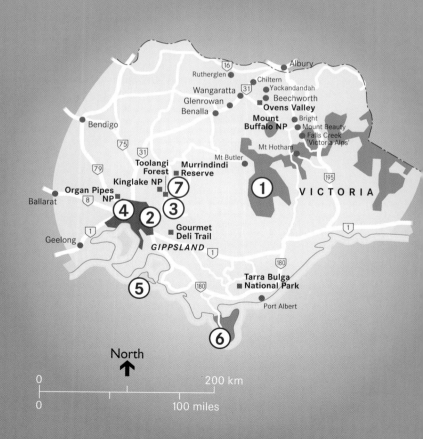

Albury

Rutherglen
Chiltern
Yackandandah
Wangaratta
Glenrowan
Beechworth
Benalla
Ovens Valley

Bendigo

Mount Buffalo NP
Bright
Mount Beauty
Falls Creek
'Victoria Alps'
Mt Hotham

Mt Butler

Toolangi Forest
Murrindindi Reserve

Kinglake NP
(7)

Ballarat
Organ Pipes NP
(4) (2) (3)

V I C T O R I A

Geelong
Gourmet Deli Trail

GIPPSLAND

(5)

Tarra Bulga National Park

(6)

Port Albert

North

| 0 | | 200 km |
| 0 | 100 miles | |

MELBOURNE AND EASTERN VICTORIA

① Alpine National Park

Victoria's highest mountains, with glorious wildflowers, and heaps of snow when it matters. The appealing ski resorts are ready to cater for everyone – from experts to family first-timers when winter comes.
Page 118

② The Dandenongs

Fern-tree gullies, rhododendrons and giant camellias, lyrebirds and kookaburras – all natural wonders, but the top attraction in this National Park is the endlessly appealing Puffing Billy steam train. **Pages 120 and 121**

③ Healesville Sanctuary

Two hundred native Australian animal species cared for in the best conditions, and the rare chance to see twin platypus youngsters, born at the sanctuary.
Page 133

④ Melbourne

The first capital of Australia, and eternally engaged in a good-natured battle with its rival Sydney, Melbourne is renowned for its arts, fine food, fashionable living and for being absolutely sports-mad. **Pages 116–17**

⑤ Phillip Island

The parade of the fairy penguins is unmissable. Watch them waddle up the beach and bustle about near their burrows, seemingly oblivious to their observers. **Page 127**

⑥ Wilsons Promontory

Very important to the local Aborigines, this National Park's 130 kilometres of pristine coastline attract 400,000 visitors every year. 'The Prom' is the perfect place for your first overnight hike. **Pages 130–1**

⑦ Yarra Valley

More than 30 wineries offer tastings in the Yarra Valley, and many have their own restaurant. Spend some time wandering round the valley, enjoying the gourmet delights. **Page 132**

Tourist information

Victoria Visitor Information Centre, Town Hall, cnr of Little Collins St and Swanston St. Tel: (03) 9790 2121.

Parks Victoria website: www.parks.vic.gov.au

Melbourne

It is widely accepted that Melbourne is the queen of Australian cities. With its superior restaurants, elegant architecture, wide streets and green, open spaces, it's been voted one of the world's most 'liveable' cities. With up to 50 per cent of its population having one parent born overseas, Melbourne has grown up to be a metropolitan, multicultural and urbane city.

One of the special joys of Melbourne is that it is a city of art, where works may be seen in the streets and in the public and commercial buildings, as well as in galleries. The glorious **National Gallery of Victoria** (*180 St Kilda Rd; tel: (03) 9208 0203; open daily 1000–1700*) has the finest collection of art in the southern hemisphere. **The Aboriginal Desert Art Gallery** (*31 Flinders St; tel: (03) 9654 2516; open Mon– Sat 1000–1730, Sun 1200–1700*) specialises in Aboriginal paintings and artefacts from the central Australian desert.

Within the city, the **Royal Botanic Gardens** (*Visitors' Centre and Gate F, Birdwood Ave; tel: (03) 9655 2300; open daily 0730–2030 Nov–Mar, 0730–1730 Apr–Oct*) is one of the glories of Melbourne. The gardens sweep down to the banks of the Yarra and are generally accepted as being among the finest in Australia.

A sporting city

Melbourne is a city obsessed by sport, particularly **Aussie Rules football**. In addition, the whole of Australia comes

to a standstill for the Melbourne Cup **horse race**. Melbourne (formerly Flinders) Park (*Botman Ave; tel: (03) 9286 1234; open Mon–Fri 0700–2300, weekends 0900–1800*) hosts the Australian Open **tennis** in January. Melbourne **Cricket** Ground (*Yarra Park, Jolimont;*

Aussie Rules

Melbourne is mad about Aussie Rules. The first recorded game took place in 1858, with 40 players a side. Now, it's slightly more civilised, but only slightly. Edward Kinglake wrote in 1891: 'There have been more brutal fights in Melbourne over football matches than in any other colony … it raises such enthusiasm, even to the point of broken heads and bloody noses.' The bloody noses may be on the pitch rather than off these days, but the Melbourne fans' enthusiasm remains undiminished.

tel: (03) 9657 8864; open 1000–1600, with guided tours conducted hourly), always referred to as the **MCG**, is a sacred shrine to the sport of Don Bradman and Dennis Lillee.

Getting there: Victoria Visitor Information Centre, Town Hall, cnr of Little Collins St and Swanston St. Tel: (03) 9790 2121.

Royal Botanic Gardens, Cranbourne

Royal Botanic Gardens, Cranbourne, Ballarto Rd, off South Gippsland Highway, Cranbourne. Tel: (03) 5990 2200. Open 0900–1700 daily except Christmas Day and Good Friday. May be closed on days of total fire ban. $.

On the outskirts of Melbourne, the Cranbourne Gardens are an annexe of the Royal Botanic Gardens. The remnant bushland and wetland was bought in 1970 to develop a

garden specialising in native Australian flowers, trees, grasses and shrubs in a natural setting. The heathland starts flowering in July, producing a carpet of pink and white; during October and November, the scene is a mass of white with the star-like flowers of the wedding bush. In summer and autumn the silver *banksia* produces a mass of golden cones. A surprising number and variety of native animals live in the gardens. Bandicoots often scuttle around the picnic area and koalas and echidnas are also common. Signs remind you to share the path with snakes. The garden has several easy walking tracks.

Alpine National Park

Visitor Information Centre, PO Box 145, Mount Beauty. Tel: (03) 5754 4718.
Access via either Harrietville and Mount Hotham (Great Alpine Road) or
Mount Beauty and Falls Creek (Bogong High Plains Road).

Banjo man

Drovers would graze their cattle on the High Plains of the Alpine National Park during summer. Their way of life was immortalised by legendary Australian writer Banjo Patterson in his famous poem The Man from Snowy River. *Many of the small wooden huts dotted across the park, now used by weary walkers and lost cross-country skiers, were built by those same cattlemen.*

This vast national park contains Victoria's highest mountains and a largely untouched alpine wilderness area. The 400-km Alpine Walking Track traverses the Bogong High Plains from Mount Hotham to Mount Bogong. (The weather can change suddenly, so be prepared.) The spring wildflowers are glorious, while the High Plains is a landscape of grassy plateaux and stunted snow gums.

Organ Pipes National Park

Organ Pipes National Park, Calder Hwy, Diggers Rest. Tel: (03) 9390 1082.

Just 20km northwest of Melbourne, the Organ Pipes National Park provides some beautiful picnic spots and walking tracks. The strange 20-m high basalt columns – the 'organ pipes' – were formed possibly two to three million years ago from deep lava flows filling creek valleys. These then cracked into hexagonal blocks as they cooled and shrank, and the cracks gradually extended and formed the columns seen today.

Festival!

Opera in the Alps, *Mount Buffalo*, January. *Food, Wine and Wildflower Festival*, *Falls Creek,* 3rd weekend in January; tel: (03) 5758 3490. *Mount Bogong Conquestathon*, early March; tel: (03) 5754 4647. *Yackandandah Folk Festival*, second weekend in March. *Winery Walkabout*, *Rutherglen,* one weekend in June. *Benalla Rose Festival*, November; tel: (03) 5762 1749.

Mount Beauty

Visitor Information Centre, Kiewa Valley Hwy, Tawonga South.
Tel: (03) 5754 4024.

The rocky face of Victoria's highest mountain, Mount Bogong, towers above the town of Mount Beauty. In the 1940s, the town provided accommodation for workers on Victoria's hydro-electric Kiewa project. Today, it is a good base for skiers, mountain-bikers and bushwalkers. The most popular way of climbing Mount Bogong is via the Staircase Spur, a steep 6-km climb that rises from 700m to 1 986m.

Skiing

Mount Buller, tel: 1800 039 049 or (03) 9809 0291; Falls Creek, tel: 1800 033 079; Mount Hotham, tel: 1800 354 555; Mount Buffalo, tel: 1800 037 038. Alpine Resorts Commission mountain information line: 190 2240 523.

From June to late September, Victoria goes ski-mad when snow settles on the Victorian Alps and the world-class ski resorts of **Mount Buller**, **Falls Creek**, **Mount Hotham**, **Dinner Plain** and **Mount Buffalo** open for business. Cross-country skiing is magnificent, with groomed tracks close to the resorts, and virgin bush snow for the intrepid to explore further afield. Mount Buller (closest to Melbourne, and the most 'jetset' of the resorts), Falls Creek and Mount Hotham are all separate villages above the snowline, nestled in the Alpine National Park. **Mount Buffalo** offers gentle skiing and young families.

Stay on the *piste*

Off-piste *skiing is not encouraged in the Victorian Alps, where the mountains are wild, empty and remote. Getting lost can lead to a quick and cold death.*

The Dandenong Ranges

Visitor Information Centre, 1211 Burwood Highway, Ferntree Gully 3156. Tel: 1800 645 505; fax: (03) 9758 7533.

Spectacular mountain-ash forests and lush fern gullies are the main features of this popular 3 215-hectare National Park. There are walking tracks to suit all levels, and the views from the Sherbrooke Forest roads are surprisingly beautiful. Many of the mountain ashes growing in the forest today are the result of regeneration following bushfires in the 1890s and early 1900s, but some of the forest giants are thought to be up to 200 years old. The park boasts more than 130 native bird species, the best known being the lyrebird. Visitors will often hear them mimicking the sounds of other birds, especially on the 7-km **Eastern Sherbrooke Lyrebird Circuit** walk. Among the pleasant picnic spots is the site of the old Doongalla homestead, where open lawns, giant camellias and rhododendrons contrast with the surrounding bush. Friendly kookaburras live in the trees.

Olinda National Rhododendron Gardens

The Georgian Rd, Olinda. Open daily 1000–1630; daylight saving closes 1730. $$.

The 40-hectare National Rhododendron Gardens are at their best in spring when the gentle slopes are covered in the brilliant colours of 12,000 azaleas and 15,000 rhododendrons, which thrive on the deep acidic mountain soil and the cooler high-altitude climate. Other features are a cherry walk, a dogwood path and an extensive alpine garden, and a spectacular view over the Yarra Valley and distant mountains.

There is more colour in the Dandenongs and Yarra Valley at **Tesselaars Tulip Farm** at Silvan, alive with swaying heads in early spring, at McCulloch's specialist **Fuchsia Nursery** at Toolangi, and at the charming **Warratina Lavender Farm** at Wandin North.

Puffing Billy

Old Monbulk Rd, Belgrave. Tel: (03) 9754 6800; 24-hr recorded timetable information: 1900 937 069; fax: (03) 9754 2513; e-mail: pbr@pbr.org.au; www.pbr.org.au. Runs daily except Christmas Day. $$.

The open carriages and closed restaurant cars of the little Puffing Billy steam train have been a favourite holiday experience for generations of Melbourne children and adults.

It was once an important link for mountain dwellers to transport timber and farm produce to the city, and it now chuffs through hills, untouched bush, fern gullies and across tall wooden trestle bridges from Belgrave Station to pretty Emerald Lake (3-hour round trip). Since 1990, volunteers have been rebuilding the track and the section from Emerald Lake to Gembrook is now open.

William Ricketts Sanctuary

Mt Dandenong Tourist Rd, Mt Dandenong. Tel. (03) 9751 1300. Open daily 1000–1600 except Christmas Day. $$.

The sanctuary of sculptor and environmentalist William Ricketts is dotted with nearly 100 intricate clay sculptures depicting Aboriginal people and animals. The figures are moulded into rocks and tree stumps, with inscriptions engraved on clay tablets. This evocative place was Ricketts' home from 1934 to 1993, and is now a memorial to his passion for the environment and to his time spent with the Pitjantjara and Aranda Aborigines of central Australia. In his sculptures, the wistful faces of dark-skinned, blond-haired desert children peer out alongside powerfully modelled Aboriginal men with flowing beards and headbands. Fountains trickle among the ferns and the image of water flows through the sanctuary. Ricketts' belief in the unity of all life is strongly evident in his work.

MELBOURNE AND EASTERN VICTORIA

Gippsland

Gippsland is a loosely defined area to the southeast of Melbourne, between the Great Dividing Range and Victoria's southern coastline. It was once covered in lush rainforest, but today it is a fertile region of rolling hills and farmland.

Gourmet Deli trail

The Gourmet Deli driving trail, through the rolling green hills and lush valleys of west Gippsland, visits farms, vineyards, bakeries, galleries and several scenic outlooks. The region's rich soil and consistent rainfall have long been known for producing fine potatoes, onions, asparagus and dairy products (including the renowned Gippsland Blue cheeses from Neerim South). Now, many more gourmet delights – from soft fruits to smoked meats – are available through farm-gate outlets and specialist shops.

Grand Ridge Road

The Grand Ridge Road winds its way along the spine of the Strzelecki Ranges, past the mountain-ash forests and steep fern gullies of Tarra Bulga National Park (*see below*).

The road has fantastic lookouts over Wilsons Promontory and South Gippsland. Mount Tassie, the highest point in the Strzeleckis, provides wonderful views of the entire LaTrobe Valley and beyond.

Port Albert

The fishing town of Port Albert is Gippsland's oldest village and one of Victoria's earliest settlements. It was the arrival point for thousands of gold-diggers heading for the rich Omeo and Walhalla goldfields during the 1860s, and the supply port for Gippsland farm pioneers until the railway from Melbourne to Sale was completed in 1878. It was also a major centre for whaling, sealing and fishing, its large old timber jetties often hosting a fleet of commercial and passenger sailing vessels from Europe and America. Today it remains an attractive, but much quieter, commercial fishing port with popular swimming and surfing beaches nearby. Its 1841 pub is a great favourite with the many fishermen who use the town to explore the excellent fishing around Snake Island and Corner Inlet marine park. Every March, Port Albert hosts the hundred-thousand-dollar Fishing Classic.

123

Tarra Bulga National Park

Information Centre, Grand Ridge Rd, Balook. Tel: (03) 5196 6166.

The 1560 hectares of Tarra Bulga National Park are all that remain of the ancient, lush Gippsland rainforest, after brutal clearing by settlers. It has a range of excellent walking tracks to suit all levels. Listen for lyrebirds singing in the mountain ash forests and look out for platypus in the mountain streams. Go quietly amid the ferns – and don't forget it can be very wet.

Kinglake National Park

Office and visitor information, National Park Rd, Pleasant Creek. Parks Victoria Information Centre. Tel: 13 1963; www.parks.vic.gov.au

Spectacular waterfalls, fern gullies and lyrebirds draw visitors to the Kinglake National Park, 21,600-hectares of eucalypt forest on the outskirts of Melbourne. The park's two main picnic areas are at Masons Falls and Jehosophat Gully; the shy lyrebird can often be seen near the Masons Falls area. There is a choice of several short or longer walks from these picnic areas.

The northern section of the park has more open forest and the trees are more stunted due to drier conditions and poorer soils. Follow the short walking trail to the Wombelano Falls, a beautiful and relatively pristine waterfall that is spring-fed and flows for most of the year.

Murrindindi Reserve

With its tumbling waterfalls, soaring mountain ash trees and damp, fern-filled gullies, the Murrindindi Scenic Reserve, just off the Melba Highway, is home to a variety of native animals including wombats, echidnas and shy swamp wallabies. A short walk along the River Walk track from the reserve car park takes you to the Murrindindi Cascades, where the river drops steeply over granite boulders, through beautiful temperate rainforest of myrtle beech and sassafras.

Toolangi Forest

Discovery Centre, Main Rd, Toolangi. Tel: (03) 5962 9314. Open 1000–1700 except Christmas Day and Good Friday. Guided tours $.

A striking building made of timber, glass and steel, the Toolangi Forest Discovery Centre (8km east of the Murrindindi Reserve) tells the story of tall forests and the timber industry in the Yarra Ranges, an area which teemed at the beginning of the 20th century with pioneers, loggers and extraordinary little timber tramways. The centre is a good starting place to begin exploring the Toolangi State Forest on a number of short forest discovery walks. The poet C J Dennis was a proprietor of a sawmill at Toolangi, and often wrote about local characters in his poems. Today, his old home, and his famous 'Singing Gardens', created in 1915, are a Devonshire tea-house (*98 Kinglake Rd; tel: (03) 5962 9282; open Sat–Thu 1000–1700, closed August and Christmas Day*).

Mount Buffalo National Park

Parks Victoria Information Line: 13 1963; www.parks.vic.gov.au

The imposing rock face of Mount Buffalo makes it quite different from the surrounding mountains. This National Park offers spectacular views over mountain valleys and huge granite walls, as well as the relaxing atmosphere of the historic **Mount Buffalo Chalet** (*tel: (03) 5755 1500*). It is a bushwalker's paradise, with many well-signposted and accessible walking tracks. In summer, the plant and animal life of the tall eucalypt forest, alpine heathlands and snowgrass plains is abundant. In winter, the landscape is marked with gentle ski *pistes* and cross-country trails. The near-vertical walls of the gorge provide some challenging rock climbs and abseiling.

Rutherglen

Rutherglen Wine Region tourism office. Tel: (02) 6032 9166.

The 16 well-established and internationally renowned wineries clustered around the historic town of Rutherglen, and along the nearby Murray River, are famed for their fortified wines. Most are open seven days a week for tasting and sales. Many have been in the same family for several generations, and some are based in historic old buildings. **Rutherglen** is an attractive town with a main street lined with old veranda-fronted buildings. It comes alive during the immensely popular Rutherglen Winery Walkabout weekend in June. Organised bike tours and bike hire are available.

Phillip Island

Phillip Island Visitor Information Centre, Newhaven. Tel: (03) 5956 7447.

Penguin Parade Visitors Centre. Tel: (03) 5956 8300; fax: (03) 5956 8394; e-mail: penguins@penguins.org.au; www.penguins.org.au. $$.

Phillip Island is best known for its **Penguin Parade**, Victoria's most popular tourist attraction. Every evening at sunset, hundreds of tiny Little Penguins come ashore at Summerland Beach and waddle across the sand to their burrows in the dunes, just as their ancestors have done for thousands of generations. Once ashore, the penguins spend time around their burrows in the spinifex tussocks preening themselves and, in summer, feeding their hungry chicks. Visitors watch from raised boardwalks.

Linked by bridge to the mainland at San Remo, Phillip Island also has spectacular beaches for surfing, swimming and fishing, as well as excellent walking. Its wildlife includes Australia's largest colony of 7 000 fur seals, about half a million short-tail shearwaters (mutton birds), which breed every year at Cape Woolamai, and a large koala conservation centre (*tel: (03) 5956 8300*).

MELBOURNE AND EASTERN VICTORIA

Ovens Valley gold rush

In the 1850s, the area around the Ovens River, along with other parts of Victoria, experienced a gold rush. The industry was based in Beechworth, where there was a huge Chinese population, but many other villages grew up around the area, including Chiltern, Bright and Yackandandah. Although the mining stopped at the beginning of the 20th century, many of the places associated with the gold industry are well preserved, and have maintained an evocative atmosphere.

Beechworth

Visitor Information, Ford St. Tel: (03) 5728 3233.

Picturesque Beechworth is one of Victoria's best-preserved gold-mining towns, with more than 30 buildings classified by the National Trust, and wide, tree-lined streets. It is surrounded by forested valleys, waterfalls and rocky gorges. The town's museum contains an interesting collection of gold-rush memorabilia and a replica of the main street of a century ago. The main street now has numerous antiques and craft shops, as well as the famous Beechworth Bakery.

Bright

Bright Information Centre, 119 Gavan St. Tel: (03) 5755 2275. Walking maps available.

Bright Outdoor Centre, 9 Ireland St, Bright 3741. Tel: (03) 5755 1818. Equipment for camping, fishing, bushwalking, skiing.

In the heart of the Ovens Valley, Bright is a good base for skiing and for the **Mount Buffalo National Park**. A spring festival (Oct/Nov) showcases many of the town's lovely gardens, while an autumn festival (late April/early May) celebrates the changing seasons, with the avenues of deciduous European trees turning red and gold. Walking trails around Bright include Canyon Walk, an easy route along the Ovens River, passing remains of the old gold workings.

Chiltern

Visitor Information Centre, cnr Conness St and Main St. Tel: (03) 5726 1395.

The pretty town of Chiltern boomed during the 1850s gold rushes, with a population of 20,000 at its peak. Today, life proceeds at a more leisurely pace, and Chiltern's historic atmosphere is in great demand as the backdrop for a number of major films. The oldest grapevine in Australia runs (literally) down the posts and shopfronts of the main street. The Chiltern Box-Ironbark Forest around the town has a number of walks and excellent displays of wildflowers during spring and summer.

Yackandandah

Yackandandah Visitor Information Centre, High St. Tel: (02) 6027 1222.

This small gold-mining town, in the scenic Indigo Valley, is home to a strong community of artists and craftspeople, whose work can be seen at the local gallery or in their own studios. Many of Yackandandah's Victorian-era buildings are listed by the National Trust. In the surrounding forest there is evidence of mining; walkers need to watch out for mine shafts and tunnels. In the early morning or late afternoon, the trees come alive with honeyeaters, rosellas and willy wagtails.

Wilsons Promontory National Park

Information Centre, Tidal River. Tel: (03) 5680 9555 or 1800 350 552. Open daily 0830–1630.

Wilsons Promontory National Park is a 50,000-hectare park featuring 130km of pristine coastline on the southernmost tip of mainland Australia. Its diverse landscape ranges from gentle coves, coastal heathland and fern gullies to wild white-sand Bass Strait beaches and spectacular rock formations, and majestic, granite peaks. Once a land bridge to Tasmania until the sea level rose 15,000 years ago, 'The Prom' has long been of great significance to local Aboriginal people. It is the state's oldest National Park and its most popular. An extensive network of day and overnight walking trails and camping grounds starts from the information centre at the small settlement of **Tidal River**. The lookout at Mount Oberon car park offers magnificent views across Bass Strait.

For many of The Prom's 400,000 annual visitors, their enduring memory of the park is of its wildlife and flora. Fish and seals abound on its protected reefs, offshore islands and waters, hundreds of tame crimson rosellas flock around Tidal River, and emus, wombats, koalas, swamp wallabies and eastern grey kangaroos often wander across the park's roads.

The camping ground at **Tidal River** fronts on to the sweeping **Norman Bay**, a popular family swimming beach, which lacks the strong currents that can make other Prom beaches dangerous (including nearby Oberon Bay). The famous white sands of **Squeaky Beach** are only a half-hour walk away from Tidal River, while the **Loo-errn boardwalk** track, named after an Aboriginal spirit, offers serene views of the river and surrounding peaks to the less active and to wheelchair users. Also recommended is the self-guided **Lilly Pilly Gully nature trail** circuit, a two- to three-hour easy walk through banksias, casuarinas and gum trees where many koalas live, before descending down into the cool verdant gully with its ferns and rainforest.

Relatively easy overnight-hiking trails give access to beaches as magical as **Sealers Cove**, **Refuge Bay** and **Waterloo Bay**. Their little bush camping grounds are set behind sheltered coves – permits are necessary and no wood fires are allowed. The northeast corner of the park has been designated a wilderness zone, with the emphasis on preserving the land, and its flora and fauna in as pristine a state as possible.

Yarra Ranges

Visitor Information Centre, The Old Court House, Harker St, Healesville 3777. Tel: (03) 5962 2600; fax: (03) 5962 2040.

The **Yarra Ranges National Park** offers bush walks for everyone. In the Black Spur and Dom Dom Saddle area, the 12-km **Morleys Track** is a walk through thick, dark and tall mountain ash forest with a rich understorey of wattles, ferns and myrtle beech. The **'Top of the Ranges'** is a spectacular 22-km one-way scenic walk linking Mount Dom Dom with Mount Donna Buang. Other popular walks include the ski trails around Mount Donna Buang, Echo Flat and Lake Mountain. The 4-km loop track near **Powelltown** leads through fern gullies, groves of ancient sassafras and other temperate rainforest species, to the Ada Tree, a towering 76-m, 300-year-old mountain ash.

Yarra Valley wineries

Less than an hour from Melbourne, more than 50 wineries have grown up in the rolling hills of the long-established farming area of the Yarra Valley. Early in the morning hot-air balloons drift over the valley before landing for a winery champagne breakfast. About 30 of the wineries offer cellar-door tasting and sales. Many also have their own restaurants or cafés – the glass-walled tasting room at **Domaine Chandon** (*Maroondah Hwy, Green Point; tel: (03) 9739 1110*) is one not to be missed for a lunchtime glass of sparkling wine. The **Yarra Valley regional food trail** takes in more than 60 epicurean delights, ranging from chutney and hand-made chocolate to lavender honey. Buy picnic provisions from the store at **Yering Station**, the oldest winery in the valley, or at the evocative **Old Dairy** near Yarra Glen. Many festivals take place at Yarra Valley wineries, including the annual Grape Grazing Festival (*first weekend in March; tel (03) 9761 8474; fax (03) 9761 9488*), outside opera performances at the Eyton on Yarra winery, and musical afternoons at Domaine Chandon.

Healesville Sanctuary

Badger Creek Rd, Healesville. Tel: 24-hr information line 1902 240 192;
e-mail: hs@zoo.org.au; www.zoo.org.au. Open daily 0900–1700. $$.

This is the most famous and natural place to see more than
200 species of Australia's unique native wildlife species. There
are excellent keeper talks and special animal exhibitions, and
the wedge-tail eagle flights are an unmissable highlight.
Behind the displays, the sanctuary is involved in veterinary,
research and education programmes that place it at the
forefront of wildlife conservation. In 1999, for the first time
in 50 years, a platypus gave birth here; the twin youngsters
can now be seen.

Eating and drinking

Melbourne is renowned as a great dining city. In a list of the 20 best restaurants in Australia, a dozen would be here. At the very top are:

Jacques Reymond
78 Williams Rd, Windsor. Tel: (03) 9525 2178. Open lunch Tue–Fri, dinner Tue–Sat. $$$. Widely considered to be the best restaurant in Australia. The only restaurant awarded five chef's hats in *The Age* guide.

Flower Drum
17 Market Lane. Tel: (03) 9662 3655. Open lunch Mon–Sat, dinner daily. $$$. Four chef's hats and widely accepted as Australia's finest Asian restaurant.

Mask of China
115 Little Bourke St. Tel: (03) 9662 2116. Open daily. $$$. Four chef's hats and seen as the rival contender for the Asian title.

Paul Bocuse
Daimaru Level 4, Melbourne Central, La Trobe St. Tel: (03) 9660 6600. $$$. Better than his French establishment near Lyon.

Stephanie's
405 Tooronga Rd, Hawthorn E. Tel: (03) 9822 8944. Open Tue–Fri and Sun for lunch, Tue–Sat for dinner. $$$. Run by a great chef.

Multi-racial Melbourne has one of the largest Greek-speaking populations in the world, more Maltese than Malta, more Asians as a percentage of the population than Sydney, and an enormous Italian community. The result of this mix is a fascinating range of markets, restaurants and delicatessens, from the cheap Turkish and Lebanese eateries of Sydney Rd to traditional Italian food in Lygon St, from Chinese in Bourke St to Vietnamese in Victoria St.

Also in Melbourne:

Adelphi Hotel and restaurant
187 Flinders Lane. Tel: (03) 9650 7555; e-mail: info@adelphi.com.au. $$. This small, contemporary hotel has a much-photographed rooftop swimming pool that juts out over Flinders Lane, and a restaurant that offers a superbly cooked, innovative menu.

135

Babka Bakery Café
*358 Brunswick Street, Fitzroy. Tel:
(03) 9416 0091. $.* The Russian
heritage of the owners is evident from
the menu – borscht and cabbage rolls.
Patrons don't mind queuing for a table
while enjoying the aroma of freshly
baked bread. Great breakfasts.

Caffè e Cucina
*581 Chapel St, South Yarra. Tel:
(03) 9827 4139. Open Mon–Sat. $$.*
Authentic Italian atmosphere, good
coffee and cakes and aloof waiters.
Breakfast, lunch and dinner.

Walter's Wine Bar
*Level 3, Southgate. Tel: (03) 9690
9211. $$.* A popular Southgate eatery
where diners can enjoy a selection of
modern Australian cuisine while sitting
on the balcony overlooking the Yarra
and sipping a glass of wine from the
extensive list.

Dandenongs

Ranges
*5 Main St, Olinda. Tel: (03) 9751 2133.
$$.* A contemporary café/restaurant
amid a plethora of tea shoppes.

Ovens Valley

All Saints Winery
*All Saints Rd, Wahgunyah. Tel: (02)
6033 1922. $$$.* Cellar door and
restaurant inside the walls of a
130-year-old castle.

Beechworth Provender
*18 Camp St, Beechworth. Open 7 days.
$$.* Café/delicatessen serving up local
cheeses, mustard, smoked meats
and relishes.

Beechworth Bakery
27 Camp St, Beechworth. $$. An
irresistible array of cakes and pastries.

Parlour & Pantry
69 Ford St, Beechworth. $$. Gourmet
deli and restaurant.

Phillip Island

Narabeen Cottage Restaurant
*16 Steele St, Cowes. Tel: (03) 5952
2062; fax: (03) 5952 3670. $$.* Quiet
location close to beach and all facilities.

Tarra Bulga Guesthouse
*Grand Ridge Rd, Balook. Tel: (03)
5196 6141.* 1930s-style guesthouse
and tearooms.

Yarra Valley

Sweetwater Café *($$)* and
Eleonore's Restaurant *($$$)*
*Chateau Yering, 42 Melba Highway,
Yering. Tel: (03) 9237 3333; fax: (03)
9237 3300.* Freshly baked snacks and
meals in magnificent surroundings.

Bianchet Winery
*187 Victoria Rd, Lilydale. Tel: (03)
9739 1779; fax: (03) 9739 1277.
Café open daily 1000–1800, dinner
Friday and Saturday.* Continuously
serving food with Mediterranean
and Asian influences.

Shopping

Melbourne

Pedestrianised **Swanston St Walk** in Melbourne city centre has a collection of upmarket shops, as well as many outdoor cafés. They say you can buy anything at the **Queen Victoria Market** (*cnr Victoria St and Elizabeth St; tel: (03) 9658 9601; open every day except Mon and Wed*), where more than 1 000 traders offer everything from live poultry to leather handbags. Melbourne also has a tradition of shopping for non-essentials, almost as a social activity, on Sunday mornings. There is a **Sunday Market** at the Victorian Art Centre (*100 St Kilda Rd*); **Sailyards market** (*cnr Lansdale St and Swanston St; open daily 1000 to dusk*) offers clothing, handicrafts and jewellery. **Chinatown**, on Little Bourke St, is Australia's only surviving area of continuous Chinese settlement since the Gold Rush. It is packed with restaurants shops housed in Victorian buildings.

The Mornington Peninsula

If you feel like heading for the beach rather than the hills, a visit to Sorrento and the Mornington Peninsula is an easy day trip from Melbourne. From Melbourne, take the Nepean Highway and Frankston Freeway to Dromana and a winding road that leads up to Arthurs Seat lookout, where the 302-m peak gives a panoramic view over Port Phillip Bay, Bass Strait and the hinterland. In summer, a chairlift up the mountain provides visitors with thrilling treetop vistas. A short drive away is the town of Red Hill, home to Victoria's oldest continuous community market (first Sat of the month, Sept to May). The area is also well known for its wineries, craft shops and restaurants. Fresh fruit from local orchards is a speciality with opportunities to pick your own berries in season.

Cape Schanck, the southernmost tip of the peninsula, and part of the Mornington Peninsula National Park, has a wild, rugged coastline. A boardwalk leads from the clifftop lookout to Pulpit Rock. One of the best coastal walks leads from the cape to Bushrangers Bay. A 27-km walking track goes all the way from Cape Schanck to Portsea, taking in spectacular and exhilarating scenery as it passes the ocean beaches of Rye, Gunnamatta, and Sorrento with access available at various points along the way.

At the entrance to Sorrento, a small memorial and pioneer cemetery marks the site of the first, doomed, white settlement in Victoria, at Sullivan Bay. Sorrento has many fine buildings, some of them made from local limestone, which has an

attractive honey colour. This popular holiday town has cafés, boutiques, galleries and other shops that cater to visitors all year round. Bottlenose dolphins frolic in the waters of the bay; one of the most delightful ways to see them, and admire the clifftop Portsea mansions, while enjoying a different perspective of Point Nepean at the same time, is to take the 40-minute passenger ferry trip to Queenscliff. Alternatively, put your car on the vehicle ferry, and cross more directly to Queenscliff and Geelong on the western side of The Heads narrow entrance to Port Phillip Bay.

The **Point Nepean** section of the **Mornington Peninsula National Park** includes historic Fort Nepean and the quarantine station. After being off limits to the public for more than 100 years, most of the tip of the peninsula was opened in 1988 and visitors can now explore the area on foot or by a transporter.

Getting there: Peninsula Visitor Information Centre. Tel: 1800 804 009; fax: (03) 5981 0462.

West of Melbourne

The main attraction west of Melbourne is the world-famous Great Ocean Road, with its huge cliffs and roaring seas on one side, and magnificent rainforest on the other. Inland are charming towns associated with the gold rush of the 1850s, Victoria's spa country, and the Grampians National Park, where you can stand suspended over nothingness on rocky outcrops, or eat your picnic with a friendly joey for company.

West of
Melbourne

Getting around: The area west of Melbourne is all about the call of the great open road, so hire yourself a car and see what all the fuss is about.

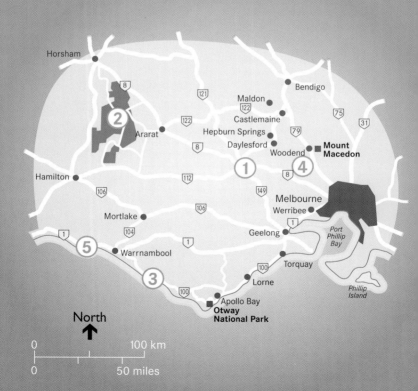

① Ballarat and Sovereign Hill

The gold rush of the 1850s brought an invasion of migrants to this area and a population boom. Sovereign Hill's constantly evolving re-creation of a gold-rush town is a fun and educational and attraction that is thoroughly deserving of the awards it's won.
Pages 144–7

② The Grampians

Bushwalking, rock art, tame kangaroos, gum trees with koalas clinging to them, and spectacular waterfalls – all within relatively easy reach of Melbourne and the Great Ocean Road. **Page 150**

③ Great Ocean Road

Victoria's spectacular coast road, built in the 1920s, attracts people from all over the world for its thrilling offshore and onshore views, and for its fun towns along the way. **Pages 148–9**

④ Hanging Rock

Have your own Picnic at Hanging Rock, and lose yourself in the mysteries of this ancient site, where the story goes that three schoolgirls disappeared one hot summer's day, never to be seen again. **Page 155**

⑤ Port Fairy

This quaint fishing village, a favourite with visitors and locals, has something of an Irish heritage. Once called Belfast, it has stone whalers' cottages and bluestone warehouses and mills.
Page 151

143

Victoria's gold fields

When a young man called Edward Hargreaves first discovered gold in his pan near Bathurst in NSW in 1851, it sparked gold fever throughout the fledgling nation and across the world. Melbourne businessmen offered a reward for the discovery of gold in their own colony – it soon paid off with some of the biggest gold finds ever, at Ballarat, Bendigo and Mount Alexander, near Castlemaine. Diggers flooded in and Victoria boomed, with Ballarat and Bendigo establishing themselves as grand gold centres by the 1880s.

Ballarat

Visitor Information Centre, 39 Sturt St. Tel: 1800 648 450.

The Aborigines used the rich countryside of this district as a resting place – Ballarat's name is derived from two Aboriginal words meaning, literally, 'resting on one's elbow'. With the discovery of gold in 1851, all kinds of people came here to seek their fortune.

The town has wide tree-lined streets, beautiful gardens and grand architecture. The city's gold heritage is evident in the ornate decoration of many of its buildings, including **Her Majesty's Theatre**, Australia's oldest purpose-built, continually operating theatre, and the **Ballarat Fine Art Gallery** (*40 Lydiard Street North; open daily 1030–1700*).

Eureka Street is filled with old miners' cottages; **Montrose Cottage** was the first bluestone dwelling to be built on the gold fields. In the forests and bushland of the **Smythedale Gold Fields**,

Gold rush!

Within five years of the discovery of gold in Victoria, more than 7 000 diggers had arrived at the port of Melbourne from England, Scotland, Ireland, America and China, seeking their fortune. In many ways, it was the gold rushes of the 1850s to 1890s that built the Australia of today, creating a sound economic base for the fledgling colony, and a population explosion.

17km south of Ballarat, the old diggings have names like Jubilee Mine, Misery Creek, Devil's Kitchen and Hard Hill. Ballarat's most famous tourist attraction is **Sovereign Hill** (*see page 146*).

Bendigo

Visitor Information, 51–67 Pall Mall. Tel: 1800 813 153 or (03) 5444 4445; fax: (03) 5444 4447; e-mail: tourism@bendigo.vic.gov.au. Open daily 0900–1700.

The city of Bendigo was laid out in 1854 with broad boulevards. **Pall Mall**, with its decorative Alexander Fountain, is a beautiful Victorian-era streetscape, and opulent gold-rush architecture is a feature. Just minutes from the city centre are **One Tree Hill** and the **Whipstick Forest**, and the Bendigo Bushland Trail provides 74km of cycling and walking tracks.

Bendigo has many fine antique shops and galleries including the recently redeveloped **Bendigo Art Gallery** (*32 View St, Bendigo 3550; tel: (03) 5444 0007; open Wed to Sun 1000–1700; $*), one of the oldest and finest regional galleries in Australia, with outstanding permanent collections of 19th-century European art, and Australian art of the 19th century to the present.

To experience the city's gold-mining history, visit the **Central Deborah Gold Mine** (*76 Violet St; tours daily from 0930; tel: (03) 5443 8322; $$*), which stopped operating in 1951. Visitors descend 61m below ground for a one-hour guided tour. Central Deborah is also the place to pick up one of Bendigo's unique vintage trams for the hop-on, hop-off **City Circle Heritage Tour** (*tel: 0500 544 169; fax: 0500 844 169; departures hourly from 1000 weekends, school and public holidays, 1000 and 1400 normal weekdays; $$; recorded commentary*).

Castlemaine

Visitor Information Centre, Mostyn St. Tel: 1800 171 888; fax: (03) 5471 1746.

The pretty town of Castlemaine, with its hilly streets and splendid old sandstone buildings, is a hub of art and folk music. At its last biennial State Festival of the Arts (*Apr/May, next in 2001*), 47 art galleries sprang up almost overnight, many of them artists' studios open for the occasion. During the gold rush, Castlemaine became the marketplace for all the gold fields of central Victoria. Unlike many of the other small towns nearby, it has survived as a regional centre.

Buda Historic Home and Garden (*Hunter St; open daily 0900–1700; $$*) has a pavilion set among flowering bulbs and an aviary that are charming examples of garden architecture from the 19th century. The best time to visit is in spring, or during Castlemaine's annual **Festival of Gardens** (*Oct/Nov; contact PO Box 758, Castlemaine; tel: (03) 5472 2086*).

Maldon

Information Centre, High St. Tel: (03) 5475 2569; fax: (03) 5475 2007.

Maldon Easter Fair, Folk Music Festival (Oct). Tel: (03) 5475 2166.

Maldon has remained largely unchanged since its days as a 19th-century gold-mining town. Banks, shops and hotels still bear their original signs but it is a real living community. The Victorian streetscape includes fine houses, pretty cottages and shops full of antiques, local arts and crafts, and homemade food. In 1966, the National Trust classified Maldon as Australia's first 'Notable Town', citing its 'most unique and well-preserved variety of historic architecture'.

Sovereign Hill

Bradshaw Street, Ballarat. Tel: (03) 5331 1944. Open daily 1000–1700. $$.

Built on the site of the old Ballarat gold diggings, the award-winning Sovereign Hill is a premium tourist attraction that is quite out of the ordinary. It authentically re-creates the bustling, hectic, rough and dirty life of the gold rush days. The hills are covered with tents, 'miners' pan for gold in the creeks, and the place hums with life as people perform their chores in costumes of the time. There are sweet shops, a funeral parlour, a Chinese Joss House, an open school and even a brothel! An evening sound and light show, 'Blood on the Southern Cross', tells the story of the Eureka Rebellion. Visitors can pan for gold, ride in a coach, dress in period costume, and tour the underground mine. The creeks are regularly seeded with gold dust, so real gold can be found – and kept.

Great Ocean Road

Torquay marks the official start of the Great Ocean Road, Australia's most spectacular and rugged coastline driving route. From here, it's a procession of sand, surf, towering cliffs, limestone formations, thick forests and resort destinations. A memorial arch at Eastern View commemorates those who built the road in the 1920s. Past Apollo Bay, the road turns inland and winds through the Otway National Park, with magnificent mountain-top lookouts. Back on the coast, the road's most spectacular stretch, near Port Campbell, proceeds past world-famous limestone rock formations – the Twelve Apostles, London Bridge and Loch Ard Gorge.

Apollo Bay

This once-sleepy fishing village is now a
popular base for tourists exploring the Otway
cool-climate rainforests and the attractions
of the coast, and the Great Ocean Road.
Colourful fishing boats fill its busy wharf
and its nearby beaches are long and sandy.
Farming and fishing are central to the local
economy – crayfish is a speciality of the area
and the fishermen's co-operative at the edge
of the wharf sells fresh fish every day.

Geelong

Visitor Information Centres:
National Wool Museum.
Tel. (03) 5222 2900; fax: (03) 5223 2069.

Market Square Shopping Centre.
Tel: (03) 5222 6126.

Geelong and Great Ocean Rd, Stead Park,
Princes Hwy. Tel: (03) 5275 5797 or toll-free
1800 620 888.

Tucked in the southwest corner of Port Phillip Bay, Geelong
was historically the export base for wool from the productive
and wealthy grazing properties of Victoria's Western District
basalt plains. The historic 1872 bluestone woolstore now
houses the **National Wool Museum** (*26 Moorabool Street;*
tel: (03) 5227 0701), which animates the sights and sounds
of an industry central to Australia's economic success. Geelong
boasts many National Trust properties and historic country
gardens, as well as fine botanical gardens on a headland
overlooking the bay. Eastern Park, with its beautifully
restored art-deco baths, on Corio Bay, is a peaceful spot
for a stroll, swim or a picnic. In recent years the waterfront,
Steampacket Place, has been given a new lease of life, with
seafood restaurants, wharf shops and a marina.

Tourist information

Great Ocean Road Visitor Information Centre, Foreshore, Apollo Bay.
Tel: (03) 5237 6529; fax: (03) 5237 6194.
Information Centre, Morris St, Port Campbell. Tel: (03) 5598 6382.

Grampians National Park

Visitor Centre, Grampians Rd, Halls Gap. Tel: (03) 5356 4381; fax (03) 5356 4446.

Stunning views, hidden valleys, waterfalls, rocky outcrops and Aboriginal culture as well as outstanding wildflower displays – the Grampians National Park is one of Victoria's best bushwalking locations. The Aborigines know the Grampians as Gariwerd and descendants of the original inhabitants continue to have a strong association with the area today. At the excellent **Brambuk Living Cultural Centre** (*Halls Gap; tel: (03) 5356 4452; fax: (03) 5356 4455; open daily; bush-tucker restaurant, display, souvenir shop and auditorium*), just south of the central hamlet of **Halls Gap**, you can learn about the culture of the Aboriginal communities of southwest Victoria and find out the location of rock-art sites. Koalas can often be seen in the gum trees around Halls Gap, and the kangaroos at Zumsteins picnic area are very tame. Walk up Mount Abrupt, overlooking Dunkeld, or drive down the magnificent Victoria Valley, especially when the wildflowers are out. The **Grampians Gourmet Weekend** is held during the first weekend in May.

Lorne

Visitor Information Centre, 144 Mountjoy Parade. Tel: (03) 5289 1152; fax: (03) 5289 2492.

With its trendy cafés, restaurants, boutiques and shops, appealing Lorne was a popular holiday town even before the Great Ocean Road was built. The mountains behind Lorne provide a photogenic background and also give the town a mild, sheltered climate. A long, protected beach provides swimming and surfing conditions for all abilities. Popular **Erskine Falls** is just a short drive away and the heathland and eucalypt forest of the **Angahook-Lorne State Park** offer many other easily accessible walks.

Otway National Park

Parks Victoria Information Line: 13 1963; www.parks.vic.gov.au

Spectacular and lush rainforest stretches inland and along the coast between Apollo Bay and Princetown. Here, the Great Ocean Road is bordered by giant trees and graceful ferns. The Otways were formed 150 million years ago, when the great southern land mass known as Gondwana began to break up. European settlers cleared much of the land, but extensive forest remains. The Mait's Rest rainforest walk meanders through a beautiful and tranquil fern garden and past huge moss-covered trunks of old beech and myrtle trees, some of them thought to be more than 300 years old. Try *Otway Eco-Guides* for an interesting range of walks (*tel: (03) 5237 7240; fax: (03) 5237 6622; e-mail: sue@otwayeco-guides.com.au; www.otwayeco-guides.com.au*).

Port Fairy

Visitor Information Centre, 22 Bank St. Tel: (03) 5568 2682; fax: (03) 5568 2833.

This seaside village is a favourite with everyone who visits. Its historic wharf, with its quaint harbourside dwellings and colourful fishing boats, transports visitors to another time. Early in the morning, local fishermen unload their harvests of crayfish, abalone and shark. The town used to be known as Belfast and the area's Irish heritage is still present in the names of local landmarks. Many of the old colonial buildings remain, including stone cottages once occupied by whalers, sealers and fishermen, and bluestone warehouses and mills, many of them now converted into accommodation. Port Fairy also boasts wide, sandy swimming and surf beaches and Griffiths Island, where tens of thousands of mutton birds (short-tailed shearwaters) land each year and nest (*Sept to Apr*).

Keen walkers can take the 22-km Mahogany Ship walking track all the way to Warrnambool. The wreck of a mysterious mahogany-coloured ship, last sighted in the 1890s, is thought to have been covered by drifting sands; its existence is believed by some to indicate that Portuguese explorers made it to this coastline long before Captain Cook. During the first weekend in March, Port Fairy bulges at the seams, for its hugely popular folk festival.

Torquay

Australia's 'surf city' and home to some of the world's best-known surfing industry manufacturers, Torquay is a busy holiday town with a mixture of styles. The front beach, with its tall Norfolk pines dotting the shoreline, offers a quiet protected foreshore while nearby the fisherman's beach attracts a wide cross-section of beach-goers; further on, waves come crashing in from Bass Strait on to the main surf beach. **Surfworld Australia** (*Surf City Plaza, Beach Rd, Torquay; tel: (03) 5261 4606; fax: (03) 5261 4756;*

www.surfworld.org.au) is a museum dedicated to surfing, packed with memorabilia. Not far away are the world-famous surfing temples of Bells Beach and Jan Juc.

Warrnambool

Visitor Information Centre, 600 Raglan Parade (Princes Hwy), Warrnambool. Tel: 1800 637 725.

Warrnambool, at the other end of the Great Ocean Road from Torquay, is a gracious town, with long beaches and historic buildings. Its coast is also the nursery for the rare southern right whale. Every year these magnificent creatures – some up to 15m long – journey from the Southern Ocean to calve in the shallow waters of Logans Beach. They often swim within 100m of the shore and can be viewed from a platform in the sand dunes. Whale-watching season begins around May and continues through till September.

The **Flagstaff Hill Maritime Museum** (*Merri St; tel: (03) 5564 7841*) effectively re-creates the sights and sounds of a 19th-century port, complete with original lighthouses and replicas of buildings of the time, including a sailmaker's loft, bank, town hall and chapel.

In January, Warrnambool celebrates with the Spirit of the Sea summer music festival, and February, the Wunta Wine and Food Fiesta takes place.

153

Werribee Park

K Rd, Werribee. Tel: (03) 9741 2444. Mansion open from 1000 daily except Christmas Day. $$.

The 60-roomed Italianate-style mansion at Werribee Park was built in the 1870s by Scottish brothers Thomas and Andrew Chirnside, owners of a massive pastoral empire in Australia. The ornate sandstone house gives visitors a good impression of what life was like for wealthy Victorian graziers in the boom years of the 1870s and 1880s. There is a working farm with animals and herb gardens, and polo matches are still played in November and February on the polo lawns. The large formal gardens include the Victoria State Rose Garden, with 4 000 rose bushes that bloom from November to May.

Spa country
Daylesford and Hepburn Springs

Visitor Information Centre, 49 Vincent St, Daylesford. Tel: (03) 5348 1339.

A large number of mineral springs flow around the charming towns of **Daylesford** and **Hepburn Springs**, set among the lakes and forests of the central highlands. The Aborigines knew about the healing properties of the mineral springs and early this century European settlers came to take the waters to treat disorders such as rheumatism and gout.

The Hepburn Spa Resort (*Mineral Springs Reserve, Hepburn Springs; tel: (03) 5348 2034; fax (03) 5348 1167; www.hepburnspa.com.au; open weekdays 1000–2000, weekends 0900–2000; $$*) is Australia's only mineral-water bath facility, with a large relaxation pool and private mineral baths. Mineral water can also be collected for free, as it gushes out of old pumps and mountain springs. Other attractions include boating on Lake Daylesford, a visit to the **Wombat Hill Botanic Gardens**, monthly Saturday markets, a Sunday afternoon train ride through the Wombat State Forest, and numerous bookshops, galleries and cafés.

Hanging Rock

This remarkable volcanic rock formation rising abruptly as a solitary peak above surrounding farmland near **Woodend** is steeped in Aboriginal – and more recent – legend. The site inspired Joan Lindsay's book *Picnic at Hanging Rock*, reputedly based on a true story. One hot summer's day, three white-frocked schoolgirls wandered off from a school picnic at the rock; one of them was to reappear three days later, but the others were never seen again. Visitors can walk to the top on several different paths – even with the map, it's easy to feel something of the mystery of the rock.

Festival!

During the last weekend in May, a Swiss Italian Fiesta takes place in Daylesford, with food, music, wine, art and film (tel: (03) 5348 3512). On New Years Day and Australia Day, Hanging Rock Picnic Races take place at mysterious Hanging Rock, near Woodend, where there is also a Harvest Picnic Festival on the last weekend in February.

Eating and drinking

Gold Fields

The Green Olive
Bath Lane, Bendigo. Tel: (03) 5442 2676. $$. Delicatessen: café and take-away cheeses, antipasto, breads, etc.

Bazzani
Howard Place, Bendigo. Tel: (03) 5441 3777; fax: (03) 5443 9995. Open daily. $$–$$$. Bar, restaurant and café: a popular and stylish eatery.

JoJoes
4 High St, Bendigo. Tel: (03) 5441 4471. Open nightly from 1700 till late. $$. From pizza and pasta to more upmarket meals, dine in and take-away.

Togs Place Café and Gallery
58 Lyttleton St, Castlemaine. Tel: (03) 5470 5090. Open 1000–1700 daily, from 0900 Saturday. Trendy salads, freshly baked pies and cakes all made on the premises. Dine in the gallery coffee shop or the leafy courtyard at the back.

Great Ocean Road

The Beach House
Eastern Beach Reserve, Geelong. Tel: (03) 5221 8322. $$. A downstairs café has snacks and take-away meals while upstairs has an interesting menu and pleasant view from the balcony across Corio Bay.

Sempre Caffe
Little Malop St, Geelong. Tel: (03) 5229 8845. $$. Casual eatery that is very popular with locals.

Kosta's Taverna
48 Mountjoy Parade, Lorne. Tel: (03) 5289 1883. $$. Well known for its fresh seafood and traditional Greek dishes.

Chris's Beacon Point Restaurant and villas
Skenes Creek Rd, Apollo Bay. Tel: (03) 5237 6411; fax: (03) 5237 6930. $$$. Enjoy the glorious views, check into the fine self-contained accommodation, or eat at Chris's excellent restaurant.

Bay Leaf Gourmet Deli
131 Great Ocean Rd, Apollo Bay. Tel: (03) 5237 6470. $$. Just as the name suggests – great picnic fodder.

Proudfoot's Boathouse
2 Simpson St, Warrnambool. Tel: (03) 5561 5055. $$. Tavern bar and bistro, tearooms and restaurant.

Portofino
28 Bank St, Port Fairy. Tel: (03) 5568 1047. $$. Offering good food and cheerful service, this pleasant restaurant is open for dinner every night and Sunday lunch all year round.

Merrijig Inn
1 Campbell St, Port Fairy. Tel: (03) 5568 2324; fax: (03) 5568 2723; e-mail: merrijig@standard.net.au. $$. Sensational breakfasts are a feature of this historic inn, which also has a fully licensed restaurant. Tall people might prefer a downstairs room.

Spa Country

The Boathouse Café
Lake Daylesford. Breakfast at weekends, lunch and dinner daily. $$. Good coffee and great views; the nearby playground makes it ideal for people with young children.

Cosy Corner Café
3 Tenth Avenue, Hepburn Springs. Open Thu–Mon for lunch and dinner, breakfast/brunch from 0930 at weekends. $$. Homely café that has become very popular. Serves brasserie-style food.

Two Rooms
27 Albert St, Daylesford. Tel: (03) 5348 2752. $$. Café, restaurant and take-away.

The Food Gallery
77 Vincent St, Daylesford. Tel: (03) 5348 1677. $$. A coffee shop and deli and a smart place for breakfast.

Shopping

Shopping in the Victoria gold-fields area is likely to centre around the fine antique shops and galleries of Bendigo and Castlemaine. At Castlemaine's biennial **Festival of the Arts** (*next in 2001*), local artists and craftspeople open up their studios to browsers and buyers. In the spa country, the **Pantechnicon Gallery** (*34 Vincent St, Daylesford*) sells local art at reasonable prices. Along the Great Ocean Road, the surfing town of Torquay is the perfect place to pick up those Rip Curl baggies, while inland the **Brambuk Aboriginal Living Cultural Centre** (*Halls Gap, Grampians National Park*) has a bush-tucker restaurant and a shop selling Aboriginal artefacts.

157

Surfing Australia

Despite Australia's image today as a nation of swimming, surfing, sun-bronzed beach lovers, until 1903 it was totally unacceptable to be seen in public in any kind of swimming gear. In that year, a Sydney newspaper editor, Harry Goocher, went in the sea at Sydney's Manly beach during daylight hours, starting a trend that eventually overcame Victorian prudery. Swimming was to become the national pastime.

The first surfboards were brought to Australia in the 1920s by Hawaiians. Their traditional, heavy longboards were difficult to master. In 1956, during the Melbourne Olympic Games, a Californian life-saving team came to Australia and gave surfing exhibitions using light balsa boards at Torquay and Manly; Australia, and particularly its teenage youth, became surfing-crazy. By 1962, Midget Farrelly had become the first Australian to win a world surfing championship at Hawaii, the Bells Beach surf competition had been born, and every young kid near a surf beach was hanging around with a short light board under his arm and bleached blond hair.

Since that time, Australia has won multiple world surfing championships, has spawned an industry around surfboard and wet-suit manufacture, and is regarded worldwide as a top surfing nation. While Sydney's Manly, Freshwater and Bondi beaches were the centre of early surfing in Australia, it is now possible to find surfies and good breaks anyway around the coast, from Perth through to Noosa.

Allied to the growth in the sport of surfing has been the increasing popularity of surf lifesaving. Teams of lifesavers, men and women, each representing their own home beach, race to steer substantial wooden boats through the pounding surf. Awesome competitions are held throughout the summer, at all the main surf beaches.

The best surf beaches and meccas of surfie culture remain Manly and Bondi in Sydney, Jan Juc and Bells Beach near Torquay in Victoria, Shark Bay near Ceduna in SA, Byron Bay and Crescent Head on the NSW north coast, and the Gold Coast and Noosa in Queensland. However, almost the entire coastline of southwest WA, Victoria and New South Wales offers magnificent surf. (There is one notable exception: north of Noosa, or, more accurately, Agnes Waters, in Queensland, the 2 300-km Great Barrier Reef shields the beaches from surf, turning the sea into a mainly flat body of water.)

The Victoria seaside town of Torquay, home to surf manufacturers such as Rip Curl, stuffed with surf shops and the location for a major surfing museum, is now the commercial surfing capital of Australia. The most famous surfing competition in Australia, the Rip Curl Pro – otherwise known as the Bells Beach Classic – is held at Torquay's Bells Beach every Easter.

WEST OF MELBOURNE

ADELAIDE AND AROUND

Adelaide and around

South Australia offers a rich variety of landscapes and experiences, from the rolling hills and European-style villages of the Barossa Valley to the rugged, majestic outback of the Flinders Ranges, and the land-locked mystery of the Coorong. Its capital, Adelaide, is an elegant city, with the feel of a large country town.

163

*Getting around Adelaide: This flat city was made for walking. Its public transport system is unusually efficient; tickets are the same for buses, trams and trains. The **TransAdelaide office** (cnr of King William St and Currie St) has bus timetables and transport maps. The hop-on, hop-off **Adelaide Explorer tram** (tel: (08) 8364 1933) tours the main attractions on a 150-minute loop.*

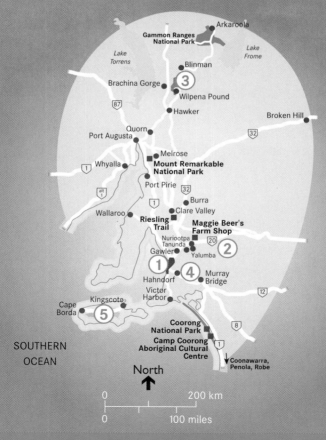

① *Adelaide*

Easy-going Adelaide has close links to its surrounding pastoral community, and an old-money elegance, with fine public buildings and old-time trams. **Pages 166–7**

② *Barossa Valley*

Jacob's Creek is perhaps the best-known name of the blessed wine-growing regions of South Australia. The rolling hills of the Barossa Valley produce delicious whites, while the *terra rossa* earth of the Coonawarra is the envy of big-red producers worldwide.
Pages 170–1 and 173

③ *Flinders Range*

It's a dry, often almost unbearably hot part of the country, but the Flinders Ranges National Park is a ruggedly beautiful and wild part of Australia, and a geologist's paradise. Aboriginal people have lived here for more than 40,000 years.
Pages 175–6

④ *German-style villages, Barossa Valley*

Settled in the 1830s by German Lutherans escaping religious persecution in their own country, Hahndorf is now SA's most popular tourist town. The influence of northern German culture is equally obvious in Tanunda. If you like a crisp Riesling, you'll love the Barossa and Clare valleys. **Pages 169–72**

⑤ *Kangaroo Island*

Just a 30-minute flight from Adelaide, this isolated spot is a haven for an enormous number of native species – expect to see sea lions and seabirds, koalas, possums, wallabies, platypus and, of course, kangaroos. **Page 181**

Tourist information

The South Australian Travel Centre, 1 King William St, Adelaide. Tel: (08) 8303 2033; www.visit-southaustralia.com.au. Open weekdays 0900–1700, weekends 0900–1400.

Barossa Wine and Visitor Centre, 66 Murray Street, Tanunda. Tel: (08) 8563 0600; www.barossa.mtx.net. Open weekdays 0900–1700, weekends 1000–1600.

Clare Valley Tourist Information Centre, Town Hall, 229 Main North Rd, Clare. Tel: (08) 8842 2131. Open Monday to Saturday 0900–1700, Sunday 1000–1600.

Flinders Ranges and Outback South Australian Tourism Centre, 41 Flinders Terrace, Port Augusta. Tel: 1800 633 060. Or 142 Gawler Place, Adelaide. Tel: (08) 8223 3991.

Information on walking in SA: *www.recsportsa.gov.au*

Adelaide

Named after William IV's queen, Adelaide was laid out in 1836 around a square-mile grid of wide streets and squares. The feeling of an elegant city of Victorian solidity prevails. The architecture reflects Adelaide's character, which is based on old values and old money.

Shocking pink

In the 1960s, Adelaide's parliament was shocked to its conservative core when Don Dunstan, then the premier, turned up in a pair of pink shorts.

The city's North Terrace boulevard is lined with museums, galleries, the university campus, Government House, Parliament House and a casino. The stylish **casino** (*tel: (08) 8212 2811; open Mon–Fri 1000–0400, weekends 24 hours*) is housed in the 1920s stone railway station. It's well worth a visit, even for non-gamblers. **Parliament House** (*cnr of North Terrace and King William St; tel: (08) 8237 9100; open on non-sitting days 1000–1400; to see parliament sitting, visit from 1400 onwards*) was built in two stages and is a solid pile of Kapunda marble on granite with Corinthian columns.

This cultured city has a significant number of art galleries and museums. The **Art Gallery of South Australia** (*North Terrace; tel: (08) 8207 7000; open daily 1000–1700*) opened in 1841. Its collection of Australian art is particularly strong and it has the world's most comprehensive collection of Aboriginal artefacts. Another place to see Aboriginal art is the multi-arts complex of **Tandanya** (*253 Grenfell St; tel: (08) 8223 2467; open daily 1000–1700*), which has galleries, a workshop and performing areas. Aboriginal guides give introductory talks (*by appointment*) on various aspects of their heritage and culture.

At the **Migration Museum** (*82 Kintore Avenue; tel: (08) 8207 7570; open Mon–Fri 1000–1700, Sat–Sun 1300–1700*), visitors can take a chronological walk through the history of immigration and settlement in South Australia since 1836.

The South Australian Maritime Museum (*126 Lipson St, Port Adelaide; tel: (08) 8240 0200*) spreads over several sites, including an 1850s bond store, the 1869 lighthouse and a wharf with vessels moored alongside.

Pie Floater

The 'Pie Floater' is an Adelaide institution for post-party munchies. Served from pie carts throughout the city, it comprises a hot meat pie with tomato sauce, sitting in a bowl of pea soup. Treat yourself as you stumble out of the casino late at night.

Adelaide is a green city with plenty of air and space. The **Adelaide Botanic Gardens** (*North Terrace; tel: (08) 8228 2311; open Mon–Fri 0800 to sunset, Sat–Sun 0900 to sunset*) were begun in 1855, almost with the founding of the city. Next door to the oldest greenhouse in a botanic garden in Australia is the Bicentennial Conservatory, built in a giant arc and containing a tropical rainforest.

The **Zoological Gardens** (*Frome Rd; tel: (08) 8267 3255; open daily 0930–1700*) are among the oldest in Australia. Animals are housed in moated enclosures, walk-through aviaries and an excellent reptile house.

Only 15 minutes from the city is the suburb of **Glenelg** (*reached by electric tram from Adelaide's Victoria Square*), where golden beaches extend to Port Adelaide in the north and to Marino in the south. The water is safe for both swimming and sailing. Adelaide also boasts Australia's largest indoor heated pool complex, at the **Adelaide Aquatic Centre** (*Jeffcott Rd, North Adelaide; tel: (08) 8344 4411; open daily 0700–1000*).

Hills and valleys

Burra

Tourist Office, Market Square. Tel: (08) 8892 1254. Burra Passport $$$.

Around the historic town of Burra, the landscape changes to treeless rolling hills – a radiant green in winter and spring, but a thirsty brown the remainder of the year. Burra is a popular tourist destination because of its fascinating history, mainly centred on the discovery of copper in this dry region in 1845. The whole of the little sandstone town is on the National Estate Register, and many buildings are owned by the National Trust. A caring community has ensured that the character of historic Burra remains intact.

The **Burra Passport** enables visitors to drive or walk an 11-km trail past 43 heritage sites, seven of which can be entered with the passport key. The **Bon Accord Mine Complex** depicts Burra's eclectic history; for a view of the large mine site, climb to the platform of the well-lit vertical mine shaft. The tiny **Paxton Square** cottages must have seemed palatial to the families who had lived in **Miners' Dugouts** along the river bed. One cottage is a museum with a mine captain's furniture. The dugouts, which housed up to 2 000 miners and their families, can be visited, and are amazing. The **Police Lockup and Stables**, and the **Redruth Gaol** depict 19th-century prison conditions; the gaol was one location for the Australian film, *Breaker Morant*.

Hahndorf

Visitors Centre, 64 Main Street. Tel: (08) 8388 2285.

Nestled in the Adelaide Hills, the unique North German-style village of Hahndorf has become South Australia's most popular tourist town. It was settled by 187 German Lutheran settlers in 1837, and is Australia's oldest German settlement. Its Main Street, lined with shady century-old trees, offers hours of entertainment, with arts and crafts shops, galleries, and museums. Original buildings feature *fachwerk* (timber framing with wattle and daub infill). Taste a variety of beers at the German Arms Hotel or sample traditional German cuisine in the many bakeries or cafés. At the Hahndorf Academy (*47 Main Street, Hahndorf; tel: (08) 8388 7250; open daily 1000–1700; $$*), you'll find local artists and artisans at work, and galleries exhibiting work by South Australian artists.

Built in 1858 on the outskirts of Hahndorf, The Cedars (*Heysen Rd, Hahndorf; tel: (08) 8388 7277; closed Saturdays; gallery open 1000–1600, free; guided tours 1100, 1300 and 1500; $$*) was home for Australian landscape artist Sir Hans Heysen from 1912 until his death in 1968. The house and chalet-style studio, maintained as a gallery, and the gardens are open to the public.

South Australia wineries

Barossa Valley

Visitor Centre, 66 Murray Street, Tanunda. Tel: (08) 8563 0600; www.barossa.mtx.net. Open weekdays 0900–1700, weekends 1000–1600.

The wine region of the Barossa Valley is just an hour's drive north of Adelaide. The valley is bordered by rolling hills, and magnificent old churches, wineries, European-style villages and farm cottages are scattered among vineyards, in a manicured landscape. Cycling is a popular way of exploring the roads and trails. Mostly, the Barossa Valley is about a gourmet journey, usually beginning at the **Barossa Wine and Visitor Centre**. About 50 wineries produce unique world-class wines, including Yalumba and the internationally known Jacob's Creek. Some offer tours, picnic facilities and restaurants, as well as cellar door tastings.

A lot of hot air

*A bird's-eye view is the perfect way to discover the beauty of the Barossa. Hot-air balloons are often seen drifting above the vineyards, particularly in May, during the Barossa Balloon Regatta (*Balloon Adventures; tel: (08) 8389 3195, fax: (08) 8389 3220; $$$*).*

Tanunda is at the heart of the Barossa Valley, and is the most German of the Barossa towns, even though its name is derived from an Aboriginal word for watering hole. A leisurely stroll through its back streets, and National Trust-classified Goat Square, Rose Bridge, Kegel Alley and four Lutheran churches instantly tell of the importance of northern German culture to this settlement.

The extensive vineyards of the Nuriootpa Plains can be viewed from the Barossa Valley Way. Nuriootpa is the commercial centre for the Barossa Valley, and just the place to stock up on local fare. Even before European settlement, it was a place of barter – its name comes from an Aboriginal word for 'meeting place'. Penfolds Winery (*Barossa Valley Way, Nuriootpa; tel: (08) 8560 9408; www.penfolds.com.au; open Mon–Sat 1000–1700, Sun 1300–1700*), the Valley's largest winery complex, is home to the world-famous Grange Hermitage wines.

Maggie Beer

Maggie Beer's Farm Shop, Pheasant Farm Rd, off Seppeltsfield Rd, Nuriootpa. Tel: (08) 8562 4477.

Maggie Beer is a household name throughout Australia. In 1973, she and her husband Colin moved to the Barossa Valley and began breeding pheasants at The Pheasant Farm. They soon opened their famous restaurant, which they operated for 15 years. The restaurant won the award for best Australian restaurant in 1991, then closed at the height of its fame, in November 1993. Since then, Maggie Beer has been making and selling her popular Pheasant Farm pâté, quince paste, mushroom pâté and smoked kangaroo through her Farm Shop at Nuriootpa. The Pheasant Farm is a foodies' heaven, a place to enjoy a glass of local wine or an espresso, and sample her products, as well as seasonal treats.

Yalumba

Eden Valley Rd, Angaston. Tel: (08) 8561 3299. Open weekdays 0830–1700, weekends 0900–1700. Guided tours daily 1015, 1045, 1315, 1415, 1515. $$.

The beautiful **Yalumba Winery**, 10 minutes east of Angaston, was founded in 1849. Its yellow sandstone baroque-style château has imposing balustrade steps, an elegant ballroom with crystal chandeliers, and period furniture. On the daily guided tours of the winery, visitors see the vast oak maturing cellars and bottle-maturing tunnels. The Garden Bistro and Gazebo adjoining the wine-tasting area is shaded by huge gums, and serves locally made German meats, breads, cheeses and seasonal Australian game. Outdoors, there are scenic walks around the lakes, deer and fauna parks, and picnic areas along the river.

Clare Valley

Tourist Information Centre, Town Hall, 229 Main North Rd, Clare. Tel: (08) 8842 2131. Open Mon–Sat 0900–1700, Sun 1000–1600.

The picturesque Clare Valley, north of Adelaide, is famous for its verdant vineyards and excellent crisp white wines, and for its old stone heritage buildings. The commercial centre, **Clare**, is set in a wooded valley, among orchards and 30 vineyards, many of which are 'boutique'-style. The **Sevenhill Jesuit Monastery**, in the tiny township of Sevenhill, is the oldest Clare Valley winery. The **Old Clarevale Museum** is a co-operative winery restored as a museum of winemaking, with a gallery and restaurant.

Riesling Trail

The picturesque 27-km Riesling Trail, which passes through the Clare Valley along old railway lines between Clare and Auburn, is suitable for recreational walkers and cyclists. It can be accessed at various points for shorter walks. Autumn and spring are good times to visit; summer can be hot and dry, but visitors will see grape harvesting and the start of vintage at the many wineries.

Coonawarra

Penola-Coonawarra Visitors Centre, 27 Arthur St, Penola. Tel: (08) 8737 2855. Open weekdays 0900–1700, weekends 1000–1600, closed Christmas and Good Friday. Winery maps available.

There are about 30 wineries in the Coonawarra region, southeast of Adelaide, close to the border with Victoria. It is most famous worldwide for its award-winning mighty red wines, especially its cabernet sauvignons. The wineries follow a straight road north from Penola, a pleasant drive through vineyards edged with roses or poplars. The secret of the great wines is the rich red *terra rossa* soil laid over limestone, pure underground water and the long, cool ripening season.

South Australian outback

Arkaroola

Arkaroola Wilderness Sanctuary and Resort, Arkaroola, Northern Flinders Ranges. Tel: 1800 676 042 or (08) 8648 4848. $–$$. Camping and lodge accommodation, restaurant, tours, flights and walks.

Known as the jewel of the northern Flinders Ranges, Arkaroola is a privately owned and run wilderness sanctuary and resort property of 610 square kilometres, adjacent to the Gammon Ranges National Park (*see page 177*). For a friendly, really remote outback experience, Arkaroola is the perfect place. There are fascinating rock formations and gorges, particularly Echo Camp and Bararranna Gorge, vast salt lakes, prolific wildlife and some lovely swimming waterholes, such as Bolla Bollana and the Paralana Hot Springs. It also has its own astronomy observatory – the stars in this remote region are magical.

Brachina Gorge

One of the most spectacular driving tours passes via Wilpena Pound, past the gnarled old Cazneux Tree river red gum, through Bunyeroo Valley to spectacular and ancient Brachina Gorge. The scenery is sensational – at times, the tall walls of the Flinders Ranges crowd around you, at others, the purple rocky spines of the Bunker and Heysen mountain ranges are away in the distance, giving a feeling of space, majesty and isolation. The road (quite rough in parts) that runs along Brachina Gorge is a complete contrast, with cliffs, rockpools and the quiet river.

Pioneers

The first white people to experience the aridity and dramatic scenery of the Flinders Ranges were the crew of the HMS Investigator, *who pushed inland from Port Augusta with Matthew Flinders in 1802. Edward John Eyre explored the length of the ranges, from Crystal Brook to Mount Hopeless, in 1839 and 1841, encouraging pioneering graziers such as Thomas Elder to bring their sheep into the district.*

Flinders Ranges National Park

Outback South Australian Tourism Centre, 41 Flinders Terrace, Port Augusta.
Tel: 1800 633 060. Or 142 Gawler Place, Adelaide. Tel: (08) 8223 3991.
www.flindersrangestourism.com.au

Flinders Ranges National Park, SA National Parks and Wildlife Service (NPWS)
office, Wilpena Pound. Tel: (08) 8648 0048.

This National Park of 93,000 hectares has ancient landscapes, soaring cliffs and ranges, geological wonders, Aboriginal culture, and prolific wildflowers and wildlife. Formed between 650 million and 700 million years ago, when the earth's crust rose above the sea, split and was pushed up to form the mountain ridges of the Elder, Chase, Heysen and Bunker ranges, the National Park is a geologist's paradise containing fossils, gold, opal, copper, quartzites, dolomites, shale and granite. Wind, water and rain have cut out deep valleys and smooth gorges over the years, giving the landscape stunning variety and some naturally formed walking trails through the rugged hills. Aboriginal people have lived here for more than 40,000 years and evidence of their occupation and art remains in many caves and rock-art galleries.

There are hundreds of walking tracks within the park, including the finishing section of the 1 500-km Heysen Trail (*details available from the Wadlata Information Centre, Port Augusta, or at the main Flinders Ranges National Park centre, Wilpena Pound*). The highlight for most visitors to

the park is a walk up into the serene beauty of **Wilpena Pound** (*see page 179*); **Brachina Gorge** (*see page 174*) and other more remote areas of the park on its northern fringe around **Blinman** are also fascinating.

Bush camping is allowed throughout the park, but permits must be obtained first from park rangers. At Wilpena Pound there is a camping and caravan ground with full facilities, as well as the Wilpena Resort. Accommodation and serviced camping is also available at the excellent Rawnsley Park Station (*Rawnsley Bluff, just south of Wilpena Pound; tel: (08) 8648 0008; accommodation, camping, horse-riding, tours*) on the southern rim of the park.

Driving note

A conventional car can drive happily along most of the good gravel tracks within the National Park, as long as the creeks and gorges are not flooded. However, this is the start of the Australian outback. It may not be far from 'civilisation', but it is a dry, often hot, empty part of the country. There are two golden rules for driving. First, if your car breaks down, stay with it – it is lack of shade that kills unwary travellers in the outback. Second, do not drive in the dark. The Flinders Ranges has huge numbers of kangaroos, and serious accidents from collisions between cars and roos at night are all too common. Leave time to get where you are going while it is still light. Flinders Ranges Road Conditions hotline, tel: 1300 361 033.

Gammon Ranges National Park

SA National Parks and Wildlife Service (NPWS) office, Balcanoona.
Tel: (08) 8648 4829.

The ancient granite peaks of the Gammon Ranges are estimated to be more than 1.6 billion years old, rearing up jagged between the two great salt lakes of Lake Frome and Lake Torrens on either side. This 128,000-hectare National Park is believed to be one of the oldest places on earth, with deep gorges, high ranges, dry, arid country and plenty of untamed wilderness. Much wilder and less developed than Flinders Ranges NP, Gammon Ranges NP is best explored on foot, with great bushwalks to places like Weetootla Gorge, with its abundant wildlife. Other popular and lovely walks are Italowie Gorge (*16km one-way*), and Grindells Hut.

NP rangers and the visitor information office are based at Balcanoona, and provide excellent maps and advice on where to go. To get to some of the walking trailheads, 4WD vehicles are needed.

Mount Remarkable National Park

National Park offices, Mambray Creek. Tel: (08) 8634 7068.

Named by explorer Edward John Eyre, Mount Remarkable National Park has lovely walks for everyone. From Melrose, the oldest town in the Flinders Ranges, a steep but rewarding climb of about four hours (*return*) through wildflowers and grassy fields along the Hans Heysen Trail leads to the top of Mount Remarkable (956m high). Alligator Gorge can be reached by car from Wilmington. From the gorge, it is a short walk downstream to The Narrows, where the walls of the gorge close in, or upstream to The Terraces. Overnight hikers can hike the 15-km Hidden Gorge and Battery Ridge Trail loop in the western Mambray Creek section of the park.

On hot days, when the threat of bushfire is high, the park is closed to all visitors and bushwalkers.

Port Augusta

Tourist Information Centre, Wadlata Outback Centre, 41 Flinders Terrace.
Tel: (08) 8641 0793.

The largest city in outback South Australia, Port Augusta is
often described as being 'at the crossroads of Australia'. From
here, the Stuart Highway heads north, the Eyre Highway
goes west towards the Nullarbor Desert, the Port Wakefield
road leads south to Adelaide, while the Barrier Highway
heads east.

The award-winning **Wadlata Outback Centre** provides
an entertaining way of learning about Aboriginal culture
and its history, the geology of the Flinders Ranges and the
environment. Just north of Port Augusta is the magnificent
200-hectare Australian Arid Lands Botanic Gardens (*Stuart
Hwy, Port Augusta; tel: (08) 8641 1049; Mon–Fri 0900–1700,
Sat–Sun 1000–1600*). The bright Sturts Desert Pea flowers
here all year round.

Quorn

Tourist Information Centre, Seventh St. Tel: (08) 8648 6419.

Quorn is the home base of the wonderful little **Pichi Richi
steam train** (*Quorn Station; tel: (08) 8395 2566 for 24-
hour recorded information, or tel: (08) 8648 6598 on train
days; Easter–Oct, weekdays and school holidays; $$*), which
chuffs along the old 1879 Great Northern Railway route,
across trestle bridges to Woolshed Flat and back – a 33-km,
2.5-hour trip. Near Quorn, the Devils Peak and Waukerie
Falls loop track (*easy, 18km*) is a popular walk, reached
from the Richman Valley Rd; watch out for fossils in the
700-million-year-old quartzite deposits.

Wilpena Pound

Flinders Ranges National Park, SA National Parks and Wildlife Service (NPWS) office, Wilpena Pound. Tel: (08) 8648 0048.

According to Aboriginal lore, the elevated Wilpena Pound (known as Ikara) was formed when a giant dreaming serpent spirit, Akurra, encircled the dancing of a corroboree being held by the local Aboriginal people, and then went to sleep. The mountain ranges were formed, and a spring was created within the sacred pound. More prosaically, geologists believe the rim is made up from the stumps of eroded mountains, once as massive as the Himalayas. Despite its appearance, it is neither a volcanic crater nor a meteorite impact site.

The Pound is now a collection of cracked, split and weathered peaks, where the colours change with the sun. The highest is St Mary's Peak, which Aboriginal people believe should not be climbed. The quiet, wooded, grassy interior of the Pound – only accessible through the narrow neck of Sliding Rock Gorge by a gentle 2-km walking track from the camping ground below – is 11km long and 8km across. To appreciate this geological wonder, take a half-hour scenic flight, or view it from the Wangara lookout, on the rim.

Within the Pound, take a look at the restored cottage of the Hill family, who farmed sheep here in the late 19th century; 12-year-old Jessie kept house all alone for five older brothers. Now, kangaroos and euros (small, wallaby-like marsupials) bound between rampant yellow wattle trees, pampas grass and wildflowers in spring. In season, there are the brilliant reds and pinks of the Sturt's Desert Pea, the Flinders Ranges Bottlebrush, the Hopbrush and the Sturt's Desert Rose. The Pound is also a birdwatcher's paradise, with 97 species of bird catalogued.

Outside the Pound's walls are the Wilpena Pound resort and camping ground (*tel: (08) 8648 0004 or 1800 805 802; www.wilpenapound.on.net; $–$$*), as well as the headquarters of the Flinders Ranges National Park office and visitor centre.

179

South of Adelaide

On the drive south, from Adelaide to the famous vineyards of Coonawarra, the scenery changes radically, from rolling hills and orchards to pounding surf beaches and unspoiled sand dunes, and, finally, the prized terra rossa *soil of the wine-producing region.*

The Coorong

Meningie. Tel: (08) 8575 1200. Camping permits and information about walking trails.

The **Coorong National Park** is a mystical place, its name spoken with reverence by those who know it. It is a land-locked sliver of water, bounded on the seaward side by blindingly white sand hills. Just under 3km wide at its widest, the Coorong's pristine white beaches stretch 145km from the mouth of the River Murray. The Park's 47,000 hectares are a wetland of international significance and, with more than 230 bird species, a mecca for bird lovers. This is Australia's largest, permanent breeding colony of pelicans. The Coorong is also home to 37 professional fishermen, as well as cocklers, who scrounge the ocean beach for cockles to sell.

Camp Coorong Aboriginal Cultural Centre

Tel: (08) 8575 1557. Cottage and dormitory accommodation. Aboriginal cultural tours and lessons.

A visit to Camp Coorong provides a glimpse into the Aboriginal heritage of the Ngarrindjeri people, the original occupiers of the mystical Coorong. Learn about the traditional life of the Ngarrindjeri, taste traditional bush tucker, listen to Dreaming stories of the Coorong, see mats and baskets being made from rushes, and discover the Aboriginal secrets of the Coorong's animals, medicine and food plants.

Kangaroo Island

Kangaroo Island Gateway Visitor Information Centre, Howard Drive, Pennseshaw. Tel: (08) 8553 1185. Open weekdays 0900–1500, weekends 1000–1600.

Kangaroo Island National Parks and Wildlife, Dauncey St, Kingscote. Tel: (08) 8554 8381.

The isolation of Kangaroo Island has protected the animals and plants of this wilderness area magnificently, making it a haven for an enormous variety of species. The 18 conservation and national parks on this large island off Victor Harbor cover one-third of the island, giving it a wild, bush feel. Rugged cliffs, roaring surf, pristine beaches and dramatic caves form the backdrop for the wildlife, which have attracted visitors for decades. Seal Bay Conservation Park, on the island's south coast, is home to about 500 rare Australian sea lions; regular guided tours take visitors close to them.

Flinders Chase National Park, with its weather-worn rocky coastline and coastal dunes, is also a haven for sea lions and seabirds. Further inland, koalas, possums, wallabies, platypus, birds and kangaroos can be spotted from the walking tracks that wind through the heath and mallee scrub.

A 30-minute flight (*Kendell, tel: (08) 8231 9567; Southern Sky Airlines, tel: 1800 643 300; Emu Airways, tel: (08) 8234 3711*) from Adelaide, or car and passenger ferry (*Kangaroo Island Sealink ferries, tel: (08) 8553 1122; 4 times daily; coach connection with Adelaide*) from Cape Jervis, 60km south of Victor Harbor, provide the only access to Kangaroo Island.

Penola

Penola/Coonawarra Visitors' Centre, the John Riddoch Interpretive Centre, and the Penola Hydrocarbon Centre, 27 Arthur St, Penola. Tel: (08) 8737 2855. Open weekdays 0900–1700, weekends 1000–1600, closed Christmas and Good Friday.

Penola is a pretty rural settlement, surrounded by flat red-gum grazing country, and the Coonawarra vineyards to the north. Its historic sandstone architecture is typical of South Australian rural towns. Blessed Mary MacKillop, destined to become Australia's first saint, opened her first school in Penola in 1867. The old schoolhouse and new Mary MacKillop Interpretive Centre are on her pilgrimage trail. Opposite, in Petticoat Lane, a row of finely restored stone and red-gum slab cottages now house boutiques and accommodation. Penola's heritage unfolds in the John Riddoch Interpretive Centre and the self-guided Penola Historic Walk and Penola Bicycle Trail (*printed guides available from the Visitors' Centre*). The Penola Hydrocarbon Centre is a comprehensive display illustrating the region's natural gas industry. It's a well-equipped town, with good hotel, restaurant and café meals, an eclectic shopping centre including galleries and antiques, and varied accommodation.

Robe

Tourist Information Centre, Mundy Terrace, Robe. Tel: (08) 8768 2465.

This pretty seaside village has been a holiday destination for 150 years. Even the colonial governors spent their summer holidays here. Robe is also a vibrant fishing port. During the warmer months, take an early-morning stroll to the port to watch the fisherman unload their lobster pots, or to buy 'spiders' (lobster legs filled with the sweetest meat). Robe has a wild and windswept back beach, where you can take an exhilarating walk in all seasons, and explore the rockpools. The town beach is sheltered and offers safe swimming. Drive along the surf beach to find the perfect spot. Walk or cycle around Robe to enjoy its quaint cottages, historic sandstone buildings, busy cafés and galleries.

Southeast of Robe, on the Robe to Penola Road (*tel: (08) 8768 2083*), at the Narraburra Woolshed, visitors can see sheepdogs working, sheep being shorn, emus and kangaroos, and try a shearer's 'cuppa'.

Invasion!

The traditional seaside resort of Robe is invaded on the New Year's and Australia Day holidays, when young people descend here to party noisily.

Victor Harbor

Tourist Information Centre, Flinders Pde. Tel: (08) 8552 5738.

The favourite summer holiday playground for Adelaide families, Victor Harbor sits on the wide sandy arc of Encounter Bay, close to pounding surf beaches. There's an enjoyable 15-minute walk across the causeway or, for a small cost, a historic horse-drawn tram to Granite Island, home to a group of **Fairy Penguins**. Every dusk, a small number of people are taken (*Fairy Penguin dusk tour, Granite Island; tel: (08) 8552 7555; daily*) to watch the penguins emerge from the ocean and return to their nests.

Now a commercial fishing port, Victor Harbor was once a whaling and sealing depot; you can still enjoy viewing the southern right whales which visit each year, and find out more at the **Whale Centre**. During the warmer months, the expansive lawn between the shopping centre and the foreshore is a favourite gathering place to have a picnic, or fish and chips. This spot is even more popular on Sundays, when a fair is held here.

183

Eating and drinking

Adelaide

Adelaide claims one eatery to every 32 citizens. O'Connell alone has over 40 restaurants, cafés and wine bars. Hutt St is said to be the place where modern Australian cuisine was born. In truth, it came into being in a number of places, but Hutt St is still an enjoyable spot to sit and eat and watch the world go by in the shade of old verandas.

Al Fresco Gelateria and Pasticceria
260 Rundle St. Open 0630 till very late. $. The place to be seen and drink superb coffee.

Aroma
108 Jetty Rd, Glenelg. Tel: (08) 8376 9222. Open daily 1800–2230. $$. Italian restaurant serving good pasta and pizzas from a wood-fired oven.

Buongiorno Caffè
145 The Parade, Norwood. Open daily 0800–0100, or later. $. Large, always lively café which reaches a noisy and crowded crescendo on Sunday nights.

Café Paradiso
150 King William Rd, Hyde Park. Open daily 0830–2200. $. Long-established favourite; great coffee and real Italian alfresco dining, from pasta to *osso buco*. Licensed.

Eros Ouzeri
275–277 Rundle St. Tel: (08) 8223 4022. Open lunch Sun–Fri, dinner 7 days. $$. Greek *meze*, or sit outside at the attached café for Greek pastries and coffee. Licensed.

Ozone Fish Café
45 Commercial St, Port Adelaide. $. Possibly the oldest chippie in Australia, having been there since 1884, and the only Australian fish and chip shop under Royal patronage – the Queen and the Duke of Edinburgh dropped in during a visit in 1977.

Rising Sun Inn
60 Bridge St, Kensington (4km out of town). Tel: (08) 8333 0721. Open lunch, dinner Mon–Sat. $$. Winner of all sorts of awards for its food. Licensed.

Barossa Valley

Linke's Bakery and Tearooms
40 Murray St, Nuriootpa. Lunch, coffee and snacks are available in the tearooms, or buy their famous breads, German cake, pies or pastries.

1918 Bistro & Grill
94 Murray St, Tanunda. Tel: (08) 8563 0405. $$$. A casual and friendly atmosphere, local wines and fantastic food. In warmer months dine on the lawns under the trees.

Skillogalee Winery and Restaurant
Hughes Park Rd, Sevenhill. Tel: (08) 8843 4311. $$. One of Clare Valley's favourite restaurants, located in a 150-year-old Cornish miner's stone cottage. Sit on the veranda overlooking the cottage garden and vineyards drinking cool Clare Valley whites.

Treetops Restaurant
Seppeltsfield Rd, Marananga. Tel: (08) 8562 2522. Open daily for lunch, and morning and afternoon teas only. $$.

Flinders Ranges

The Prairie Hotel
Cnr High St and West Terrace, Parachilna. Tel: (08) 8648 4844. $$. Great Australian gourmet food and accommodation.

The Old Ghan Restaurant
Leigh Creek Rd, Hawker. Tel: (08) 8648 4176. $$. Open Wed–Sun for lunch and dinner.

South of Adelaide

Penguini's Bistro
Granite Island, Victor Harbor. Tel: (08) 8552 8311. $$. Meals with a pleasant view of Victor Harbor.

Whalers' Inn Resort
The Bluff, Encounter Bay, Victor Harbor. Tel/fax: (08) 8552 4400. $$$. Base yourself in Victor Harbor to explore the Fleurieu Peninsula. All rooms at this resort overlook Encounter Bay, as does the restaurant.

The Barn
Main Rd, McLaren Vale. Tel: (08) 8323 8618. Open daily for lunch and dinner. $$. This is one of South Australia's best-known restaurants and galleries. A popular day outing for Adelaide dwellers.

Grey Masts Restaurant and Guesthouse
1 Smyllie St, Robe. Tel/fax: (08) 8768 2203. $$$. Built in 1847, and listed on the National Heritage register, this boutique guesthouse really pampers. The food is excellent, and the coffee invigorating. It is certainly worth stopping here for a meal; if time is short, coffee and cake will suffice.

Shopping

Adelaide has a wonderful asset in the **Jam Factory Craft and Design Centre** (*cnr North Terrace and Morphett St; open Mon–Fri 0900–1730, Sat–Sun 1000–1700*), which sells the high-quality work of local craftspeople.

Many of the wineries throughout the **Barossa Valley** sell their wine from the cellar door, but some also specialise in other gourmet treats. **Maggie Beer's Farm Shop** (*see page 171*) is something of an institution in the area, selling this famous chef's pâtés and other delights. For picnic fare, try **Nuriootpa**'s delis, and especially the renowned Linke's Central Meat Store and Linke's Bakery and Tearooms.

Australia's wine industry

Grapes have been grown commercially in Australia since first being established on the fertile flats of the Hunter Valley north of Sydney in the 1830s, but Australia's wine industry experienced its real boom in the late 20th century. Its wines have won top awards worldwide, its young progressive winemakers are employed across the globe, and the export wine industry is now worth more than a billion Australian dollars a year.

Now almost every state in Australia has large wine-growing areas – the best known, with reputations for fine wines, are the Hunter Valley in NSW, the Yarra Valley and Rutherglen in Victoria, the Coonawarra, Barossa and Clare valleys in SA and the booming viticulture industry around Margaret River in WA. Yet nearly half of Australia's grapes are grown nowhere near these famed districts – actually, the Murray River between Mildura and Renmark, and the

ADELAIDE AND AROUND

Murrumbidgee Irrigation Area around Griffith in NSW produce the bulk of Australia's wine grapes, which are then blended in the major wineries with grapes grown from the prestige boutique districts.

For the novice to Australian wines, the best and most dependable are full-bodied hearty red wines from the Coonawarra district, crisp dry Rieslings from the Clare Valley, dry Sémillon and Chardonnays from the Hunter Valley, fortified ports, Tokays and Muscats from Rutherglen, Shiraz from SA's McLaren Vale, Pinot Noirs and young light reds from the Yarra Valley and almost any wine from the Barossa.

But the best way to find out what style and taste of the plethora of Australian wines available suits your palate is to taste them. Wine-tasting and wine-touring through some of the major wine-growing districts is something of a national hobby. Almost all of the wineries, from the largest corporate-owned establishment to the smallest boutique winery, are open for tastings and cellar-door sales of new vintages. Tasting is either free or costs a couple of dollars for multiple sips. It's a great and fun way to visit and get to know a region and some of its more colourful characters. If you do want to buy, most wineries will ship wine overseas, or have agents abroad, so it is not usually necessary to have to cart any cases with you.

Don't forget that Australia has strict drink-driving laws – ride a bike on a special wine-tasting trail, or take a wine-tasting bus tour to avoid having to limit yourself!

Perth
and the
southwest

Perth, the most isolated major city in the world, enjoys mild winters and sun-washed sandy beaches. It is beautifully set around the wide Swan River, which flows into the ocean at the historic port of Fremantle. Australia's southwest corner is an extraordinarily diverse region of intense natural beauty, from towering native forests to rolling farmland. In spring and early summer, millions of wildflowers create a blaze of colour.

189

Getting around: Perth very sensibly allows free bus travel in the central zone, so no cars are needed. The Perth Tram is a fun way to see the city on 1½-hour guided tours.

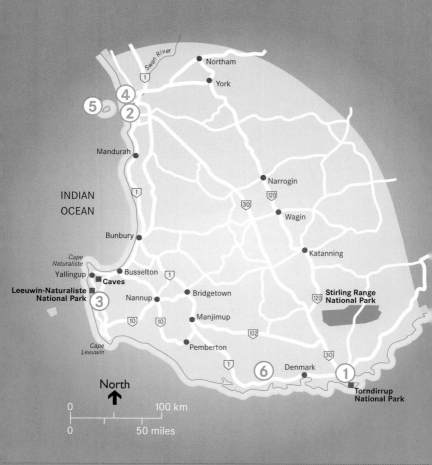

INDIAN
OCEAN

Swan River

Northam

York

Mandurah

Narrogin

Wagin

Katanning

Bunbury

Cape
Naturaliste

Yallingup

Busselton

Caves

Leeuwin-Naturaliste
National Park

Nannup

Bridgetown

Stirling Range
National Park

Manjimup

Cape
Leeuwin

Pemberton

Denmark

Torndirrup
National Park

North

0   100 km

0   50 miles

① Albany

This, the 'Gem of the Southern Ocean', was nearly a French settlement. In the end, the Brits got here first, and found a Mediterranean-type climate, and one of the best natural harbours in the world. **Page 198**

② Fremantle

Historic yet dynamic, the working port of Fremantle had a successful facelift in time for Alan Bond's 1987 America's Cup defence. Now, it offers streets of enjoyable cafés, undercover markets, and the freshest fish. **Pages 193–5**

③ Margaret River

Surf's up at some great spots along the WA coast south of Perth, and some eclectic communities have grown up around the Aussies' national pastime. Make a date with the setting sun at Margaret River. **Pages 198–9**

④ Perth

Particularly popular with Europeans, this efficient and agreeable place is the most isolated major city in the world. It does have skyscrapers, but it also revels in the wide-open spaces of the Swan River and Kings Park, right at its heart. **Pages 192–7**

⑤ Rottnest Island

This delightful island off the coast of Perth is something of a secret holiday destination, enjoyed by in-the-know Western Australians for a number of generations. Hire a bike and do it from end to end in a day. **Page 196**

⑥ Valley of the Giants and Pemberton

Don't miss the chance to drive around WA's tall tree forests. If you want to climb one of the trees, the Gloucester Tree has 153 steel and wooden rungs driven into its trunk in a spiral pattern, leading up to the world's highest fire lookout. **Pages 200–1**

Tourist information

Western Australian Tourist Centre, *Perth. Tel: (08) 9483 1111.*

191

Perth

Perth is believed to have the best weather in Australia, with a difference in mean temperatures between summer and winter of just 10 degrees centigrade. There are occasional heatwaves, when the air is almost unbearably hot, but these are rare. And there is just enough rain to ensure that the city remains lush and verdant. Undoubtedly, the climate makes a major contribution to the agreeable – if not positively hedonistic – style of living enjoyed here.

The city

A free bus service, Central Area Transit (CAT), operates around the central Perth area. Red CAT buses do an east–west loop and blue CAT buses run north–south. Travel on the TransPerth bus service is also free to passengers who board and alight within the city area.

Perth is an unashamedly modern city but a walk around its shopping and business area reveals glimpses of its past. Founded in 1829, it was the first settlement in Australia entirely made up of volunteers from England rather than convicts. However, that lasted only until 1850, when labour shortages forced the delayed introduction of convicts, who were immediately put to work constructing roads and public buildings.

Perth's **Town Hall** on the corner of Hay and Barrack Sts was built by convict labour in the 1870s, as was the Gothic-style

Government House in St George's Terrace. Also sandwiched among the Terrace's skyscrapers are the beautiful **Cloisters**, the first boys' secondary school in Western Australia, and the **Old Perth Boys School**, built in 1853, which now houses a National Trust information centre. The main shopping precinct is bounded by Hay, William, Wellington and Barrack Sts. Further west, **King St**, once a shabby home for wholesalers and warehouses, has been transformed over the past decade into one of the city's swankiest areas, lined with galleries, cafés and boutiques.

Cottesloe Beach

Cottesloe is Perth's icon beach, with a sandy glamour and two famous watering holes: the Cottesloe Beach Hotel, which has a legendary summer beer garden, and the Ocean Beach Hotel, which has expansive views to Rottnest Island. A string of good cafés includes The Blue Duck and the North Cott Café.

Dalkeith

Riverside Dalkeith has the distinction of being the most expensive suburb in Perth in which to live, owing to its beautiful location overlooking the Swan River and its relative proximity to the city and the beach. Its most famous street is Jutland Parade, christened 'millionaires' row' in the late 1980s, when seven-figure sums regularly began to change hands for its mansions. The less well-heeled can enjoy the same outlook from **Point Resolution** reserve at the end of Jutland Parade, a pretty foreshore park and picnic spot that gives views across to Point Walter.

Fremantle

The port of Fremantle is a beautifully preserved heritage precinct in a state that has often shown scant respect for its architectural history. But what makes it more fascinating is that it remains a vibrant working port and city. Its streets and buildings received a complete facelift in the lead-up to 1987, when it was the host port for the international yachting America's Cup, won four years earlier by Perth's most notorious businessman, Alan Bond. The cup was lost, but Fremantle has not looked back.

A walk along Fremantle's pavements will pass galleries, museums, terraced houses, sidewalk cafés, markets and many fine examples of architecture from the decades immediately after the first British settlers established the Swan River Colony, in 1829. **The Round House**, a 12-sided stone building at the end of High Street, is Western Australia's oldest building, constructed in 1830 as the colony's first civil gaol. Fremantle's **West End**, flanking the harbour, is rated one of the best Victorian port streetscapes in the world.

After a stroll through the past, **South Terrace** offers wall-to-wall sidewalk cafés and pubs, many reflecting Fremantle's more recent history as home to Italian immigrants.

Fremantle's popular **undercover markets**, a lively mix of stalls selling everything from incense to fresh fish, are open all day Friday to Sunday on the corner of South Terrace and Henderson St.

Refreshment in Fremantle

South Terrace is packed with sidewalk cafés and pubs, a number with an Italian flavour. The Sail & Anchor was Australia's first pub brewery and continues to serve speciality beers, while The Norfolk has a delightful beer garden. There are more cafés and restaurants on the waterfront at Fishing Boat Harbour.

Fremantle Gaol

1 The Terrace. Tel: (08) 9430 7177. Open daily 1000–1800.
Tours every half-hour; candlelight tours Wed and Fri at 1930.

On the edge of the city centre, the former Fremantle prison provides a fascinating if chilling insight into the city's history and an alternative to its prevailing image as a fun seaside town. Built from limestone rock by British convicts sent to the colony, it received its first inmates in 1855 and remained Perth's major maximum-security prison until November 1991. Its cold, damp cells and cement exercise yards are evidence of a punishment system no longer considered to be acceptable and it is now classified as an important cultural heritage site.

Kings Park

Kings Park Board, Fraser Avenue. Tel: (08) 9480 3600 (general enquiries and info on guided tours).

In 1872, Perth's forefathers preserved 172 hectares on Mount Eliza overlooking the city as permanent parkland. Today, Kings Park covers 400 hectares and is the largest park within the confines of a major city in Australia. It is a peaceful blend of natural bushland, landscaped gardens, walking trails, ponds and playgrounds, in addition to offering a panoramic view over the city of Perth and the Swan River. The park supports 250 species of wildflowers. Something is always in bloom but in spring it is transformed into a mass of colour. Visitors can drive through the park, hire a bicycle or simply wander along its many tracks. The major lookout has recently been enhanced to double as a performance area for Aboriginal music and dance, and underneath it is an Aboriginal-owned and run gallery.

Aussie Rules

Perth's *West Coast Eagles* **are one of the most successful teams in the national Australian Rules football league, and a subject of obsession for most Western Australians from April to September. The district of** *Subiaco* **is perhaps best known as the home of the team's stadium. Tickets for Eagles games are hard to come, but try Red ticket booking agency on (08) 9484 1222.**

Northbridge

Northbridge lies over the railway tracks from Perth city and is the centre of much of the city's cultural and night life. It was originally home to many Europeans who migrated after the Second World War. Over the past two decades a multicultural abundance of cafés, restaurants, pubs and clubs, has sprung up from these origins – some are good, some mediocre. The **Re Store** in Lake St and **Kakulas Bros** in William St are examples of the fine European grocery stores which remain, while **Kailis Bros** fish market at 100 Roe Street gives local consumers access to some of the best seafood caught off Western Australia.

Northbridge is also home to the **Perth Cultural Centre** complex (*James St; tel: (08) 9492 6600; open daily 1000–1700; no charge, except for special exhibitions*), including the **Art Galley of Western Australia**, which has a number of significant Australian works. Northbridge can become crowded and a little sleazy on Friday and Saturday nights.

Rottnest Island

Rottnest Island Authority. Tel: (08) 9432 9300.

Boat Torque (08) 9221 5844 or Rottnest Express (08) 9335 6406. Ferry services all year, several times a day. Mainland departure points are Perth, Fremantle or Hillarys in the northern suburb.

Rottnest, 20km west of Fremantle, was named in 1696 by a Dutch explorer who mistook the island's unique marsupial resident, the quokka, for a huge rat. From 1838 to 1903, it served as a harsh Aboriginal prison. It became a tourist resort in 1917; development since then has been strictly limited. No cars are permitted, and hired bicycles are the main form of transport. Its beautiful rocky bays, white sandy beaches and turquoise waters have made it a low-key holiday playground for generations of Western Australians.

Subiaco

One of Perth's most popular eating, drinking and shopping areas, Subiaco is an interesting atmospheric blend of conservative high street and inner-suburban hip strip. Within a few hundred metres, it ranges from the intimidating outlets of Australia's top designers, to pet shops, antique dealers, dusty drapers and undercover markets. It is also home to one of Perth's best-regarded Aboriginal art galleries, Indigenart (*115 Hay St*).

Swan River

Captain Cook Cruises (tel: (08) 9325 3341) is one of a number of different companies offering river cruises down to Fremantle or up to the Swan Valley from Perth's Barrack Street Jetty.

Perth is often described by visitors as a beautiful city and the major reason undoubtedly is its setting on the Swan. The river glides from the Swan Valley down through the city's eastern suburbs before widening into a vast body of water in front of the Central Business District skyline. It then curls its way through the cliffs of Perth's wealthy western suburbs before emptying into the Indian Ocean at Fremantle. In between it is enjoyed by sailors, windsurfers, rowers, canoeists and water-skiers, while along its edge, cyclists, joggers and walkers make use of a network of riverside paths. A scenic 10-km circuit connects the city and South Perth via the Narrows Bridge and The Causeway, the main bridges linking Perth's northern and southern suburbs. Other tracks run all the way to Fremantle. The less energetic can just watch it all from a number of riverside cafés, like **Jo Jos** at the end of the small Nedlands jetty or **Moorings** at Barrack St jetty at the bottom of the city.

Surf's up

Albany

Tourist Bureau, Proudlove Pde (Old Railway Station). Tel: (08) 9841 1088. Open daily.

Albany, WA's oldest city and port, overlooks the vast, island-studded Princess Royal Harbour. The first settlers came in 1826, and the town retains good examples of colonial architecture. More recently, Albany was the last site for commercial whaling in Australia – the whaling station at Cheynes Beach is now a museum, **Whaleworld** (*Frenchman's Bay Rd*). Southern right whales can be seen from July to November calving in the calm waters of sheltered bays in the Bremer Bay area. They can be observed from many vantage points along the coastline, at times as close as only 6m from the shore. Occasionally, humpback whales can be seen from a distance, as well as other marine mammals such as dolphins and seals.

The town has good local beaches, and plenty of secluded spots further afield.

Margaret River

Margaret River Tourist Bureau, cnr Tunbridge Rd and Bussell Highway. Tel: (08) 9757 2911. Open daily.

Margaret River, 10km inland from where the river flows into the Indian Ocean, developed slowly between 1910 and 1920. In the early 1970s, wine-growing was attempted – successfully – and since then the district has boomed. It was once a mecca for alternative lifestylers, but has recently taken a distinct turn from hippie to yuppie. But its natural attractions remain intact – spectacular surfing, sandy beaches, towering stands of native forest, vast underground caves, and vineyards producing some of Australia's best wines. At **Prevelly**, some of the best wave breaks in Australia draw surfers from around the world. The sheltered beach and open-air café at **Gnarabup** is a great spot for a morning swim and breakfast.

One of Margaret River's attractions away from surfing is **Eagles Heritage** (*south of Margaret River, on the Boodjidup*

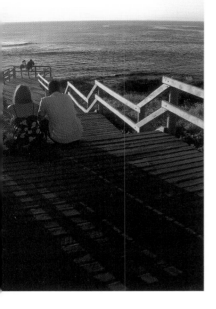

Rd; open daily 1000–1700; $), which cares for birds of prey that are injured, orphaned or displaced. The centre, which now boasts the largest collection of raptors in Australia, is located on 12 hectares of bushland. Visitors can enjoy a 1-km walk to see an abundance of wildflowers and orchids, in season.

Ellensbrook House (*long walk from the town; open Mon–Fri 1000–1500, daily in school holidays*) is the National Trust-listed homestead of the prominent local Bussell family. It was built in the 1850s from available materials – a ship's mast found as driftwood acts as the ridge beam; for the framework, bush poles and paper bark were gathered from the riverbanks with the help of local Aboriginal people, and then sealed with a plaster made by burning limestone from nearby dunes. The house has changed little over the years.

About 500m from Ellensbrook is the **Meekadarribee Waterfall** (the 'moon's bathing place'). It is surrounded by tall peppermint trees that arch over a limestone cave behind the falls.

The Bussell family

Bussell is a recurrent name in the history of the area around Margaret River. In 1834, the family settled along the Vasse Valley; their homestead, Ellensbrook, was named after Mrs Bussell. Their family name was given (against their wishes) to Busselton, and Margaret River was named after Margaret Wicher, a family friend.

Yallingup

Yallingup's rolling swells attract surfers from around the world; it is close to many of the Margaret River region's renowned vineyards and wineries; it is home to fine art and craft galleries; and it is a speleologist's paradise (*see page 202*, the **Ngilgi Caves, Leeuwin-Naturaliste National Park**). South of Yallingup, **Smiths Beach** is popular with surfers, swimmers, fishermen and walkers.

199

Big trees

Pemberton

Pemberton Tourist Centre, Brockman Street. Tel: (08) 9776 1133. Open daily.

Pemberton – the Kingdom of the Karri Tree – is surrounded by magnificent stands of the pale, smooth-barked giants. **Warren** and **Beedelup National Parks** (*off Vasse Hwy*) contain 3 000 hectares of old-growth karris. The trees, the third-tallest in the world, mature at 200 years but some live for more than 1 000. The tallest tree felled here was 104m high. The 60-m high **Gloucester Tree** (*2.4km east of the town*) is said to have the highest tree-mounted fire lookout in the world; the tree can be climbed by the more adventurous.

Tip

The Tree-Top Walk has become one of southwest WA's top tourist destinations. With safety requirements restricting the number of people to 20 per span, delays can occur during the holiday season. An early start will beat the crowds, and give the added bonus of better birdlife.

Pemberton is first and foremost a timber town. In 1913, the local mills supplied half a million sleepers for the rail line across the Nullarbor Plain. For an idea of working life in the forest before the 20th century, the **Brockman sawpit** (*Pemberton–Northcliffe road*) has been restored to its original state of around 1865. In those days, lengths of timber were cut by hand with a cross-saw.

On the **Pemberton Tramway** you can ride in a 1907 replica tram through towering karri and marri forests along one of the most scenic rail lines in Australia, crossing rivers and streams on rustic wooden bridges. It's an ideal way to enjoy the quiet beauty of the forest (*tel: (08) 9776 1322; departs daily at 1045 and 1400*).

Although Pemberton's timber industry has diminished, the town has resurrected itself in the past decade on tourism and a rapidly growing wine industry. **Salitage** (*Vasse Hwy*) and **Gloucester Ridge** (*100m from the Gloucester Tree; open daily 1000–1600*) are among the better wineries in the region and also have excellent restaurants. Bus tours of the wineries are a good way to enjoy the tasting without worrying about drink-driving laws. Pemberton also has a number of good woodcraft galleries, including **Fine Woodcraft** (*Dickinson St; open daily*), which showcases work by nearly 200 woodworkers.

Valley of the Giants

Tree-Top Walk, off Valley of the Giants Road. Open daily 0900–1700 Mar to Nov and 0900–1800 Dec to Mar. Last ticket sold 45 minutes before close. $$.

This area gets its name from giant red tingle trees, which occur only in this very wet, cool part of the state. Visitors can explore the forest canopy via a 600-m tree-top walkway – an engineering marvel made of steel trusses on steel pylons. There is also a ground-level boardwalk through a grove of old tingles dubbed the 'Ancient Empire'; some are up to 16m in diameter. In many ways the grandeur of the forest is much more overwhelming at this level.

PERTH AND THE SOUTHWEST

National Parks

Leeuwin-Naturaliste National Park

Ngilgi Cave, Caves Rd, Yallingup. Tel: (08) 9755 2152. Open daily from 0930. $$.

The small peninsula marked by the **Cape Naturaliste lighthouse** is one of the most beautiful coastal strips in the southwest. The stretch facing **Geographe Bay** has both a northern and an eastern outlook, creating an arc of sheltered, pristine bays perfect for swimming, snorkelling, fishing and diving. **Meelup Bay** is one of the prettiest, with an extensive lawn area under shady peppermint trees. At Cape Naturaliste, the environment changes dramatically. Sandy trails leading from the lighthouse give breathtaking views south to Sugarloaf Rock. In winter and spring, migrating southern right and humpback whales can often be sighted from here.

Around 360 of the oldest and most valuable archaeological caves in Australia have been discovered beneath **Leeuwin-Naturaliste National Park**. The best-known cave, **Ngilgi**, is at Yallingup and is one of four in the park where visitors can be guided through vast limestone caverns spiked with stalactites and stalagmites.

Stirling Range National Park

The magnificent blue granite peaks of the Stirling Range rise abruptly out of surrounding farmland about 80km north of Albany. The National Park offers well-maintained climbing trails and dramatic views on clear days as far as the Southern Ocean. More than 1 500 species of spring and early summer wildflowers are found here, most notably eight species of *Darwinia* or 'mountain bells' that cannot be found outside this park. At 1 073m, **Bluff Knoll** is the tallest peak in the southwest and a strenuous challenge for walkers. (*Be aware that it can frequently and suddenly be covered in streaming low cloud.*) The unsealed 42-km **Stirling Range Drive** is a less arduous way of seeing the park.

Torndirrup National Park

The Torndirrup Peninsula gives easy access to some of the wildest coast in Western Australia. On the peninsula's southern side, the Southern Ocean surges against giant formations of granite rock formed more than 1 000 million years ago when Australia and Antarctica collided. **The Gap**, a sheer-sided deep gorge in the cliffs, and a 24-m drop to the sea, is awesome even on calm days. **Natural Bridge** is a granite arch over the sea and, at the **Blowholes**, air and spray shoot up through a crack in the granite. Respect the signs that warn of the danger of freak 'king' waves, which have been known to surge up to 9m high and to take lives.

WA on the *WWW*

WA Department of Conservation and Land Management has an excellent website with detailed information on most of the state's national parks. Find it at www.calm.wa

National Park passes

A variety of National Park passes can be bought from Department of Conservation and Land Management stations to reduce the cost of regular visits. A holiday pass gives entry for four weeks to all WA national parks for around $20.

Eating and drinking

Perth and Fremantle

Subiaco, and **Oxford Street** in **Leederville**, 3km northwest of the city, are two of Perth's best eating, drinking and shopping areas. Leederville is popular with students. Its eating places range from the long-standing Asian budget diner, **Hawkers Hut**, to such ultra-contemporary establishments as **Fourteen 7** noodle bar and **Nucastle** in Newcastle St.

Altos
424 Hay St, Subiaco. Tel: (08) 9382 3292. $$$. Modelled on the best cafés of Melbourne or New York, Altos serves fresh, quality produce with skill and style, in a smart environment.

Coco's Restaurant
The Esplanade, South Perth. Tel: (08) 9474 3030. $$. Seafood and steak restaurant located on the South Perth foreshore.

Doing Lunch
44 King St. $$. Serves, among other things, the King Street Plate, which consists of bits and pieces of savoury dishes.

Dusit Thai
249 James St, Northbridge. Tel: (08) 9328 7647. $$. One of Perth's longest-established Thai restaurants.

Fraser's
Kings Park. Tel: (08) 9481 7100. $$$. This restaurant defies the conventional wisdom that superb views and great food seldom go together. Some of the best contemporary menus in Perth, with an emphasis on seafood.

Hung Long Coffee House
344 King William St, Northbridge. $. Vast range of Asian dishes, many of which are served up as a form of delicious, fragrant stew. BYO.

Indiana Teahouse café and restaurant
99 Marine Parade, Cottesloe. Tel: (08) 9385 5005. $$$. Cottesloe's grand 1920s changing rooms and surf lifesaving club transformed into a very smart establishment.

The Individual Thai Restaurant
101 Edward St, East Perth. Tel: (08) 9227 6122. $$. Award-winning top Thai tucker.

Jessica's
Hyatt Centre. Tel: (08) 9325 2511. $$$. Claims to be Perth's finest seafood restaurant, overlooking the Swan River.

Gino's Café
1 South Terrace, Fremantle. Tel: (08) 9336 1464. Considered by many to serve the best coffee in the port.

The Left Bank
15 Riverside Rd, East Fremantle. Tel: (08) 9319 1315. $$. Restored two-storey mansion alongside the Swan River, now one of Perth's most popular bars and cafés. There are few better-located beer gardens in the city.

Prickles
408 South Terrace, Fremantle. Tel: (08) 9336 2194. Australian bush tucker including many native Australian foods as crocodile, kangaroo, emu, witchetty grubs and buffalo.

Albany

Celo's Restaurant

Churchlane Rd, Upper Kalgan (follow the Chester Pass Rd from Albany for about 22km). Tel: (08) 9844 3370. BYO. $$. Celo's, in a restored stone homestead, is one of WA's great country restaurants and cafés. Not only very good food but a wonderful view over a wooded bend in the Kalgan River.

Meelup Bay

Wise Winery and Restaurant

Eagle Bay Rd, Meelup. Tel: (08) 9755 3311. Open for lunch daily, dinner Fri and Sat.

Yallingup

Caves House

Caves Rd, Yallingup. Tel: (08) 9755 2041. $$. One of the southwest's most historic getaways, dating from 1903, four years after Yallingup's caves were discovered. The main house retains its art-deco features, and beautiful gardens lead down to Yallingup Beach. Caves House is also a great spot for a drink; the Sunday session draws large, noisy crowds.

Shopping

Perth offers the usual shopping opportunities of any biggish city, but also the **Craftwest Centre for Contemporary Craft** in the old Perth Railway Station (*Wellington St; open Mon–Fri 1000–1700, Sat 1000–1600, Sun 1400–1700*), a gallery and retail outlet for fine contemporary work by leading WA craftspeople. On weekends, wander round the popular undercover markets at **Fremantle**, where you may find anything from incense to fresh fish. Back in the city, in **Northbridge**, there are two fine traditional European grocery stores – the Re Store (Lake St) and Kakulas Bros (William St) – a legacy of post-Second World War migration. Hip **Subiaco** has all sorts of shopping, from designer outlets to second-hand treasure troves.

205

WA's wildflowers and tall trees

Wildflowers and Western Australia belong together. In the spring, between August and November, more than 11,000 species of flowers burst into brilliantly coloured blooms, carpeting dry deserts, rocky plains, beach dunes and the forests of Australia's southwest corner with blazing reds, yellows, purples, pinks and blues. More than three-quarters of these unusual flowers are unique to WA, and the state has one of the richest ranges of flora in the world.

Evolution has taken its own course in Australia's western region, resulting in some remarkable plants such as the Kangaroo Paw – WA's floral emblem – the Donkey Orchid and Cowslip Orchid, the dry pom-pom-like Mulla Mullas of the north and the brilliant blue and pink Leschenaultia.

With such a profusion of native flowers, WA's breeding and cut-flower export industry is booming. Many specialist nurseries and flower farms can be found around Albany, selling both seeds and cut flowers. The excellent **Banksia Farm**, south of Mount Barker, grows and shows all of the *banksia* species known in Australia.

Although there are fabulous displays in Kings Park in the heart of Perth, bushwalking or driving further afield among the flower carpets of WA is an experience not to be missed. Most WA wildflowers bloom in spring, but the exact time varies in different parts of the state, given its enormous size and varying climates. As a rough guide, the wildflower season begins in the northern red dry mountain ranges of the **Pilbara** in July, and commences slightly later further

south, culminating in the magnificent flowering around the **Stirling Ranges** and the south coast in late October and November.

To ensure wildflower tourists are in the right place at the right time, to see the best of the breathtaking displays, the Western Australian Tourism Commission (*tel: (08) 9483 1111*) has produced a special *Wildflower Country* booklet. This divides the state into seven flower 'trails' or driving routes, all starting from Perth, advising on the type of flowers that will be seen, in which national parks and at what time of the season. Information about current wildflower conditions can also be found on the Internet at *www.casair.com.au./tour-no 19*. For those travellers without cars, many tour companies also run specialist flower tours during the spring.

Remember: take only photographs, leave only footprints. The picking of wildflowers is prohibited.

207

Another unusual species in WA is the extraordinary carnivorous, insect-eating Albany Pitcher Plant. The region is also renowned for its unique trees, especially its tall jarrah, karri and red tingle giants. These towering tree species can be seen around **Pemberton** and **Albany** on the south coast, particularly in the **Valley of the Giants**, in the **Walpole-Nornalup National Park**, and in the **Warren** and **Beedelup National Parks**. The pale, smooth-barked karri tree is the third-tallest tree in the world behind California's redwood sequoia and Tasmania's mountain ash.

Brisbane and around

The Gold Coast is a world of sweeping sand beaches and the classic Aussie surfer lifestyle, close to beautiful rainforest-clad mountains, where tumbling waterfalls feed delicate ecosystems. A paradox of natural beauty and man-made fun, this stretch of coast south of Brisbane has become a tourist mecca. Along the Sunshine Coast, north of Brisbane, tourism has more of an environmental focus; here, the great outdoors means camping on the largest sand island in the world, whale-watching at Hervey Bay, or canoeing in Noosa Everglades.

209

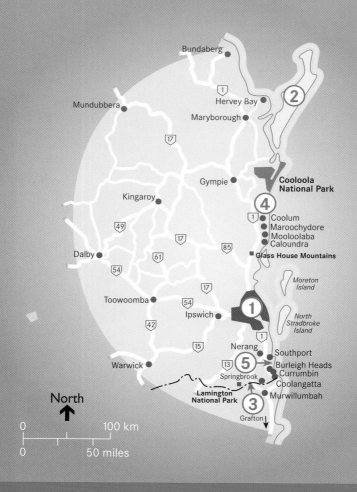

BEST OF
Brisbane
and around

*Getting around: **Brisbane** is a small city, easy to explore on foot. It also has an excellent public transport system (to midnight). The **Roverlink** allows unlimited travel (on bus, tram and ferry) for one day.*

Bundaberg

Mundubbera

Hervey Bay

1

Maryborough

2

17

Gympie

Cooloola
National Park

Kingaroy

4

49

1   Coolum
     Maroochydore
     Mooloolaba
     Caloundra

17

85

Dalby

61

Glass House Mountains

54

Moreton
Island

17

Toowoomba

54

1

North
Stradbroke
Island

Ipswich

42

1

15

Nerang

Southport

Warwick

13

5

Burleigh Heads
Currumbin

Springbrook

Coolangatta

3

Murwillumbah

Lamington
National Park

Grafton

North

0   100 km

0   50 miles

BRISBANE AND AROUND

(1) Brisbane

Queensland's capital city is small, but certainly a pleasant, open and accessible place to visit. Its stylish and outward-looking approach has developed over the years since Commonwealth Games and Expo regeneration in the 1980s. **Pages 212–13**

(2) Fraser Island

Hire a 4WD to explore the largest sand island in the world, with its tall rainforests, long white beaches where dingoes wander, crystal-clear streams and unique perched mirror lakes. **Pages 216–17**

(3) Natural Bridge

This rock archway near the Springbrook Plateau is a lovely spot, and a favourite place to spy glow worms, who have a colony here. **Page 223**

(4) Noosa Heads

Australia's very own St Tropez, with sophisticated bars, shops and restaurant, and no building 'higher than a palm tree'. Secluded Alexandria Bay is the location for the annual Nude Olympics. **Page 220**

(5) Surfer's Paradise

It's big, brash and glitzy, and its architecture is high-rise rather than low-impact, but Surfer's is a holiday playground like no other. With 300 days of sunshine a year, and unbeatable beaches, for some Australians it's a place of annual pilgrimage. **Page 215**

Tourist information

Queensland Tourist and Travel, *123 Eagle St. Tel: (07) 3833 5400.*

Queensland Government Travel Centre, *cnr of Edward St and Adelaide St. Tel: (07) 3833 5412.*

211

Brisbane

Brisbane, the third-largest city in Australia, lies inland on the Brisbane River. In 1982, it smartened itself up for the Commonwealth Games, and then, in 1988, the city hosted Expo – buildings were refurbished, restaurants opened and the ugly industrial area of South Bank was brought to life. Today, it's an enjoyable, outward-looking city.

Some of Brisbane's appeal is undoubtedly due to its traditional 'Queenslanders'. These timber bungalows on stilts, with lattice screens, shutters and corrugated-iron roofing, are eminently functional in a warm, wet climate, and many have been the subject of restoration. Its other trump card is the Brisbane River, which meanders through the centre of the city, giving it shape and character.

City Hall, in King George Sq (*open daily from 0700*), contains an art gallery, museum, 2 000-seat concert hall and public library. It was built in the 1920s and 1930s, using Queensland marble, granite and native timbers. The observation platform on the clock tower – there is a lift to the top – gives panoramic views of the city and the surrounding countryside.

On your bike

Brisbane has 300km of bike paths. If you want to explore the city in a healthy and green way, Backpackers Mountain Bike Hire (tel: 1800 635 286) will deliver a bike to your hotel, complete with the essential helmet (a legal requirement in Australia) and maps.

Parliament House (*cnr George St and Alice St; tel: (07) 3406 7637; guided tours Mon–Fri 1000 and 1400*), opened in 1868, is a fine example of French Renaissance architecture. The public gallery is open to visitors when parliament is sitting. The building is set in parkland opposite the glorious **Botanic Gardens** (*Alice St; open daily, sunrise to sunset; free tours Tue–Sun 1100 and 1300*), designed in 1855 by Walter Hill.

Brisbane has a wide range of museums and art galleries. The **Queensland Cultural Centre** (*South Bank; tel: (07) 3414 7303; open daily 1000–1700, Wed late closing at 2000*) is one

of the landmarks of the city. Covering two blocks on either side of Melbourne St, it contains the **Queensland Art Gallery** the **Queensland Museum** the **State Library** and a performing arts complex. The **Art Gallery** has serious collections of Australian art, paintings, sculpture, prints and ceramics. The **Queensland Museum** (*tel: (07) 3840 7635; open daily 0900–1700, Wed late closing at 2000; $$*) houses a vast range of exhibits relating to anthropology, geology, zoology, history and technology.

The regenerated area of **South Bank Parklands** (*tel: (07) 867 2020*) consists of 16 hectares of landscaped parklands on the south bank of the river, with restaurants, a 'beach' area facing on to the Brisbane River, boat rides and entertainment. Within the park, the **Gondwana Rainforest Sanctuary** (*tel: (07) 3846 4155; open daily 1000–2200*) has a pool containing crocodiles, plus koalas, green tree frogs, lizards and Tasmanian devils. Also in the park is the world's largest collection of Australian butterfly species at the **South Bank Butterfly House** (*tel: (07) 3844 1112/1137; open daily 1000–1800; $*).

Islands everywhere

At Moreton Bay, where the Brisbane River enters the sea, there is said to be an island for every day of the year. Some of them are large enough to shelter the coast from incoming storms.

Getting there: Brisbane City Council Information Booth, Queen St Mall. Tel: (07) 3229 5918. www.brisbaneonthenet.com; www.brisbane-online.com

Just outside Brisbane, the **Lone Pine Koala Sanctuary** (*Jesmond Rd, Fig Tree Pocket, 11km from the city; tel: (07) 3222 7278; open daily 0845–1700*) is the oldest, the largest and one of the best of the Australian wildlife parks, with crocodiles, dingoes, Tasmanian devils, kookaburras, kangaroos and, of course, koalas.

The Gold Coast

Burleigh Heads, Currumbin and Coolangatta

Information Booth, Beach House Plaza, Marine Pde, Coolangatta. Tel: (07) 5536 7765. Open weekdays 0800–1400 and 1500–1600, or 0800–1500 on Sat.

Burleigh Heads National Park, Gold Coast Hwy near Tallebudgera Bridge, Burleigh Heads. Tel: (07) 5535 3032. Open daily 0900–1600.

The popular 'towns' of Burleigh Heads, Currumbin and Coolangatta serve some 20km of the world's finest beaches, internationally renowned for their surf breaks. Cheap accommodation is easy to find, and these places are relaxed and unpretentious. The river inlet at **Currumbin Beach** has a relatively sheltered swimming area, ideal for less experienced swimmers. **Burleigh Heads National Park** has good walks and views. The well-loved wildlife park at **Currumbin Sanctuary** (*Tomewin St, Currumbin; tel: (07) 5534 1266; open daily 0800–1700; $*) is filled with rainbow-coloured lorikeets and other bird life. **Coolangatta** has a sleepy small-town ambience thanks to classic surf beaches, such as Kirra, Point Danger and Greenmount.

Grafton

Clarence River Tourist Association, Pacific Hwy, South Grafton. Tel: (07) 6642 4677.

Following a council bye-law set up in 1866, encouraging the planting and preservation of trees, the pleasant garden town Grafton now has more than 7 000 trees lining its streets. A **Jacaranda Festival** has taken place on the last weekend in October since 1935 – the jacarandas are a glorious sight in season. Since 1994, Grafton has also hosted an **Easter Jazz and Blues Festival**, now a **Festival of Music** that animates the entire town.

Surfer's Paradise

Gold Coast Tourism Bureau, Cavill Ave, Surfer's Paradise. Tel: (07) 5538 4419.

Glitzy Surfer's Paradise is brassy, brash and vibrant – and seemingly not at all Australian. Its population is increasing at four times the national average.

The site was known to the Aboriginal people as Kurrungul (after the hardwood used to make boomerangs) and is said to have been a meeting place for Aborigines from as far away as Maryborough. The resort began to be developed when a James Cavill of Brisbane paid $80, in 1923, for a plot of land, and built the Surfer's Paradise Hotel. Some years later the area was renamed, mainly through Cavill's efforts.

Surfer's Paradise today is at the heart of the Gold Coast: a compact strip of land dominated by spectacular beaches and oceanfront high-rise apartments and hotels. **Cavill Ave Mall** is a vibrant pedestrian district filled with shops, duty-free stores, and several themed restaurants. Running perpendicular to the Mall is Orchid Avenue, the coast's leading nightclub quarter.

Stroll along The Esplanade for a crash course in Australian beach culture – bronzed surfers, beach bums and visiting sun-worshippers. Several major international surfing and surf lifesaving championships are held here every year, with more than 5 000 competitors.

Southport

The northern end of the bleached Gold Coast is based around **Southport**, on a sparkling river estuary, with its picturesque 'Seaway' opening into the Pacific. On the **Broadwater Spit** lie luxurious resorts, endless shops and delightful restaurants. **Marina Mirage Shopping Centre** (*Broadwater Spit, Main Beach; tel: (07) 5577 0088; www.marinamirage.com.au*) is a prime example of Gold Coast high life. On the eastern side of the spit is **Main Beach**, the start of almost 40km of beaches stretching south.

The Sunshine Coast

Fraser Island

Fraser Island–Great Sandy National Park, National Parks and Wildlife Service, Rainbow Beach Rd. Tel: (07) 5486 3160 (for permits).

Fraser Island NPWS, Eurong, Fraser Island. Tel: (07) 4127 9128.

Getting there: *Fraser Island is reached by boat barge and ferries from either Hervey Bay (Urangan and Mary River Heads) or Rainbow Beach (Inskip Point). Only 4WD vehicles are allowed on the island. Visitors can drive their own or hired 4WDs but must pay a permit fee ($30 per vehicle), and a $30 one-way ferry charge. Inskip Point and 75-Mile Beach can be safely driven on only two to three hours each side of low tide. Alternatively, see Fraser Island with one of the tour companies operating from Noosa or Hervey Bay.*

Fraser Island Adventure Tours, Noosa Heads. Tel: (07) 5444 6957.

Fraser Island Excursions, Noosa Heads. Tel: (07) 5474 8622.

Fraser Island Suncoast Safaris, Noosa Heads. Tel: (07) 5474 0800.

Fraser Island 4x4 Getaway Tours, Tewantin. Tel: (07) 5474 0777.

Trailblazer Tours, Noosaville. Tel: (07) 5474 1235.

Inskip Point to Hook Point ferry/barge. Tel: (07) 5486 3154.

Mary River Heads to Kingfisher Bay resort ferry/barge. Tel: (07) 4125 5511.

Urangan to Moon Point ferry/barge. Tel: (07) 4125 3325.

Getting to World Heritage-listed **Fraser Island** is an effort, but it's well worth it. It is one of the great natural wonders of the world – the largest sand island in the world, at over 120km in length and 163,000 hectares in size. It was probably named after a Mrs Eliza Fraser, who was shipwrecked here in 1836. It was declared a native reserve in 1860, but the Aboriginal population had dispersed to the mainland by 1903.

Mineral sands leases were granted in 1949, but conservationists, under the umbrella of **FIDO** (Fraser Island Defenders Organisation), fought long and hard to stop mining. It effectively ended in 1976.

The dune systems of the Great Sandy Region, of which Fraser Island is a part, are the largest and oldest in the world, dating back more than 30,000 years. The dunes rise to 200m in height, and at least 72 different colours of sand have been identified. The dunes are best seen along the 35-km stretch of ocean beach north of **Happy Valley**, which lies on **75-Mile Beach**. Driving on the beach is great fun (*speed limit 60km/h; keep 4WD engaged to stop wheel-spin*), but swimming off it is dangerous because of the currents and sharks.

Pile Valley has massive 1 000-year-old satinay trees, the only place in the world where rainforest trees grow on sand dunes. The lovely little fern and palm-studded **Wanggoolba Creek** has its boardwalk at Central Station. The beautiful freshwater mirror lakes, with white-sand fringes, paperbark trees and clear water that is lovely for swimming, include dazzling **Lake McKenzie**. **Lake Wabby** on the island's east coast is a tea-coloured perched lake. Clear **Eli Creek** is a popular picnic and swimming spot. Stop and admire the coloured-sand cliffs at **The Cathedrals**, and the rocky bluff named **Indian Head** in 1770 by Captain Cook. Beyond Indian Head are the wave-splashed **Champagne Pools** for exhilarating low-tide swimming.

Glass House Mountains

Glass House Mountains National Park. Tel: (07) 5494 6630.

The mountains were named by Captain Cook as he sailed past on 18 May 1770; because of their domed, conical structure, he thought they resembled glass kilns and foundries. Rising out of the flat plains to 556m, these 13 old volcanic plugs are an extraordinary sight and have great Aboriginal Dreamtime significance. The easiest family walk is up Mount Ngungun (253m); Mount Beerwah and Mount Tibrogargan are tougher. The best viewing points are from Mary Cairncross Park near Maleny or from the spectacular glass Wild Horse Lookout off the Bruce Highway, with free shuttle trips every hour from Moby Vic's Mobil service station (*Bruce Highway; tel: (07) 5496 9666, for buses*).

Gympie

Cooloola and Gympie Information Centre, Bruce Highway, Gympie. Tel: (07) 5482 5444. National Park permits (for Fraser Island and Cooloola National Park) available.

Gympie is the major centre in this region on the Bruce Highway, servicing the surrounding rural district. Its history dates from the 1860s, when it was a rich gold-rush town. Thousands of campers descend on nearby **Amamoor Creek State Forest Park** during the last weekend in August for the famous **National Country Music Muster** (better known as the Gympie Muster), to enjoy great country music concerts under the stars, among the gum trees, bush and mountains.

Hervey Bay

Fraser Coast–South Burnett Regional Tourism Office, 388–396 Kent St, Maryborough. Tel: (07) 4122 3444 or 1800 444 155.

Hervey Bay Central Booking Office, 363 Charlton Esplanade. Tel: (07) 4124 1300, for whale-watching enquiries and bookings.

Relaxed, sunny Hervey Bay has a reputation as one of Australia's favourite holiday spots, particularly with families and retired caravanners. The area's main claim to fame, however, is as one of the **whale-watching capitals** of Australia. Between August and early November, giant humpback whales move from their breeding grounds in the warm Pacific down the inner east coast of Australia to feed in Antarctic waters during the southern summer. Platypus

Festival!

Festivals in this region include the famous Hot and Spicy Food Festival at Noosa every June, the Woodford Folk Festival in late December, the Hervey Bay Whale of a Festival in August and the Noosa Festival of Surfing in March.

Bay, between Hervey Bay and Fraser Island, provides a safe area for the humpback giants to regroup before continuing their 12,000-km journey south. During September and October, many mothers with calves can be seen here.

The best time to watch whales is the early morning; most operators leave from the Urangan Pier and Boat Harbour from 0700–0800. Some have underwater hydrophones that allow passengers to hear whales singing. There are about 20 whale-watching operators at Hervey Bay, with more than 80,000 customers a year. In the first two weeks of August, Hervey Bay comes alive with its special 'Whale of a Festival'.

Mooloolaba

Underwater World, The Wharf, Mooloolaba. Tel: (07) 5444 2255.

The attractive beachside town of Mooloolaba is a popular place with yachties, with an excellent and large marina and harbour. Each March, it sees the finish of the Sydney to Mooloolaba yacht race. The famous surf beach of **Alexandra Headland** is just nearby. Mooloolaba is best known for the award-winning Underwater World, Australia's largest tropical oceanarium and an excellent mix of education and family fun. The twin highlights of Underwater World are the 80-m walk-through glass tunnel, around which sharks, rays and a myriad of ocean fish glide, and the performing seals of Marine Mammal Cove.

New agers note

219

Don't miss the little new-age weather-boarded village of Eumundi in the hills behind Noosa. On Saturday mornings and Wednesdays it holds a special and thriving market, selling good-value crafts, clothing, woodwork, knick-knacks, candles, crystals and food. It's all good quality, and there's a great atmosphere. Try the cooked breakfast at the Imperial Hotel on Saturdays, and the local Eumundi Lager beer. Buses leave regularly from Noosa Heads every Saturday from 0630.

Noosa

Noosa Heads

Noosa Information Centre, Hastings St roundabout, Noosa Heads.
Tel: (07) 5447 4988.

Noosa National Park, Noosa Heads. Tel: (07) 5447 3243.

Noosa Heads, one of Australia's premier holiday resorts, is a bustling little village gloriously positioned between the main surf beach, a lagoon and the Noosa river mouth. Relatively unspoilt, it still offers the hedonism of good coffee, food and conversation, combined with an enviable outdoor lifestyle.

Above all, Noosa is regarded as the culinary capital of Queensland, with many top-quality and ever-innovative restaurants, bistros, bars and cafés (particularly around **Hastings St**). The majority of places are informal and fun, in casually elegant outdoor surroundings.

A world away from the bustle, the unspoilt **Noosa National Park** just down the road offers a gentle and popular coastal walk to the plunging Hells Gate gorge, and back via the broad sweep of Alexandria Bay (good surf and nudism).

Noosa Everglades and Cooloola

Cooloola National Park, Queensland National Parks and Wildlife Service.
Tel: (07) 5449 7364.

The magnificent 56,000-hectare **Cooloola National Park** is the largest tract of natural coast and bush on Queensland's southern coast, and is virtually untouched by development. It includes the long, golden 40-Mile Beach, the vast sand mountain of the Cooloola Sandpatch, the rusty red and yellow cliffs of the Teewah Coloured Sands, patches of verdant green rainforest, and the inky waters of the **Noosa Everglades**, an extensive part of the Noosa river system. Much of the saw-tooth sedge grass on the edge of the rivers grows in floating patches – rare in Australia. Hire a canoe from Boreen Point or Elanda Point and paddle gently upstream to Harry's Hut, an old logging camp for a swim, fish and lunch.

Ever-reddy Everglades

*The waters of the Noosa Everglades, an extensive section of the Noosa
river system, are a dark reddy-black. The colour is due to the tannins
from the paperbarks and bloodwood trees that grow alongside the water.*

National Parks

Lamington National Park

Lamington NP Ranger Station, Green Mountains, Lamington. Tel: (07) 5545 1734. Best reached via Nerang on the Gold Coast.

Lamington National Park has over 150km of walking trails, including a suspended canopy walk through the forest crown. The forests shelter abundant wildlife, from small forest wrens and bush turkeys to irresistible wallabies known as pademelons.

The O'Reilly family pioneered the rugged landscape of **Green Mountains** in the early 1900s, and still runs the famous **O'Reilly's Guesthouse** mountain retreat (*Green Mountains; tel: (07) 5544 0644; fax: (07) 5544 0638; $$*), a beautiful lodge that serves as a base for Lamington's famed walks. On the eastern side of the park, the **Binna Burra Mountain Lodge** (*Canungra Rd, Green Mountains; tel: (07) 5533 3622, or toll-free 1800 644 150; $$*) is popular with escaping city-dwellers. Both retreats also offer camping grounds, and they are joined by a 20-km forest walk.

Springbrook

Springbrook National Park Information Centre, Springbrook Rd. Tel: (07) 5533 5147. Open daily 0800–1600.

In startling contrast to the razzle-dazzle of the Gold Coast, Springbrook is a fertile plateau, with a distinctly European feel, bounded by moist temperate rainforests, escarpments of volcanic rock and rolling fields. **Springbrook National Park** is known for its lush walks, breathtaking views and the beautiful 100-m **Purling Brook Falls**. Springbrook has an annual rainfall of roughly 3 000mm, most falling during the summer, and the plateau is often shrouded in spectacular mists.

Natural Bridge

Numinbah Valley Rd, between Nerang and Murwillumbah. Tel: (07) 5533 6156.

A hidden gem – a rock archway spanning a creek buried deep within lush rainforests. Discovered by timber workers around 1893, it remains in pristine condition, and is well known for its colony of glow worms. Miniature wallabies, diverse birdlife and friendly goannas inhabit the rainforest here, which is filled with ferns, vines and orchids. There is a welcome swimming hole at the bottom of the waterfall that gushes through the bridge.

Theme parks

Dreamworld, Pacific Hwy, Coomera. Tel: (07) 5588 1111. Open daily 1000–1700. $$$.

Movie World, Pacific Hwy, Oxenford. Tel: (07) 5573 8485. Open daily 0930–1730. $$$.

Wet 'n' Wild, Pacific Hwy, Oxenford. Tel: (07) 5573 2255. Open daily 1000–1600 in winter, to 1700 in summer and 2100 in late Dec and Jan. $.

Sea World Broadwater Spit, Main Beach. Tel: (07) 5588 2222. Opens daily 0930–1700. $$$.

The northern reaches of the Gold Coast boast a fantasy world for families and the most jaded of thrill-seekers.

Dreamworld buzzes with rides and variety shows; highlights include the stomach-churning 'Tower of Terror', which reaches speeds of up to 160km/h in a 38-storey plunge. It also has a small zoo and IMAX theatre. At **Movie World**, a host of oversized cartoon characters vie for the attention of more than one million visitors a year. The main attraction is Australia's only suspended looping rollercoaster, called 'Lethal Weapon'. Next door, **Wet 'n' Wild**, with its adrenalin-soaked water slides, and 1-m waves, is definitely worth a visit on hot days. Special family passes are available for all three parks.

At **Southport** (*see page 215*), further south, the **Sea World** theme park offers daily dolphin feedings, Australia's first monorail system and the obligatory rollercoasters and water slides. During its 'shark encounters', divers hand-feed sharks, rays and giant groupers. Sea World's water-ski spectacular claims to be Australia's longest-running live show.

Eating and drinking

Brisbane

Bush Tucker Dinner
Tel: (07) 3207 5838. $$. Break O'Day
Nature and Heritage Tours take you
out of town for a three-course dinner
prepared from delicacies such as bunya
nuts, wattle seed, crocodile and emu.

Café San Marco
*South Bank. Tel: (07) 3846 4334.
Open Mon–Sat 0800–2300, Sun
0700–2230. $$.* Mediterranean cuisine
with the stunning city skyline across
the Brisbane River.

Casablanca
*52 Petrie Tce, cnr Caxton St, 1km
from city centre. Tel: (07) 3369 6969.*
Licensed restaurant serving pizza, and
the only one in town that offers tango
and salsa lessons (*Sun–Thu*).

Il Centro
*1 Eagle Street Pier. Tel: (07) 3221
6090. Lunch Sun–Fri. Dinner daily.*
Italian cuisine.

Dashing Food
*97 Ekibin Rd, Annerley. Tel: (07) 3892
5200. Open Mon 0900–1800, Tue–
Sun 0900 till late. $.* Modern Pacific-
Rim innovative cuisine with an Italian
leaning. Good stuff.

Iron Road Restaurant
Tel: (07) 3371 4231. $$. Runs dinner
trips according to demand, with a four-
course meal on an old steam locomotive
that chugs around Brisbane during
the evening.

Michael's Riverside
*Waterfront Pl, 123 Eagle St. Tel: (07)
3832 5522. $$$.* Perhaps the best
restaurant in Brisbane.

Mt Coot-Tha Summit Restaurant
*Sir Samuel Griffith Drv. Tel: (07) 3369
9922. Open daily 1100 till late. $$.*
Restaurant with wonderful views.

Oshin
*256 Adelaide St. Tel: (07) 3229 0410.
Lunch Mon–Fri, dinner Mon–Sat.*
Japanese.

Squirrels of Newmarket
*184 Enoggera Rd. Tel: (07) 3856
0966.* Vegetarian.

Tortilla
*26 Elizabeth Arcade, off Charlotte St.
Tel: (07) 3221 4416. Open daily for
dinner, weekdays for lunch.* Spanish
cuisine.

Wang Dynasty
*South Bank. Tel: (07) 3844 8318.
Open Mon–Sun 1100–1500, 1700–
2230. $$.* Generic Asian fare and a
panoramic view from the terrace.

The Gold Coast

Oscars on Burleigh
*Goodwin Terrace, Burleigh Heads.
Tel: (07) 5576 3722. $$.* Pleasant
varied menu on an open deck perched
over the sea, with long coastal views.

Lyrebird Ridge Café and Gallery
*Lyrebird Ridge Rd, Springbrook
Mountain. Tel: (07) 5533 5195.
Open Mon–Fri 1000–1700 and Sat
evening. $.* Great food in a magnificent
rainforest setting, offering glimpses
of the coast.

Surfer's Paradise

Catering for the mass tourist trade does not usually lead to high culinary standards, but there are dozens of places to choose from on practically every street. Orchid Ave and the beach end of Cavill Ave offer a wide range of al fresco cafés, restaurants and snack bars. Broadbeach Mall is more upmarket and international, but still not serious gourmet territory.

Aztec Food Court
Marine Pde. Tel: (07) 5599 2748. $$. Mexican.

Casa Mia Piccola
Marine Pde. Tel: (07) 5599 2336. $$. Italian.

Melba's Café Restaurant
46 Cavill Ave Mall. Tel: (07) 5592 6922. $. A good, wide-ranging menu, served up in the heart of the Gold Coast.

Omeros
Cnr of Frederick St and the Gold Coast Hwy. Tel: (07) 5538 5244. $$. Terrific seafood and very popular.

Hard Rock Café
Cnr of Cavill Ave and the Gold Coast Hwy. Tel: (07) 5539 9377. Open daily 0900–1100. $.

Noosa

Seen as a second home by some wealthy Sydneysiders, Noosa is a sophisticated dining resort. Hastings St alone has more than 30 top-quality cafés and restaurants, while there is further choice in Noosa Junction.

Artis
Noosa Hill. Tel: (07) 5447 2300. $$$. The top restaurant in Noosa, stylish, expensive modern Australian cuisine, often using Asian and Pacific flavours.

Eduardo's on the Beach
25 Hastings St. Tel: (07) 5447 5875. Open daily for breakfast, lunch and dinner. $$. International cuisine.

Filligan's
Munna Point. Tel: (07) 5449 8811. $$. Casual restaurant in the old wooden general store, serving Carabin food and always bursting with fun and laughter. Open late.

The Jetty Restaurant
Boreen Point. Tel: (07) 5485 3167. $$. On the edge of Lake Cootharaba at Boreen Point, ebullient owner Edi Brunetti serves long and elegant set five-course lunches. Return home to Noosa by romantic boat.

Laguna Bay Beach Club
Hastings St. Tel: (07) 5449 4793. Open daily. $$. Ocean views and great Greek-Italian cuisine.

Ricky Ricardo's
Noosa Wharf. Tel: (07) 5447 2455. $$. A casual bar and light bistro on the edge of the Noosa Sound, perfect for sunset, wine and *tapas*.

Saltwater
Hastings St, Noosa Heads. Tel: (07) 5447 2234. $$$. The best seafood at Noosa Heads.

PROFILE

Australia's World Heritage areas

Australia's size, its isolation and its enormously diverse landscapes, flora and fauna, as well as its ancient Aboriginal culture, mean that it has a significant number of special places that have been accorded Unesco World Heritage protection. The Great Barrier Reef, Kakadu National Park and the Willandra Lakes region in NSW were the first places in Australia to be listed, in 1981. The environmental importance of Fraser Island off Queensland's Sunshine Coast, the world's largest sand island, was recognised with its listing in 1992. In all, 13 extraordinary ecosystems, places and sites around the continent are listed.

According to the international agreements relating to World Heritage listing, the Australian government is obliged to have special guidelines in place for the environmental protection of each area. It must also restrict the types of activity – such as mining – that are allowed within the area's boundaries.

International funding for special research projects, extended ranger services, site protection and cultural enhancement usually comes with a World Heritage listing. So too does an immediate interest in

these locations, which are often remote, both from locals and from travellers. The increased visitor pressure brings its own problems, and in some cases numbers have to be restricted. Currently there are no restrictions on the number of vehicles and people allowed on Fraser Island, for example, at any one time, but a quota limit may soon be imposed.

Australia's 13 World Heritage areas:

- Great Barrier Reef, Queensland (1981)
- Kakadu National Park, Northern Territory (1981)
- Willandra Lakes region (includes Mungo National Park), New South Wales (1981)
- Tasmanian Wilderness (includes Cradle Mountain and Franklin River area), Tasmania (1982)
- Lord Howe Island Group, offshore from New South Wales (1982)
- Uluru Kata-Tjuta National Park (Ayers Rock and the Olgas), Northern Territory (1987)
- Central Eastern Rainforest Reserves (includes Barrington Tops), New South Wales (1987)
- Wet Tropics of Queensland (includes Cape Tribulation, Daintree and Mount Bartle Frere regions), Far North Queensland (1988)
- Shark Bay (includes Ningaloo Reef), Western Australia (1991)
- Fraser Island, Queensland (1992)
- Australian Fossil Mammal Sites (Riversleigh/Naracoorte), Queensland/South Australia (1994)
- Heard and McDonald Islands, extreme southern oceans (1997)
- Macquarie Island, extreme southern oceans (1997)

Best of
the rest

Far North Queensland (or 'FNQ', as the locals like to call it) is known as the place 'where the rainforest meets the reef'. It offers an unrivalled range of experiences – from snorkelling on the Great Barrier Reef to discovering unique rainforest animals.

The Red Centre, based around Alice Springs, is steeped in Aboriginal history, and offers much more than the big red rock that is recognisable the world over. The Top End is like nowhere else in Australia – tropical and lush in some places, red, rocky and ancient in others.

Best of the rest

Getting around: It is possible to travel around the Red Centre desert area in your own vehicle, but it's a harsh environment, and adequate preparation – such as water, spare tyres and a good understanding of outback driving – is essential. There are many excellent organised trips to the main sites from Alice. In the Top End, there is a good sealed road from Darwin to Kakadu; seek advice from the Bowali Visitor Centre (Jabiru; tel: (08) 8938 1121; open daily 0800– 1700).

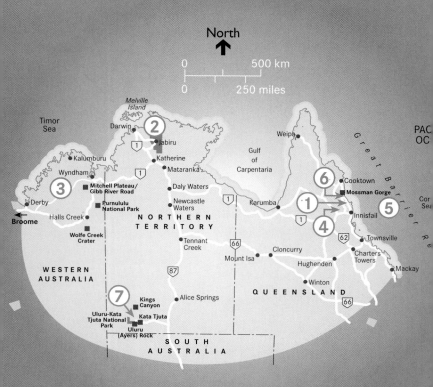

(1) Cairns

This is a modern, thriving and relaxed city that acts as the base for loads of life-affirming activities, from snorkelling and diving on the Reef to flying over a World Heritage-listed rainforest in a tiny gondola. **Page 234**

(2) Kakadu National Park

The reason why most visitors come to Australia's Top End – a massive ancient area where natural sights of great scenic beauty blend superbly with a cultural and spiritual experience. **Pages 248–9**

(3) Kimberley

The two major roads crossing the Kimberley region couldn't be more different from each other – the Great Northern Highway is sealed all the way to Perth, while the east–west rough-dirt Gibb River Rd is one for the more intrepid. **Pages 250–5**

(4) Kuranda

Shop for a T-shirt, hire a canoe, see Aboriginal dancing – and, above all, revel in the journey up (on a little train, over rickety bridges, with fantastic views), and in the journey down (by cable car, with a bird's-eye view of the rainforest). **Page 235**

(5) The Outer Reef

Just 30km out from Cairns, the outer part of the eighth wonder of the world has brilliantly coloured corals and a huge range of living characters, including tropical fish, sharks, turtles and giant clams. Diving here is a once-in-a-lifetime experience. **Pages 236–7**

(6) Port Douglas

The place to sip cocktails in the company of holidaying politicians and other bigwigs, who come here for the laid-back, community atmosphere, and the fragrant air and blue skies. **Page 238**

(7) The Red Centre

Brilliant blue skies, grey ghost gum trees, green tufts of spinifex grass, all stand in stark contrast to the red sandstone cliffs and rocks, which range from bright orange to deep ruby, depending on the time of day. **Pages 240–5**

Tourist information

Tourism Tropical North Queensland Visitor Information Centre, 51 The Esplanade, Cairns. Tel: (07) 4051 3588.

Northern Territory Tourist Information Centre, 38 Mitchell St, Darwin. Tel: (08) 8981 4300; fax: (08) 8981 0653; www.nttc.com.au. Open 7 days a week.

Northern Territory Tourist Commission, tel: (08) 8999 3900. For information, brochures and maps.

Cairns

Tourism Tropical North Queensland Visitor Information Centre, 51 The Esplanade, Cairns. Tel: (07) 4051 3588.

Queensland Tourism: www.queensland-holidays.com.au

Cairns is the heart of the Tropical North, and an ideal base for exploring the rich, varied pleasures of North Queensland, particularly the Great Barrier Reef. Founded in 1876 as a service centre for the northern goldfields, it is now a thriving and fun city. Walk along The Esplanade path by the mangrove mudflats of Trinity Bay at early morning or at dusk. Then explore The Esplanade's shops, restaurants and night markets, the hub of Cairn's activity. Grafton St has some of the best cafés and restaurants. Johno's Blues Bar – along with the reef and rainforest – is one of three places that must be visited while in town. Cairns may lack its own town beach, but the golden stretches of sand in the northern suburbs more than make up for that.

Atherton Tablelands

Atherton Tablelands Tourism, Yungaburra. Tel: (07) 4095 2111.

A trip to the fertile and rich farming area of the Atherton Tablelands is a cool relief when it's hot and muggy on the coast. Above the rainforest escarpment you will find blue volcanic lakes, waterfalls and pretty little villages – **Tolga**, **Atherton**, **Yungaburra**, **Malanda** – among the coffee, sugar-cane, tea-tree, mango and lychee farms. The tablelands can be reached from either Kuranda and Mareeba to the north or via Gordonvale, just south of Cairns. **Lake Tinaroo** has year-round barramundi fishing, volcanic **Lake Barrine** has wildlife cruises and Devonshire tearooms.

Hot 'n' humid

North Queensland is high in the tropics of Australia. It is very wet and humid between the months of December and the end of March; in 1979, Mount Bellenden Ker near the sugar town of Babinda recorded Australia's highest annual rainfall – 11.2m! The best time to travel in FNQ and to enjoy its warm waters and swimming holes is between May and October.

Kuranda

Don't miss the chance to spend a day 'doing' Kuranda, the little rainforest village in the cool hills behind Cairns. Since 1891, the enchanting Kuranda Scenic Railway train (*Cairns Station and Kuranda Station, tel: (07) 4093 7115*) has meandered its way for 34km up the steep mountain slopes of the MacAlistair Range, passing through 15 tunnels and crossing several high wooden trestle bridges. Kuranda has wonderful markets on Wednesday, Thursday, Friday and Sunday, as well as a butterfly sanctuary (*8 Rob Veivers Drive; tel: (07) 4093 7575*), and many art shops.

Return by the new Skyrail cable car (*Caravonica Lakes, Cooks Hwy, Smithfield; tel: (07) 4038 1555*), for a bird's-eye view of the fabulous wilderness of the World Heritage-listed rainforest.

Also at Kuranda, with frequent bus shuttle services from the station, is Rainforestation (*Kennedy Highway; tel: (07) 4093 9033*), 40 hectares in the midst of thick rainforest, with a wildlife park, Aboriginal Dreamtime dancing and a rainforest exploration trip aboard an amphibious Army Duck.

Great Barrier Reef

Queensland National Parks and Wildlife Service information centre, McLeod St, Cairns. Tel: (07) 4052 3096.

Reef trips:

Quicksilver, Port Douglas marina (large catamarans with their own pontoons on the reef). Tel: (07) 4099 5500.

Friendship Cruises, Clump Point jetty, Mission Beach (good for families). Tel: (07) 4068 7262.

Quick Cat, Mission Beach and Dunk Island (good for families). Tel: (07) 4068 7289.

Every visitor to Far North Queensland should take a boat trip to snorkel – or at least to see from a glass-bottomed boat – the magnificent corals and bright tropical fish of the 2 300-km Great Barrier Reef.

The best way to appreciate this marvellous World Heritage feature is to take a full day trip, so that the most spectacular Outer Reef can be reached. Around the closer coastal islands and reefs, the coral can be disappointing. The best Outer Reef expeditions leave from **Mission Beach** and **Port Douglas**

A place of remarkable ecological variety, and great underwater beauty, the Great Barrier Reef is the only living organism on Earth that can be seen from space. Protected by the Great Barrier Reef Marine Park, it comprises the world's largest collection of coral reefs – a wonderland of 2 900 individual coral reefs intertwined with idyllic bush islands, white-sand coral cays, and 350,000 square kilometres of turquoise seas.

To most Australians, the Great Barrier Reef is a true Aussie icon of incomparable beauty and rarity. Its flashing fish, brightly coloured corals and palm-fringed island resorts attract each year 1.6 million visitors and more than $1.5

billion tourist dollars to Queensland's tranquil tropical coast. The waters are warm, and the snorkelling, diving and fishing incomparable.

Tourism to, and on, the Great Barrier Reef is well developed, with a variety of experiences available in all price brackets. There are more than 30 resort islands, varying from the exclusive resorts of Lizard and Bedarra, to places like magical Whitehaven Beach in the Whitsundays where bush camping is allowed for a few dollars a night. Up and down the coast, hundreds of tour operators – all of whom have to operate within strict permit guidelines, in order to preserve the reef – offer sailing, diving, cruising, snorkelling and fishing adventures out to the reef.

Be warned: some parts of the reef close to the coastline have recently suffered from severe coral bleaching (whitening) because of too-warm sea temperatures It pays to check in advance the health status of the reef or cay area each tour operator is visiting, before picking a day trip out to snorkel the reef.

237

BEST OF THE REST

Port Douglas

Tourism Tropical North Queensland: www.tnq.org.au

*Port Douglas Visitors' Centre, 23 Macrossan St, Port Douglas.
Tel: (07) 4099 5599.*

Dazzling blue skies, long white beaches, old-fashioned charm, wide tree-shaded streets and warm perfumed air – picturesque Port Douglas is a popular and sophisticated resort beside the sea. Set on the sweeping **Four Mile Beach**, the village has managed to retain a relaxed community atmosphere. The beach is its day playground; early in the morning, the rich and famous mingle with backpackers and campers jogging and strolling. During the day, sunbathers and families take over.

The Rainforest Habitat wildlife sanctuary (*Port Douglas Rd, Port Douglas, tel: (07) 4099 3235*) is home to the elusive cassowary, green tree frogs, crocodiles, bright parrots, the red and black Cape York cockatoo, and tree kangaroos. A little steam cane train shuttle for tourists connects many of the resort hotels along the beach with the town and marina, while the bustling Sunday markets are a great place to taste tropical cane juice, or to buy some local art or a new T-shirt.

Mossman Gorge

Just north of Port Douglas is the sugar-cane town of Mossman and the road leading to beautiful Mossman Gorge, part of Daintree National Park. Here, the crystal clear waters of the Mossman River tumble over moss-covered boulders, the blue Ulysses butterfly flits across the deep rockpools, and huge strangler figs drop through the dense canopy to the dimly lit forest floor. An easy loop track across the swing bridge over Rex Creek gives an excellent feel for the ancient forests, as well as providing a great opportunity for swimming in the cold creek.

Tropical dangers

Estuarine or saltwater crocodiles *inhabit many river and creek estuaries in the Far North, even far inland. Take care when walking along mangrove-fringed beaches or across creek mouths, especially on more remote beaches. Keep an eye on any* coral cuts, *as they can fester. Deadly* stonefish *can lie hidden in water near rocks or coral – wear sandshoes, as their spines can be fatally poisonous.* Sea-wasps *deliver savage, occasionally fatal, stings from November to April – look for the signs before swimming in the warm seas.*

239

The Red Centre

As impressive and significant as Uluru (Ayers Rock) is, the Red Centre region of Australia is so much more. Steeped in Aboriginal and geological history, this outback region around the desert town of Alice Springs combines vast stretches of desert with dramatic rock formations like the MacDonnell Ranges, Finke Gorge, Kings Canyon, Uluru and Kata Tjuta (The Olgas). The brilliant blue skies provide a stunning contrast to the rich-red sandstone cliffs and the white trunks of ghost gum trees. Spectacular natural waterholes are a welcome relief from the desert heat.

Watersports without the water

The 'Henley-on-Todd Regatta' is a riotous festival with locals and visitors running along the dry river in bottomless 'boats', held each year in September/October.

Climate note: it is best to avoid the extreme dry heat of midsummer. April to September are better months for exploring Central Australia, although the nights can be cold. The walks in the National Park are along rocky paths and in some cases quite steep. Emergency water is available but you should carry one litre of water per hour and aim to walk during the cooler morning hours. A fly net to wear on your head is strongly recommended – otherwise, the flies may drive you mad.

Alice Springs

Visitor Information Centre, 60 Gregory Terrace. Tel: (08) 8952 5800; fax: (08) 8953 0295; www.northernterritory.com

The modern, bustling town of Alice Springs – or The Alice, as it is affectionately known – is at the heart of the Red Centre. It gets part of its name from a waterhole or spring close to the site of a telegraph station 4km north on the Stuart Highway. **The Telegraph Station Historical Reserve**, established in 1872 to relay messages across Australia between Darwin and Adelaide, was the original site of the first European settlement in Alice Springs. The

Todd River, a sandy strip through the town where the water flows more than half a metre underground, was named after Charles Todd, the superintendent of telegraphs in Adelaide at the time. Alice was his wife.

Alice Springs is the base for a range of tours including Aboriginal bush-food, camel treks and ballooning. Remember, summer temperatures reach 45°C while winter nights are often below zero. The **Aboriginal Art and Culture Centre** (*86 Todd Street; $*), Aboriginal-owned and operated, combines desert discovery tours, didgeridoo lessons, art exhibitions and a museum.

Kings Canyon

A dramatic red, sandstone chasm plunging 300m. On the rim of the canyon, extraordinary and seemingly endless beehive-shaped rock domes create the 'Lost City'. It is a steep climb to the rim (*accessed several hundred metres on the left from the car park*), but the views of the surrounding countryside, into and across the canyon, and of the weathered domes are breathtaking. The walk around the canyon (*3.5 hours; shorter walk possible on the canyon floor*) leads down into an exotic oasis of palms and ferns around a permanent water hole, known as the Garden of Eden. Rich in fauna and flora, rockpools, sand plains and gullies, Kings Canyon has played an important role in Aboriginal life for more than 20,000 years.

Uluru-Kata Tjuta National Park

This National Park, with its changing colours and sacred sites, is as fascinating as it is mysterious. Discover its rocks and breathtaking gorges and outcrops by car and on foot, and feel the presence of the Aborigines, whose connection with the region dates back more than 30,000 years.

The National Park is established on Aboriginal land which, following a landmark agreement in 1985, is leased back to the Commonwealth's National Parks and Wildlife division. Its major attractions are **Uluru (Ayers Rock)** and **Kata Tjuta (The Olgas)**. Many traditional Aboriginal owners, the Anangu people, still live in the park, mainly around the eastern base of Uluru and play a key role in its management. In 1987, it was added to the World Heritage list.

Please, no pictures

Visitors should note that it is forbidden to take photographs of the Cultural Centre and of the Anangu people. The Anangu also have a traditional duty of care for others' safety, and request, therefore, that tourists do not climb the monolith of Uluru. The memorial plaques at the bottom of the rock attest to the danger of the activity, which results in more than one fatality a year.

243

The park's Cultural Centre (*open 0700–1730; free*) provides an excellent history and Tjukurpa (traditional law) of the Pitjantjatjara and Yankunytjatjara, or Anangu, people, and contains the Maruku Arts and Crafts Galley and Initi Souvenirs and Café. This is the only place to buy food and drinks in the park.

Uluru: this is the Aboriginal name for Ayers Rock, the 3.6-km long and 348-m high reddish-brown iconic rock. It has great significance for its traditional owners, the Anangu people. A self-guided tour of the **Mala Walk** (*2km*) and the **Mutitjulu Walk** (*1km*), or an Aboriginal-guided tour around the base (*9.4km, 3 hours; tel: (08) 8956 2123; $$*), will offer an excellent insight into the Anangu, their sacred sites, water holes, initiation ceremonies and rock paintings.

At least one sunset and one sunrise must be spent at the specially marked spots near Uluru. As the sun sets, the huge rock turns a series of brilliant, deeper and darker reds before it fades into a dull purple while the sky forms a vibrant pink and blue curtain in the background. The parking area gets packed, so arrive half an hour before sunset (*times are shown everywhere at Ayers Rock Resort*), with a bottle of champagne.

Alternatively, try the **Sounds of Silence Dinner** (*tel: (02) 9360 9099; $$$; limited numbers*), which offers a five-star meal under the stars, with an astronomy talk.

The eco-friendly, low-impact tourist village of Yulara is the only place to stay near Uluru. There is accommodation to suit every budget, from the Sails in the Desert Hotel to the grassy campground (which has a policy that it won't turn people away, however busy it is).

Kata Tjuta: the name of this group of 36 gigantic domes of rust-red sedimentary rock, better known as The Olgas, means 'many heads'. The rocks appear eerily out of nowhere, and span 35km. The largest dome, Mount Olga, is a staggering 546m high.

Much of Kata Tjuta is still used by the traditional owners for meetings. The site is associated with ritual activities that remain the exclusive domain of initiated men; information about what goes on is restricted. Because of this spiritual significance, very little has been written about the rock formations, which are conglomerates of pebbles and boulders cemented by sand and mud, believed to have formed about 900 million years ago.

The Kata Tjuta Dune viewing area located 25km along the Kata Tjuta Rd inside the National Park gives a magnificent view of these extraordinary formations, which are believed by geologists to extend beneath the ground as far as 6km. The prolific tufts of spinifex grass and mulga trees, both important sources of materials to the Aborigines, stand in stark contrast to the orange rock. There are two signposted walks at Kata Tjuta. The longer 7.4-km Valley of the Winds route is the best opportunity to walk into some of the spectacular landscape and capture views of the surrounding country beyond the towering domes. A few short climbs can make it hard going and for safety reasons it is partly closed when temperatures are forecast above 36 degrees centigrade. Walpa, or the Olga Gorge Walk, is 2.6km to the end of the gorge, where spearwood vines flourish.

The Top End

The Top End of Australia is a land of Aboriginal culture, ancient landscapes, great rivers, towering sandstone cliffs, plunging gorges, dry plains and verdant green wetlands. It's home to great crocodiles, and a mass of colourful birds. Mythical Aboriginal spirits, Dreamtime ancestors and ghostly hands crowd on the walls of ancient cliff-face art galleries, creating the greatest and oldest collection of rock art in the world. Who could forget a dawn cruise among the crocodiles and lotus lilies at Yellow Water, in Kakadu National Park, or a dip in the clear thermal pools of Mataranka?

Climate Note: the Top End can be a seductive place, but it is also the Tropics. Travel is preferable in the cooler, drier months from April to August ('the Dry'), although the wet, humid months of January to March give a magnificent alternative view of Kakadu National Park in all its wet season splendour.

NT Police Road Report, tel: 1800 246 199 or (08) 8922 3394. For recorded message on current road conditions.

Darwin

Darwin Tourism Information Centre, 38 Mitchell St. Tel: (08) 8981 4300; fax: (08) 8981 0653.

Darwin, named in 1839 after biologist Charles Darwin, is perched on a beautiful peninsula, surrounded by turquoise seas, palm trees, warm air and lush growth. Although it seems to have a permanent holiday atmosphere, it has had to fight hard to survive – it has suffered extreme isolation, 64 direct bombing attacks in the Second World War, and obliteration by the fearful force of Cyclone Tracy in 1974.

Darwin is now a flourishing, multicultural modern city, with a relaxed tropical atmosphere. Its cafés and restaurants are among the best in Australia, while its closeness to Asia adds significantly to the cultural mix. At the twice-weekly outdoor Asian food markets (*Thu and Sun, 1700–2200*), at **Mindil Beach**, everyone takes tables and chairs and holds impromptu dinner parties. The **NT Museum and Art Gallery** (*Conacher St, Fannie Bay; tel: (08) 8999 8201; weekdays 0900–1700, weekends 1000–1700; free*) houses the best collection of traditional and contemporary Aboriginal art.

The best way to see the other tourist attractions around Darwin is by the **Tour Tub** (*tel: (08) 8985 4779*), an open-sided trolley bus that does an hourly circuit of tourist attractions.

Darwin Crocodile Farm

Stuart Highway, Noonamah, just south of Arnhem Highway turn-off, about 37km south of Darwin. Tel: (08) 8988 1450. Open daily 0900–1600. $$.

The Darwin Crocodile Farm has about 15,000 saltwater and freshwater crocodiles in residence, including many of the big 'salties' that have been taken out of NT rivers and seas by park rangers after becoming a nuisance or a threat. Crocodiles are farmed here for their meat and their skin, which makes good leather. Feeding time is at 1400 daily.

247

Kakadu National Park

Kakadu National Park and Bowali Visitor Centre, Jabiru. Tel: (08) 8938 1121. Open daily 0800–1700.

Kakadu National Park is spectacular, acquiring World Heritage listing in 1981 for its unique natural and cultural values. Its 20,000 square kilometres are filled with stunning diversity – lush wetlands and waterways teeming with fish, crocodiles and birdlife, red escarpment cliffs cut by plunging waterfalls, grassy green flood plains crossed by big twisting rivers meandering out to the mangrove coastal flats, and dry scrub country lined with paperbarks and eucalypts.

But Kakadu is not just a beautiful place full of scenic wonders. It also offers the visitor the opportunity to learn a little of the rich and ancient culture of the local Gagudju Aboriginal people, who own the land and lease it back to the Commonwealth government. They have lived there for at least 50,000 years and 300 of them still engage in traditional hunting, fishing and ceremonial activities at certain times of the year within its boundaries. There are huge galleries of ancient Aboriginal rock art painting throughout the park (several of which can be accessed by tourists), the excellent Aboriginal **Warradjan Cultural Centre** at **Cooinda**, many interpretive signs that tell the stories of the landscape through Aboriginal eyes, and cultural walks and tours run by Aboriginal rangers and guides employed within Kakadu National Park.

Start at the award-winning Bowali Visitor Centre, near the centre of the park at Jabiru, which features excellent displays describing the animals, Aboriginal culture and geology of Kakadu, and provides detailed information sheets and brochures. Next, take a sunrise cruise on the wetlands of Yellow Water at Cooinda (*Yellow Water Cruises, Cooinda; tel: (08) 8979 0111*) and see Kakadu in all its glory, with lotus lilies, crocodiles, blue-winged kookaburras, magpie geese, jabirus and hundreds of other bird species reflected in the still waters. About 50km north of Jabiru, Ubirr Rock is an elevated rocky outcrop – a magnificent spot

Flora and fauna

Kakadu National Park has an enormous variety of habitats and wildlife. More than one-third of all bird species recorded in Australia live here, as do more than 1 200 plant species, at least 10,000 insect species and 60 mammal species. At least 10 per cent are estimated to be unique to Kakadu and its surrounding region.

from which to watch the sun set over the East Alligator River wetlands. At its base are many rock-art galleries. Boat trips on the East Alligator River, with a local Aboriginal guide, reveal some of the secrets of traditional Aboriginal medicine, law, sacred ceremonies and creation stories.

Nourlangie Rock shelters a great collection of Aboriginal galleries, including the famous paintings of Namarrgon the Lightning Man and the dangerous spirit Namondjok. Nearby Angbangbang Billabong is a magical picnic spot with a carpet of water-lilies. Twin Falls and Jim Jim Falls are spectacular waterfalls thundering over the edge of the Arnhem Land stony plateau after the summer rains, down into deep rockpools and on to the billabongs and flood plains of the South Alligator River. The large swimming hole at the base of Gunlom waterfall, in the southern and drier end of Kakadu, was featured in the film *Crocodile Dundee*.

The Kimberley region

Kimberley Tourism Association, PO Box 554, Broome. Tel: (08) 9193 6660; www.ebroome.com/kimberley

Geographically, the Kimberley is divided into two sections – the East Kimberley region based around the Ord River scheme, Lake Argyle, Kununurra, Halls Creek and the Bungle Bungles, and the rest of the Kimberley, centred on Broome, Derby, the Mitchell Plateau, Fitzroy Crossing and the Dampier peninsula. Connecting these two distinct parts is the Great Northern Highway, sealed all the way from the NT border to Perth. The second great road of the Kimberley is the rough-dirt Gibb River Rd, beloved of adventure travellers and an essential link between east and west across the northern section of the Kimberley. Both roads can be impassable during the wet season; travel in the tropical Kimberley is best between April and August.

The remote north coast of the Kimberley is almost impossible to access by road. But with its rugged red cliffs, cooling waters, untouched white-sand beaches, thousands of islands and plunging cliff-face waterfalls, it is a magical place to visit by plane or by charter boat. Most tour operators up into this region are based in **Derby**.

Broome

Tourist Bureau, cnr Broome Highway and Bagot St. Tel: (08) 9192 2222; fax: (08) 9192 2063; e-mail: tourism@broome.wt.com.au. Open 7 days a week.

The little tropical paradise town of Broome has a quaint, slow-moving charm. It has a fascinating history as a major pearl-diving centre from the 1880s, when more than 400 luggers and their crews from Japan, China, Arabia and Europe were based there. Their legacy exists today in an old Chinatown area in the town, now the centre for pearl showrooms, and many locals of mixed-race origin. Its vibrant pearl industry provides most of the tourist highlights, such as a tour of a modern pearl farm, or a champagne cruise on an old wooden pearl lugger out on Roebuck Bay. **Sun Pictures**, dating from 1916, with its large movie screen and deckchairs, is the world's oldest outdoor picture gardens. Weekly Saturday morning markets are held in the gardens of the Old Courthouse, featuring local Aboriginal arts and crafts, and the work of a flourishing white artistic community.

Cable Beach is a pristine stretch of white sand on the clear blue waters and gentle surf of the Indian Ocean, about 5km from Broome. At the exclusive but relaxed Cable Beach Resort (*Cable Beach Rd, Broome; tel: (08) 9192 0400 or 1800 199 099; fax: (08) 9192 2249; $$$*), visitors can lie on the warm sand, ride camels across the sandflats, and enjoy the sunset from Gantheaume Point, where the 130-million-year-old footprints of a dinosaur are visible on the tidal rockshelf at low tide.

At the excellent **Broome Bird Observatory**, more than 250 species of birds can be watched from special hides, especially the long-distance migratory wading birds that fly from here in autumn, to summer in Siberia and northern Japan. In August, the **Pearl Festival** or **Shinju Matsuri**, is held in Broome, celebrating the town's Chinese, Malaysian and Japanese communities.

Aboriginal identity

More than two-thirds of the Kimberley population is Aboriginal. White settlement is only two to three generations old, and the Aboriginal culture is at its most intact here. Aboriginal children are educated with a strong sense of their Aboriginal identity. Many of the communities are determined to reduce welfare dependency and alcoholism, in order to regain control of their own future, and some now own their own land and cattle stations.

Gibb River Rd

Kimberley road conditions and floods, tel: 1800 013 314.

The Gibb River Rd sure is a rough, outback experience, a not-to-be-tackled-lightly alternative to the sealed Great Northern Highway linking Derby and Kununurra. Highlights include stylish **El Questro** (*Gibb River Rd via Kununurra; tel: (08) 9169 1777; fax: (08) 9169 1383; $–$$$*), a million-acre cattle station and wilderness park, spoken of in terms of reverence by anyone who knows it. Its magnificent gorges, fishing, deep pools, thermal springs and red, rocky, rugged country can be roamed freely, and visitors can stay in anything from its $600-a-night elegant cliff-top homestead, to their own tent in its camping ground.

Further along the Gibb River Rd are Manning Gorge, the rampart-like sandstone cliffs of the Cockburn Ranges, the old coral Napier Range and the gorges of Windjana, Bell Creek, Mitchell and Barnett River. This road is gravel only for 586 kilometres and can be extremely corrugated. It is only usually open from April to November, is always impassable after heavy rain and is not suitable for caravans. Great care must be taken to carry sufficient water, supplies, fuel and breakdown equipment, but this remains one of Australia's great adventure drives.

Halls Creek and Wolfe Creek Crater National Park

Halls Creek Tourist Information Centre, Great Northern Highway, Halls Creek.
Tel: (08) 9168 6262; fax: (08) 9168 6467.

Halls Creek is perched on the edge of the Great Sandy Desert, an oasis town in a hot, dry land, established in 1885, when it was the site of WA's first gold rush. About 150km from Halls Creek, on the start of the Tanami desert track, is the **Wolfe Creek Crater National Park**. This is the place where the second-largest meteorite known to have hit earth crashed some 250,000 years ago, creating the extraordinary circular rim of the Wolfe Crater, some 850m in diameter. The access road crosses the rim and ends up inside the large sheltered interior of the impact site, where it is easy to imagine yourself on the moon! There are no facilities in this park, so water must be carried.

Mitchell Plateau and Kalumburu

The Mitchell Plateau is one of Australia's last untouched wildernesses and an area of significant Aboriginal heritage. Reached via dirt track and in a high-clearance 4WD only, from the Gibb River Road, its highlights are the Wandjina Aboriginal art sites around the King Edward River, the spectacular Mitchell Gorge multiple waterfalls, and the small remote Aboriginal settlement of Kalumburu, renowned for its local Aboriginal artists. All Aboriginal art sites are protected and must not be touched. Beware of dangerous estuarine crocodiles in all rivers in this region, even above major waterfalls.

Purnululu (Bungle Bungle) National Park

Purnululu National Park, CALM Rangers, Halls Creek. Tel: (08) 9168 0200.

These 'tiger-striped beehive mountains', 'discovered' by the international world only in the 1980s, rank as one of the great geological wonders of the world. Now protected as the Purnululu National Park, the lumpy, weathered, moulded mounds of the Bungle Bungle range – 33km long and 23km wide – are most easily viewed by air from Kununurra or Halls Creek. From the ground, the site is both fascinating and spiritual; narrow gorges are lined with tall palms, and the places around clear pools of water are covered with Aboriginal handprint and rock art.

The orange and black tiger stripes of the Bungle Bungle mounds are only skin-deep and very fragile; they are simply a 10-mm thick layer of orange silica and black lichen and organic deposits protecting the soft white sandstone below.

The stuff of legend

According to Aboriginal legend, the Bungle Bungles were formed when a galah bird was fighting with an echidna, which dug holes in an attempt to hide, thus forming the mounds and hollows. Finally, the echidna raised its quills in protection, which fell out, becoming the tall livistonia palm trees scattered among the massif.

Camping is allowed within the Bungle Bungles at designated sites, but the access road is frequently impassable except to high 4WD vehicles. The isolation of Purnululu, as well as the harshness of its spring and early summer heat, are other reasons why it may be best to take an organised tour into the park.

Eating and drinking

Far North Queensland

Cairns Game Fishing Club
Marlin Pde, Cairns. Tel: (07) 4051 5959. Waterfront location on Cairns harbour, fresh seafood.

Perrotta's
Cairns Regional Art Gallery. Tel: (07) 4031 5899. The trendy spot to be seen for an outdoor drink.

Red Ochre Grill
Shield St, Cairns. Tel: (07) 4051 0100. Award-winning modern Australian food with bush tucker touches.

Nautilus
17 Murphy St, Port Douglas. Tel: (07) 4099 5330. $$$. Best, most exclusive and expensive fresh seafood and mudcrab restaurant in North Queensland.

Tree House Restaurant
Silky Oaks Lodge, Finlayvale Rd, Mossman. Tel: (07) 4098 1666. $$$. Fresh tropical foods, barramundi and mudcrabs. Served overlooking the river in rainforest treetop serenity.

Salsa Bar and Grill
38 Macrossan St, Port Douglas. Tel: (07) 4099 4922. $$. Trendy spot to hang out either before or during dinner.

Wharf St Café
Rydges Resort, Port Douglas. Tel: (07) 4099 5885. $$. Views over the sea, top spot for brunch or champagne at sunset.

Nick's Restaurant
Gillies Highway, Yungaburra. Tel: (07) 4095 4266. Award-winning traditional Italian food, with some Swiss touches.

Red Centre

Gecko's Café
Resort Shopping Centre, Yulara. $$. One of the cheaper eating places, with a lively atmosphere.

Outback Pioneer Barbecue
Yulara Drive. Tel: (02) 9360 9099. $. Cook your own food at this budget hotel complex.

The Top End

Hanuman Restaurant
Mitchell St, Darwin. Tel: (08) 8941 3500. $$$. Like no other Thai restaurant, Hanuman melds exquisite flavours and ingredients from Indonesia, Malaysia and Thailand, all in a classy setting.

Christos on the Wharf
Stokes Wharf, Darwin. Tel: (08) 8981 8658. $. A classic Darwin dining experience, eating seafood outside on the end of Stokes Wharf, overlooking the harbour and city.

Cornucopia Museum Café
NT Art Gallery and Museum, Conacher St, Fannie Bay, Darwin. Tel: (08) 8981 1002. $$. A great spot for a light lunch or Sunday brunch, dining outside on a covered deck next to the art gallery and museum and overlooking the tropical headland and bay.

Gagudju Crocodile Hotel
Flinders St. Tel: (08) 8979 2800. $$$. Built in the shape of a saltwater crocodile, this modern Aboriginal-owned hotel has all the luxuries of any major hotel, and the best restaurant in Kakadu. Guess what's on the menu?

Shopping

*The markets at **Kuranda**, just north of Cairns, are a wonderful place to spend a day browsing among the craft stalls and tiny shops. You can pick up all sorts of things, from T-shirts of original design to essential oils. Alternatively, have your fortune told, or your runes read.*

Alice Springs is a good place to buy Aboriginal art and souvenirs (*see Profile, pages 258–9*). Todd Mall's shops sell many examples, of varying quality. The Cultural Centre at the Uluru-Kata Tjuta National Park contains the Maruku Arts and Crafts Galley and Initi Souvenirs shop.

257

Aboriginal art

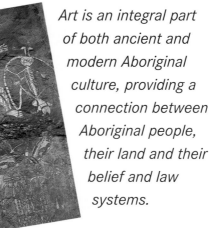

Art is an integral part of both ancient and modern Aboriginal culture, providing a connection between Aboriginal people, their land and their belief and law systems.

Rock engravings and Aboriginal paintings more than 20,000 years old have been found in many parts of Australia where Aborigines have lived for the past 50,000 years and possibly longer. Arnhem Land, Cape York, the Kimberley and the region around central Australia have the strongest ceremonial art heritage and traditions.

Rock paintings appear to fulfil at least three or four different purposes in traditional nomadic Aboriginal life. Paintings that depict different types of fish and animals that live on the land around the galleries, caves and cliff shelters where tribes often lived and visit, are thought to be 'menu' or 'hunting' boards, giving other travelling tribes an idea of what food is around the area to catch and eat. Other simple paintings, such as the commonly seen hands that are 'blow-painted' or stencilled with ochre spat from the mouth on to gallery walls, may be a way of teaching children about their identity and their own home places, or may be a type of 'visitors' book' to record people who arrive and stay at different times. Other paintings, especially more modern ones from the last two centuries, some of which depict white men with guns and boats with sails, are records of major events in each tribe or family's lives.

The more complex Aboriginal artworks of mythological beings, spirit figures, giant and strange animal shapes and land forms usually depict 'Dreamings' – particular stories involving supernatural spirits and ancestral beings who created the land and its people, and whose travels, antics and battles provide the 'law', and dictate the framework and structure of Aboriginal society even today, by guiding Aboriginal people through their everyday lives. Each Aboriginal person has his or her own 'skin' Dreaming, and 'totem', and is traditionally ruled by the obligations and responsibilities bestowed by these Creation Beings. These affect all aspects of life, from marriage and other social activity, and the pieces of land and landscape features for which they are responsible.

Art styles vary considerably in different parts of Australia, and these traditional differences are still clear in modern Aboriginal art. So-called 'dot art' predominates in the Central Deserts area around Alice Springs and is the most internationally recognisable Aboriginal art today. In Arnhem Land, paintings of mimi spirits and X-ray style fish, crocodiles and animals predominate, while in the Kimberley, the distinctive Wandjina figures who represent fertility spirits from the sea and sky can be found.

The best place to view and learn about a wide selection of Aboriginal art and styles from ancient to modern is the Museum and Art Gallery of the Northern Territory in Darwin (*Conacher St, Fannie Bay; tel: (08) 8999 8201; open Mon to Fri 0900–1700, weekends 1000–1700; free*), which has the best collection of its kind in the world.

Lifestyles

Shopping, eating, children and nightlife in Australia

Shopping

Shopping in Australia is infinitely varied. Large shopping malls in the major cities house everything from snazzy homewares to funky fashions under one roof. Weekend markets offer great opportunities to pick up alternative souvenirs with a twist of hippie chic. Glorious galleries, filled with Australian art the colour of the sea and sun, nestle in rural backwaters. Whatever your budget, there's plenty to choose from and much that is different and unusual.

Nationwide stores

There are several discount department stores such as **Woolworths**, **BigW** and **Target**, which sell everything from CDs and books to homewares and stationery at cheap prices. At the exclusive end of the scale is **David Jones** and, one notch down, **Grace Brothers**, which offer a superb selection of clothes, sportswear and homewares. David Jones' food hall in Sydney is second to none in variety and quality. For ordinary food shopping, **Coles** or **Franklins** supermarkets are everywhere.

Shopping customs

Prices are fixed in shops and even at markets haggling is rare unless you're buying several things from the same stall, when you might be able to knock off a few dollars. Many tourist-orientated stores, such as Australian souvenir, jewellery and fashion shops, offer tax-free shopping. To benefit, you will need to show your airline ticket and passport.

What to buy

Jewellery

Australia's rich mining territories provide 90 per cent of the world's opals. The most valuable are red on black, but there are many variations. They're on sale everywhere, although **The Rocks** in **Sydney** is famed for its opal jewellers. Make sure you pick a solid gemstone, not a doublet or triplet, which are thin veneers of opal magnified by a quartz dome. Sapphires are also good quality, and South Sea pearls from the west coast are some of the finest in the world. Western Australia's gold is good value and comes in 9 or 18 carats.

Fashion

Fashions in Australia range from the high-street casual to boutique chic, with many Australian designers gaining an international following. For affordable high-street fashion, popular chain stores include Sussans, Sportsgirl, Katies, Events, Jag and Jeans West. Upmarket Australian designers to look out for are Carla

Driza-Bone, which sells oiled jackets and coats. For bushwalkers, **Akubra** hats with their sun-beating brims are an essential purchase. The excellent olde-worlde **Strand Hatters** in the Sydney arcade of the same name is a good starting point.

Arts and crafts
Australia has a burgeoning arts and crafts scene, with the best buys in olde-worlde colonial towns and villages, which lend themselves perfectly to browsing afternoons. Recent years have seen a move away from the dull greens and reds that characterised colonial art towards the bright blues, yellows and oranges that reflect the colours of Australia's vibrant landscape. Pottery and ceramics are great value, ranging in style from chunky earthenware bowls to refined lacquer noodle dishes.

Arts and crafts are a major focus for tiny towns such as **Berrima**, **Byron** and **Bellingen**, but even one-horse villages may have at least one wonderful gallery. Countryside craft shops pop up all over the place, attached to motorway service stations, cafés and tourist attractions. Unsurprisingly, arty souvenirs tend to be significantly cheaper outside the main cities.

Zampatti, Anthea Crawford, Saba and Collette Dinnigan (particularly for lingerie). For one-off creations by Sydney's up-and-coming fashion gurus, head to the **Fashion Emporium** in Paddington.

For beach wear, bikinis, sarongs and the super-trendy Quiksilver, Rip Curl and Mambo surf gear, **Byron Bay** on NSW's north coast and **Torquay** on the Great Ocean Road are difficult to beat.

For fashion statements that scream Australia, the stores to look out for are **R M Williams**, which specialises in 'bush clothing' such as moleskin trousers and riding boots, and

263

Weekend **markets** have become a great tradition in Australia. It is said that you can buy anything at the Queen Victoria Market in **Melbourne** (*see page 136*), while the atmospheric Saturday market at **Eumundi**, in the hills behind Noosa, is a special experience, where you can buy all manner of things, from crystals to clothing. **Brisbane** has the climate and style for markets; its best are the arts and crafts Brunswick Market and the Riverside Market.

Junk shops requiring real determination abound in out-of-the-way places, full of farm implements, commemorative tins, battered jewellery, old pots – the phrase 'One man's meat is another man's poison' often springs to mind.

Aboriginal art is increasing in popularity and distinctive hand-painted pottery, ceremonial seed and bean necklaces, animal carvings, statues, traditional paintings, boomerangs and beautifully decorated digeridoos are widely available. Many city galleries have an Aboriginal section, but there are several specialist outlets in **Sydney** – **Blue Gum Designs** and **New Guinea Primitive Arts**

(*in the QVB*), or the **Hogarth Gallery/Aboriginal Art Centre** (*7 Walker Lane, Paddington, closed Sun–Mon*) for more serious collectors – and in the **Todd Mall** in **Alice Springs**

The **Maruku Arts and Crafts Centre** at the foot of Uluru, in the **Uluru National Park**, was established in 1984 to cater for the growing demand for the work of Aboriginal craftspeople. Today, in addition to sales at the centre, Maruku exports more than half a million dollars' worth of unique and original art. It now provides a selling service to about 800 Aboriginal craftspeople from over 19 communities.

Food and drink

In the 1960s, the food in Australia, despite the quality of the produce, ranged from dire to dreadful. Anyone arriving here now expecting a slab of beef or prawns on the barbie, swilled down with a bucket of beer, is in for a pleasant surprise. Despite the stereotyping, Australian cuisine is very cosmopolitan, particularly in Sydney, Canberra and Melbourne, and in special coastal towns such as Noosa.

Styles of food

Australia opened its doors to immigrants from Europe after the Second World War, leading to the development of strong Mediterranean influences in the national cuisine. The influx of immigrants from Asia, Africa and South America made a similar mark in the 1970s and 1980s. Consequently, what has become known as **modern Australian cuisine** is a distinctive blend of Pacific and Mediterranean flavours, with a strong leaning towards clean, fresh tastes.

The immigrant populations have also established their own **ethnic** restaurants. More than a quarter of **Sydney**'s residents were born overseas, and the city has large Lebanese, Greek, Spanish, Italian and Chinese communities. Authentic Chinese is plentiful in Chinatown at Haymarket, and Spanish restaurants cluster around Liverpool St, near Darling Harbour. In **Melbourne**, a significant community of Italians dispenses marvellous coffee, pasta and pizza from authentic cafés and restaurants along Lygon St, and

Greek eating places abound in Fitzroy. Its proximity to Asia has had a marked effect upon **Darwin**, in the Northern Territory, where the Mindil Beach Sunset Markets (*Thu and Sun, 1600–2200*) feature 60 outdoor food stalls serving specialities from Indonesia, Malaysia, Vietnam, Thailand and beyond.

Over the last few years, '**bush tucker**' has become fashionable, with native Aboriginal foods such as berries, seeds and herbs creeping on to menus in the form of bush tomatoes, lemon myrtle and Illawarra plums.

On the menu

Australian seafood tends to be exceptional and specialist restaurants are plentiful, particularly, of course, in the cities along the coast. Dishes to try are **barramundi**, a large tropical fish with delicate white flesh, the heavier, slightly oily **jewfish**, the flat, round **John Dory**, with firm, white flesh or the light, delicately flavoured **mahi mahi**. Shellfish enthusiasts will enjoy **Moreton Bay Bugs** (a saltwater crustacean from the Brisbane region), **Sydney Rock Oysters** and freshwater crayfish, known as '**yabbies**', as well as the wonderfully succulent **lobster, king prawns** and **blue swimmer crab**.

Meat in NSW is extremely good and inexpensive. NSW's milk-fed **lamb** is particularly tender and all manner of **beef** from steaks to roasts is very tasty. Many restaurants, and particularly pubs, will offer meat simply chargrilled; others will dress it up with a variety of sauces. The **barbecue** is still a prominent feature of Aussie life and most national parks, popular beaches and picnic spots have a barbecue area where you can cook your own. In some restaurants, they supply the meat for you to cook on a communal barbie, which is great fun, not least because Australians vie with each other to share their barbecuing wisdom with visitors! Other tasty alternatives include low-fat, low-cholesterol **kangaroo**, **emu** and **crocodile**.

Australia benefits from an extremely varied range of fruit and vegetables, often sold from roadside stalls at tiny prices. Look out for the delicious **sun-roasted tomatoes**, rich green **rocket salad** leaves and exotic **tropical fruits** available all year round.

267

Eating out

Eating out in Australia is not just totally marvellous; it is also immensely affordable.

Breakfast is a celebrated part of the day, with many workers starting at their neighbourhood café (probably run by an Italian family) with frothy coffee, freshly squeezed juices, muffins, pancakes or even the full monty fry-up. **Lunchtime** fare revolves around soups, salads and door-stopping *focaccias* – Italian olive oil bread with a variety of Mediterranean toppings. Shopping malls in the main cities usually have a large food court with take-away counters ranging from Italian, Chinese and Thai, to Indian, seafood and organic dishes eaten in a large communal area.

Picnic fans can turn upmarket in the wonderful delis. In some areas, **cheese-tasting rooms** are becoming popular. The combination of the cheese of your choice and the other delicacies on offer – *prosciutto*, stuffed olives, sun-dried tomatoes, hummus, king prawns – makes for a gourmet pack-up. **Bakeries** sell a mind-blowing choice of bread – rye, pitta, baguette, coffee and date, muesli, mustard and cheese twirls – plus calorific meat pies and pasties for traditional die-hards. **Markets** provide an excellent opportunity to stock up on eucalyptus honey, macadamia nuts and locally harvested fruit.

Restaurants vary enormously in price and setting – anywhere with a waterfront/beach view is likely to be on the pricey side. Cheaper restaurants nestle alongside exclusive ones, so don't be put off if you find yourself in a swanky area. All except the *most* upmarket restaurants have relaxed dress codes – no tie or jacket. Restaurants in Australia encompass everything from the fast-food hamburger chains to beach cafés, fun informal bistros, pub grub and formal, linen-tablecloth, fine dining. Restaurants in cities are usually open at least six days a week, and often seven. Eateries in country areas may be closed on Monday or Tuesday. Lunch is generally served 1230–1430 and dinner 1830–2230 (2130 in country areas). Many restaurants in seaside areas offer weekend brunches 1000–1600. It's a good idea to book for popular restaurants.

One of the best quirky elements of Australian restaurant culture is the **BYO phenomenon**. Many restaurants are unlicensed and encourage you to bring your own wine or beer to drink with your meal for a negligible corkage charge. There will almost always be a 'bottle shop' (off licence/liquor store) near by. This practice keeps the restaurant bill down with the added bonus of being able to drink great wines at supermarket prices. Some licensed restaurants may still allow you to BYO for a slightly increased corkage fee.

Drinks

Coffee is complex in Australia. It comes in a variety of forms – **flat white** (milky coffee), **short black** (espresso), **cappuccino**, **caffè latte**, and more. **Smoothies** – thick milkshakes with real fruit – are popular and healthy daytime drinks, and freshly squeezed fruit juices such as carrot and ginger are definitely in. Fizzy drinks such as coke and lemonade are available everywhere, although sparkling mineral water is the exception rather than the rule.

Considering the climate, it's not surprising that the Australians are big beer drinkers, or that they insist on their beer being served *very* cold. In many 'hotels', or pubs, you will frequently see big bruisers drinking beer from a dainty little glass – that way, it's gone before it has a chance to get even slightly warmer than completely chilled. Among the most common beers in the country are **VB** (Victoria Bitter), which, despite its name, is similar to British lager, **Swan** lager, brewed in WA, and **Toohey's**, from the largest NSW

brewer. Other popular brews include **Carlton Cold**, **Hahn Ice**, **Reschs** and **Coopers**. Low-alcohol beers have become increasingly popular owing to the stringent drink-driving laws and most major breweries produce 'light' versions of mainstream beers. A small beer is a '**middy**', a large beer is a '**schooner**'.

Australian wine is so good that imported wines are usually reserved for only the finest wine lists. **Hunter Valley** wines are excellent, as are those from the **Barossa** and **Clare valleys** in South Australia, from the area around **Margaret River** in WA, and from the **Yarra Valley** in Victoria, where the wines have a very distinctive strong Yarra flavour. An agreeable wine can easily cost less than $10 and $15–$20 will buy you a really good bottle. Sémillon, Chardonnay and a blend of the two are popular whites, while reds tend to be Cabernet Sauvignon, Shiraz and blends of several grape varieties. All spirits are widely available, although **rum**, from Queensland, is a particular speciality – look out for the dark version from **Bundaberg**.

Australia with children

Australia prides itself on being an egalitarian, relaxed society where families tend to entertain with their children alongside, at casual picnics, barbecues and outdoor events. Children are generally welcomed at all but the poshest restaurants. For visitors, Australia is an easy destination to enjoy as a family. There's no shortage of beaches, parks and child-friendly museums, while in the rural areas the National Parks have wildlife – kangaroos and koalas, of course, but also parrots and emus, crocs and dingoes – within easy reach. And surely a dolphin cruise or a whale-watching boat trip would delight even the sulkiest teenager?

Sydney and NSW

Museums in Sydney have eschewed the 'look and label' approach in favour of vibrant interactive displays. Children love Eric the dinosaur and the displays of hairy spiders and slippery snakes at the **Australian Museum** (*page 35*), the spine-tingling sharks and touch pools at the **Sydney Aquarium** (*page 32*) or **Manly Oceanworld** (*page 31*), and the beauties and the beasts at **Taronga Zoo** (*page 33*).

The **National Maritime Museum** (*page 37*) runs special children's events such as swash-buckling pirate musicals and all-night sleepovers on the HMAS *Vampire* during the school holidays (*tel:(02) 9552 7777*), while the **Powerhouse Museum** (*page 39*) has locomotives to clamber on, space shuttles to explore and lots of interactive technology.

A ride on the **monorail** (*see page 23*) is an enjoyable way for children to see over Sydney. A day at the **beach** (Bondi, Bronte) is always fun and a **ferry ride** (to Watson's Bay or Manly) makes it even more enjoyable. Children *must* swim between the flags – in the area that is patrolled by lifeguards – at all times. **Bondi**'s skateboard basin, **Centennial Park** and the

seafront at **Manly** all offer a suitable playground for rollerbladers and skateboarders.

The coast from **Port Stephens** to **Byron Bay** offers **dolphin- and whale-spotting** cruises (*see pages 64–70*).

Canberra

Canberra's child-friendly activities include **Questacon**'s Science and Technology Centre (*page 92*) and

Tidbinbilla Nature Reserve (*page 94*). Cycling on the city's extensive bike paths – perhaps on a tandem – is a great way to enjoy Canberra, and there is also boating on the lake (*page 87*).

South Australia

All children – from the very young to the not so young – will enjoy the wonderful little **Pichi Richi** steam train, based at Quorn (*see page 178*). It makes its way along the old 1879 Great Northern Railway route, across trestle bridges, for a 2.5-hour trip. The entire area may appeal to slightly older fossil-hunters, or budding geologists; there are 700-million-year-old quartzite deposits here, as well as gold, opal, copper, dolomites, shale and granite elsewhere in the **Flinders Ranges National Park** (*see pages 175–6*).

Within **Wilpena Pound** (*see page 179*) stands the restored 19th-century cottage of the Hill family, where 12-year-old Jessie kept house all alone for her five older brothers. You're sure to see kangaroos and euros (small, wallaby-like marsupials) here, as well as many bird species.

Victoria

Melbourne's seaside suburb of **St Kilda** has a seafront rollerblading track, and rollerblades for hire, as well as the traditional funfair of Luna Park. Generations of children have adored the **Puffing Billy** steam train (*page 121*), which chuffs its way from Belgrave Station in Victoria's Dandenongs to Emerald Lake. At the **Healesville Sanctuary** (*page 133*), they will be delighted to see the twin platypus youngsters, born at the sanctuary, as well as eagle flight displays and rare species, such as the helmeted honeyeater. **Port Phillip Bay** and the **Mornington Peninsula** have clean, safe, sandy beaches for family days out, as well as the chance to spot dolphins (*see pages 138–9*).

After dark

Whether you want post-dinner drinks to a background of mellow music, a night at the ballet or an energetic dance to the loudest, latest techno beats, the after-dark entertainment in Australia's main cities offers something for everyone. There's also a wide variety of free entertainment, such as lunchtime concerts in city centres, and other performers in the streets, particularly during the many festivals.

Finding out what's on

The Metro section of Friday's *Sydney Morning Herald* lists cultural and fun events on around the city. Free magazines such as *3DWorld*, *Beat* and *On the Street* offer a guide to the latest gig, club, film and music events. The *Sydney Arts and Cultural Guide* (*free from tourist info centres*) is an excellent bi-annual guide to the best of Sydney's performing arts, galleries and exhibitions.

Adelaide has a reputation for being dead after dinner, but a browse through *The Guide* in the Thursday edition of the *Adelaide Advertiser*, *Rip it Up* or the *Adelaide Review* will prove otherwise.

Bookings for most events in Sydney can be made through **Ticketek** (*tel: (02) 9266 4800*) and **Ticketmaster** (*tel: (02) 9320 9000*).

The *Canberra Times* lists music events every Thursday.

Cinemas

One of the unique pleasures of summer evenings in Australia is the outdoor cinemas or movie screenings. There is a very special 'picture garden' in Broome, claimed to be the first theatre of its kind, opened in 1916. It is immensely popular and has often attracted crowds of more than 600 in the past.

The main cities all have multi-screen cinemas of chains such as **Greater Union** and **Hoyts**, many of which have a cut-price night (often Tue). Foreign and 'alternative' films are shown at various venues. One favourite is Sydney's **Movie Room** (*112 Darlinghurst Rd; tel: (02) 9380 5162*), where for a couple of bucks more than your average cinema ticket, the entry fee includes dinner at **Govinda's** veggie restaurant below.

> **"** *Remember you're here to sweat and look fabulous so you want that fabric to cling to your butt like fungus.* **"**

Sydney Sidewalk website review of DCM club

Clubbing

Sydney is the clubbing mecca of Australia, and **Oxford St** (and close environs) the clubbing mecca of Sydney. Many are exceptionally trendy and, in some places, the fashion police at the door decide who's in and who's out – so no jeans. Most have one night (or several) a week which are particularly gay-friendly, plus themed music nights so it pays to check in advance. Some are free, others have moderate entry fees, rarely more than the cost of a round of drinks.

Gambling

It's been said that an Australian would bet on two flies crawling up a wall, and, following a relatively recent relaxation in the law on gambling, there is now a **casino** in all the main cities. Most of them lack style, looking as though they were designed to dazzle rather than

273

entertain. **Adelaide Casino** (*North Terrace, Adelaide*) is the exception. Housed in what was the old railway station, it is rather elegant, and worth a visit. All casinos in Australia enjoy a huge turnover, often flying in known 'high rollers', and putting them up in luxurious accommodation, in order to boost their reputation – and their takings.

The **Melbourne Cup** is Australia's top gambling event, run at the Flemington Racecourse on the first Tuesday in November. Everyone in Australia has a bet – mostly an uninformed and illogical one – and the whole country comes to a standstill while it's being run.

Live music

Throughout Australia, rock bands mainly play the pubs, and perhaps the local RSL clubs. In Sydney, many of the pubs around **The Rocks** area have live bands most evenings and on Sunday afternoons. Sydney has probably the liveliest pop music scene in the country, with specialist

Towns all over NSW, and often quite small villages, have RSL clubs, which put on concerts, dances and films at low prices, subsidised by money made from their poker machines. They are often member-only, but most will allow entry to overseas visitors on production of a passport or driving licence (phone beforehand).

Opera Australia. Keep an eye open for special events linked to the Sydney Festival in January such as outdoor jazz, symphony and opera in the Domain. The **Australian Ballet** and the city's leading contemporary dance group, the **Sydney Dance Company**, both perform at the Opera House too.

Melbourne still has what might be called 'old money', and seriously patronises music and the ballet, with exclusive performances that are not held anywhere else in Australia. The **Sidney Myer Music Bowl** is Melbourne's main outdoor concert area. The other principal venue is the **Victoria Arts Centre**.

venues, and never less than 70 bands playing at weekends.

Performing arts

Sydney has a very strong classical music scene. Names to look out for are the **Australian Chamber Orchestra**, **Musica Viva**, one of the world's largest chamber-music organisations and **Sydney Symphony Orchestra** – all three play frequently at the Concert Hall at the Opera House. The Opera House is also a base for the innovative

275

Practical
information

ROSE BAY-WATSONS BAY

Mc Mahons Point
Milsons Point
Cremorne Point
Darling Point
Double Bay
Rose Bay
Watsons Bay

WHARF
4
08:20

NEUTRAL BAY

Kirribilli
Nor to North Sydney
Hams to Neutral Bay
Kurraba Point

HARBOUR BEACHES

Transfer at Manly for
Balmoral
Quarantine Station
Watsons Bay

WHARF   WHARF
4   **8**
08:30

MOSMAN

Cremorne Point
Taronga Zoo
Mooney to Mosman South
Old Cremorne
Avenue to Mosman

ZOO

Taronga Zoo
Cremorne Point

WHARF   WHARF
4   **2**
08:20   08:15

MANLY

Manly FERRY

Manly JETCAT

WHARF   WHARF
3   **2**
08:35   08:25

You are now on Wharf No. 5

Tickets

Practical information

Airports

Australia's major international air gateways are Sydney's Kingsford Smith, Melbourne's Tullamarine, Brisbane, Cairns and Perth, with some direct international flights to Darwin and Adelaide as well. Immigration and customs formalities are undertaken at these airports, with domestic flights linking them to other major city destinations such as Hobart and Canberra. Most Australian airports are within a half-hour taxi ride from the city centre, and also offer good shuttle-bus services.

Climate

Due to its vast size and geographical location, Australia has a wide range of climates. During winter (June to August), you can ski in the southern states one day and dive on the Great Barrier Reef in Queensland the next. Australia's seasons are the opposite of the northern hemisphere. Summer starts in December (Christmas is hot), autumn in March, winter in June and spring in September. In the south of Australia, from Sydney south, the climate is generally Mediterranean, with hot, dry summers and wet, cool winters. But north of Brisbane, way up to the tropical Darwin and Broome, November to March is the wettest, hottest most sticky time of the year; this is the true tropics.

Travel planning is important. At the Great Barrier Reef, most rain falls from December to June, while in northern Queensland and parts of the Northern Territory and Western Australia, roads may flood during the 'wet' season (January to April). The ski season lasts from June to October in New South Wales and Victoria, and the best warm, glorious sunny days in this region are most likely from December to March.

Currency

The Australian currency is the dollar, which is divided into 100 cents. Notes are plasticised, and come in $5 (purple), $10 (blue), $20 (orange), $50 (yellow) and $100 (green) denominations. Coins include 5c, 10c, 50c, $1 and $2. Travellers' cheques will generally be accepted in large hotels, otherwise they should be changed in a bank (take your passport). Credit cards are widely accepted, although their use in smaller towns and country areas is more restricted. The most popular are American Express, Visa, MasterCard, Diner's Club and Bankcard. Credit cards and ordinary bank cards bearing an international symbol such as Cirrus, plus PIN number, can be used to withdraw cash from ATMs, which operate 24 hours a day. High-street banks include Westpac, ANZ, National Australia Bank and Commonwealth Bank.

Customs regulations

Travellers arriving in Australia need to complete a customs declaration form, which is handed in at immigration. Apart from the usual bans on bringing in plants and animals, you cannot bring in any fresh food. Passengers over 18 can bring in 1 125ml alcohol and 250 cigarettes or 250g tobacco

duty free, plus $400 worth of gifts ($200 for people under 18). There's no limit to how much currency you can bring into Australia, although more than A$10,000 or the foreign currency equivalent must be declared on arrival. This total doesn't include travellers' cheques.

Disabled travellers

Provision for disabled travellers is generally good in the main cities. Many museums, cinemas, theatres and tourist hot spots have wheelchair facilities, although public transport remains a challenge. The two main bodies that provide information for the disabled are **NICAN**, which offers information on recreation, tourism, sport and the arts, and **ACROD**, the national industry association of disability services. They can be contacted as follows:

NICAN: *PO Box 407, Curtin, ACT 2605. Tel: (02) 6285 3713; e-mail: nican@spirit.com.au*

ACROD: *33 Thesiger Court, Deakin, ACT 2600. Tel: (02) 6281 3488.*

Publications
Easy Access Australia – A Travel Guide to Australia by Bruce Cameron (Easy Access Australia Publishing ISBN 0-646-25581-9): this comprehensive guide contains info on accessible accommodation, tourist facilities as well as general tourist information. Also at *www.vicnet.net.au/~bruceeaa*

Accessing Sydney: A handbook for people with disabilities and those who have problems getting around, by ACROD NSW (ISBN 0-646-21255-9) is a useful guide to the city.

The Australian Tourist Commission's website (*www.australia.com*) also has a wide range of information under its 'special interest' section.

Electricity

Australia's electrical current is 220–240 volts. Plugs are flat, two or three pins (not the same as the British three-pin varieties), so most travellers will need an adaptor plug. Most hotels have 240- and 110-volt shaver sockets.

Entry formalities

All visitors to Australia must have a valid passport and, with the exception of New Zealand passport holders, a visa issued in their own country. In 1996, the 'invisible' visa of the Electronic Travel Authority (ETA) was introduced. Details are entered on to travel industry-booking systems without any form filling or stamps in your passport. The visa is verified when you check in for your flight and when you arrive. Tourist visas for stays of up to three months each over a 12-month period are free. Longer stays and business visas incur a processing fee. Visitors from countries that do not participate in the ETA scheme must apply for a visa from their nearest Australian consulate. South Africans can apply to the **Australian High Commission**: *292 Orient St (cnr Schoeman St), Arcadia, Pretoria 0083; tel: (012) 342 3740*. For ETA services, contact **Rennies Travel** in Johannesburg (*tel: (011) 407 3343*), Cape Town (*tel: (021) 418 5626*) or Durban (*tel: (011) 304 9971*).

Festivals

Late January
Australian Open tennis, Melbourne
February/March
Adelaide Arts Festival, even-numbered years; Barossa Valley Vintage Festival, odd-numbered years
Mid-March
Formula 1 Grand Prix, Melbourne
Easter
Bells Beach Surf Classic, Torquay, Victoria
June (last weekend)
Laura Aboriginal Dance and Cultural Festival, odd-numbered years, Cape York, FNQ
August
Mount Isa Rodeo

September (last Sat)
Grand Final, Aussie Rules Football League
November (first Tue)
Melbourne Cup, Fleminton Racecourse
December (Boxing Day)
Sydney to Hobart Yacht Race departure

Health

Australia has excellent medical facilities and a good national health insurance scheme called **Medicare**. Visitors from New Zealand, the UK, Ireland, Malta, Sweden, Italy, Finland and the Netherlands are eligible, under a reciprocal agreement, for free emergency medical and hospital treatment. To exercise this right, you need to register at any local Medicare office (look in the *Yellow Pages*). Dental treatment, ambulance services or repatriation in case of injury or illness aren't covered, so health insurance is still essential. No vaccinations are needed for entry into Australia unless you have visited a yellow fever-infected area within six days prior to arrival in Australia.

> *" [Certain countries] are entitled to free emergency medical treatment under reciprocal agreements. Anyone else has two options: take travel insurance or don't fall ill. "*
>
> **Sydney tourist publication**

Health hazards

Australia has its fair share of bronzed sun gods and goddesses, but the high incidence of sun cancer means that many people prefer to stay relatively pale. Overseas visitors should protect themselves from the strong Aussie sun by wearing a long-sleeved T-shirt and a wide brimmed hat and applying a hefty dose of factor 15-plus water-

resistant sun-tan lotion. Make sure you drink plenty of water and keep out of the sun 1100–1500 during daylight saving (end of October–end of March) and 1000–1400 at other times.

Another common hazard for visitors, particularly those unused to ocean beaches, are the rips and undertows. The lifeguards who patrol most of the popular beaches around Sydney pull out an average of 11,000 people a year. Red and yellow flags mark safe swimming areas up and down the coast, and you should always try to swim between them. If you do get into trouble, don't try to swim against the current, float with it and raise your arm for help.

Bush fires are very common in the summer. Indicators along the road show the fire risk for the day. Some days are designated 'total fire ban'

days, which means exactly that – no barbies, no camping stoves – and never throw cigarettes out of the car window on any day. Fires spread like lightning, so leave the area as soon as you see smoke, even if it's in the distance. If you're planning a camping trip or setting off on a long bushwalk, phone the **Country Fire Authority** (*tel: 131 599*) to check on conditions.

Despite Australia's deserved reputation for poisonous spiders and snakes, it's quite possible that you will finish your trip without bumping into one, poisonous or otherwise. You are very unlikely to be bitten, but sturdy boots when bushwalking are a good idea. Be careful when gathering wood for barbecues, and never put your hand into crevices or tree hollows. If you are bitten, seek urgent medical attention – antidotes are available for most bites.

281

Information

You're never far away from an information source in Australia. These can range from well-equipped official centres with books, leaflets and maps to volunteer-run kiosks overflowing with helpful advice, to cafés, newsagents or junk stores in one-donkey towns with a couple of dog-eared leaflets and lots of local charm. Wherever you end up, it's usually a friendly and helpful experience, particularly when run by volunteers.

Some of the popular national parks and nature reserves have visitor centres, while others are limited to a couple of walking trail and wildlife information boards.

Australia on the Internet:
www.australia.com
Australian Tourist Commission

www.wineries.tourism.net.au Winery tours and tastings all over Australia

www.oztourism.com.au
Information on all the states

www.npws.gov.au
National Parks and Wildlife Service

www.country-wide.com.au

www.cowleys.com.au
A really comprehensive guide to everything, especially accommodation

www.walkabout.fairfax.com.au
An excellent, informative site run by the Sydney Morning Herald

www.citysearch.com.au and
www.sydney.sidewalk.com.au
The Sydney social scene

www.tourism.nsw.gov.au
Tourism New South Wales

www.sydney.com.au

www.sydneycity.nsw.gov.au

www.sydney.olympics.org
Official site for the 2000 Olympics

www.canberratourism.com.au

www.melbourne.com.au

www.melbourne.citysearch.com

www.ballarat.com

www.greatoceanrd.org.au
Guide to the Great Ocean Road

www.southaustralia.com.au/tourism/barossa Barossa Valley tourist info

www.tourkangarooisland.com.au
Kangaroo Island visitors' guide

www.freonet.net.au Fremantle online

www.holiday-wa.net WA tourism site

www.brisbane-online.com

www.brisbaneonthenet.com

www.maxlink.com.au/bcl/
Brisbane city life

www.barrierreef.net

www.greatbarrierreef.aus.net

www.queensland-holidays.com.au

www.alicesprings.net.au

www.nttc.com.au
Northern Territory site

www.northernterritory.com

www.ebroome.com Broome online

Insurance

Take out travel insurance before setting off on your trip to cover your luggage, valuables and medical care (including repatriation). If you're planning to indulge in any potentially dangerous activities such as whitewater rafting, mountain climbing, hang-gliding or skiing, make sure these are covered by your policy.

Opening times

Shops are generally open Mon–Fri 0900–1730, Sat 0900–1700 and Sunday trading is becoming more popular, with major stores open 1100–1600. In some areas, large supermarkets such as Coles or Woolworths stay open until 2200 or midnight.

Banks are open Mon–Thu 0930–1600, Fri 0930–1700, and some open Sat morning.

Petrol stations are plentiful and are usually open seven days a week, from early till late, with shorter hours in less populated, rural areas. On major roads such as the Pacific Highway, many stay open till midnight; some are 24-hour.

Restaurants are usually open seven days a week in the main cities; some close on Sun, Mon and/or Tue in quieter areas. Restaurants that depend heavily on office workers for lunchtime trade are often open for dinner only at weekends.

Pubs usually shut at 2300 during the week, midnight on Sat and 2200 on Sun. In rural areas, many pubs open early and close around 2130.

Public Holidays

1 Jan	New Year's Day
26 Jan	Australia Day
Third Mon in Mar (ACT only)	Canberra Day
Mar/Apr	Good Friday, Easter Saturday and Easter Monday
25 Apr	Anzac Day
Second Mon in June	Queen's Birthday
First Mon in Aug	August Bank Holiday
First Mon in Oct	Labour Day
First Tue in Nov	Melbourne Cup Day – not officially a holiday, but many businesses close early to watch the race
25 Dec	Christmas Day
26 Dec	Boxing Day

Reading

Eating out

The *Sydney Morning Herald* publishes an annual *Good Food Guide*, the ultimate gourmet bible, a lively, witty, sometimes scathing collection of restaurant and café reviews, heavily focused on Sydney, but with a good chunk of recommendations all over NSW.

The Age newspaper in Melbourne, surely a strong contender for the best dining city in Australia, gives out awards to restaurants every year. **Jacques Reymond**, in Windsor, is the only restaurant to have received its top prize of five chef's hats.

History

The Oxford Illustrated Dictionary of Australian History, Jan Bassett (1996, Oxford University Press Australia), is an easy, dip-in, dip-out reference book to piece together all those names and events which you've heard bandied about and feel you should know. For a comprehensive history of the colony's early days, *The Fatal Shore 1787–1868*, Robert Hughes (Collins Harvill), is an accessible read.

Travel writing

Places in the Heart (1997, Hodder Headline) is an anthology of travel 'memories', a collection of 30 prominent Australians' favourite places. Destinations include many in Australia, some in far corners of the globe. All are brought to life through childhood memories, witty anecdotes and enchanting descriptions, which offer an insight into Australian cultural values and social mores.

Sydney, Jan Morris (1992, Penguin), is a mixture of social comment, historical fact and personalities served up with perceptive insights into Sydney life, intellect, mentality and style. Her last book on Sydney back in the 1960s earned her hate-mail for five years; this one is infinitely more affectionate and entertainingly informative.

Safety and security

Generally, Australia has a low crime rate. However, the usual sensible precautions apply – keep to well-lit areas at night, don't flash wads of cash in public, use the safe in your hotel and keep a close eye on your wallet

and handbag at all times, especially in crowded places and on public transport. In the car, don't leave valuables on display and don't advertise the fact that you're a tourist by leaving maps and guidebooks on the seats. Visitors to small towns in rural areas will usually be welcomed, although you may stand out like a sore thumb. Women travelling alone should book accommodation ahead and try to arrive before dark. Bear in mind that pubs in these areas tend to be fairly rough and ready and the domain of men.

Off peak, you could easily find that you have walking trails in national parks to yourself – for women in particular, it's best not to go wandering off alone. Bushwalking presents other dangers. Conditions can change very quickly and when the sun sets, it can turn very chilly. Make sure you're carrying plenty of water, sun cream, a hat plus warm clothing. If you're setting off on a long trip, check conditions first at information centres, make sure you've got a good map and tell staff your intended route.

Public transport is pretty safe. It's worth knowing that the Sydney underground has carriages designated for safe night-time travel, marked by blue lights.

Telephones

Public telephones are plentiful. Many accept coins and phone cards, others credit cards only, some take everything. **Telstra** phone cards ($5, $10, $20, $50) can be bought at newsagents, chemists and other retail outlets. Local calls cost a flat rate of 40c; $10 should buy you enough time to check on the dog/kids/granny back home *and* tell them where you've been. The cheapest time to

call is 2200–0800, or between 1800 Saturday and 0800 on Monday.

International code: dial 00 11 + country code + city code (minus initial zero) + telephone number. Country codes are (44) for the UK, (64) for New Zealand, (1) for US/Canada, (27) for South Africa.

Time

There are three time zones within Australia. New South Wales, the ACT, Victoria, Tasmania and Queensland are on eastern standard time (EST), 10 hours ahead of GMT. South Australia and Northern Territories are half an hour behind EST and Western Australia is two hours behind. Daylight saving runs from the end of October to end of March which adds an hour to the time differences. Queensland doesn't change, so check local times if you're flying north.

Tipping

Australia is a very egalitarian society and tipping is *not* generally expected. It's fine to tip porters, taxi drivers and hairdressers if you want to, but there's no obligation to do so. In most cafés and restaurants, it's customary to round the bill up to the nearest easy figure, although the more upmarket you go, the closer you should aim to 10 per cent.

Toilets

Public toilets are pretty thin on the ground in cities, but plentiful on the highways, in national parks and in all tourist attractions. In the main cities, the best conveniences are in cafés, restaurants and large department stores.

Index

Editorial, design and production credits

Project management: Dial House Publishing Services
Series editor: Christopher Catling
Copy editor: Jane Franklin
Proof-reader: Gill Colver

Series and cover design: Trickett & Webb Limited
Cover artwork: Wenham Arts
Text layout: Wenham Arts
Cartography: Polly Senior Cartography

Repro and image setting: Z2 Repro, Thetford, Norfolk, UK
Printed and bound by: Artes Graficas ELKAR S. Coop., Bilbao, Spain

Acknowledgements

We would like to thank Ethel Davies for the photographs used in this book, to whom the copyright belongs, with the exception of the following:

Australian Tourist Commission: pages 44, 76, 77, 104, 107, 108, 125, 128, 134, 137, 148, 150, 154, 168, 173, 201, 218, 222, 224, 225, 257 and 269

Domain Chandon: page 186

Parks Victoria: page 79

Photo Index: pages 251, 252 and 254

Bruce Postle: pages 121, 122, 133, 217 and 221

Sandy Scheltema: pages 119, 139 and 270

South Australian Tourist Commission: pages 131, 175, 176, 178, 179 and 180

Telegraph Colour Library: page 241

Tourism New South Wales: page 126

Tourism Queensland: page 236.